Chicago School Traditions

*Deductive Qualitative Analysis
and Grounded Theory*

A Reader

Volume 2
2008-2013

Jane F. Gilgun, Ph.D.

Chicago School Traditions:
Deductive Qualitative Analysis
and Grounded Theory
A Reader
Volume 2, 2008-2013

by Jane Gilgun

ISBN-13: 978-1499512779
ISBN-10: 1499512775

Key words: Chicago School of Sociology, Deductive Qualitative Analysis,
Grounded Theory, Qualitative Research, Research Methodology

CONTENTS

INTRODUCTION:
THE LEGACY

THERE ARE MANY different ways to generate theory. I have spent much of my academic career attempting to understand and share with others how to use qualitative methods to generate and test theories and to do theory-guided research. The work of Ruben Hill, Wesley Burr, and others (Burr, Hill, Nye, & Reiss (1979a & b) in theory-building inspired me when I was a graduate student in child and family studies at Syracuse University. These scholars headed efforts to build theory through the codification of existing research and theory. As a social worker, I knew through experience the importance of theory in understanding complex human situations. I also had a natural inclination to want to interact with other people and to understand them in their own terms. I was intrigued to see how research and theory worked in real-world situations. In addition, I wanted to contribute new understandings of how people view and deal with their life circumstances.

In graduate school, I also learned about the methods and methodological traditions of the Chicago School of Sociology and was delighted to learn that we can do research by talking to people, through participant observation, and through document analysis. My dissertation research more than 30 years ago was based on principles associated with the Chicago School, such as life histories, understanding persons' accounts of their experiences in context, immersion of researchers in research settings, and research as action-oriented. I have been a scholar and researcher in this tradition ever since.

As Becker (1999) pointed out, however, the Chicago School was "open to various ways of doing sociology" (p. 10). The ideas that I have worked with over the years are part of the tradition but do not represent the entire tradition. I elaborate on these ideas in the essays in this collection, especially in chapter 19 about enduring themes. My interests are only one stream of several research traditions. Urban ethnographies, survey research, and race relations are also part of Chicago School traditions (Fine 1995), but I have not studied them in any detail.

The traditions of the Chicago School have endured. The ideas are not fixed, but are flexible, open-ended, and subject to revision, as many early researchers have stated, including Cressey (1950, 1953), Lindesmith (1947), Angell (1936), and Znaniecki (1934). My purpose is putting this collection of essays together is to share the many generative ideas associated with the Chicago School of Sociology, to show their evolution over time, and to illustrate their applicability to contemporary social issues. As a social worker and a family scholar, I wrote these essays for publications in family journals and in social work journals. The fields are related and have shared audiences with other disciplines, too, such as psychology, sociology, and nursing. This collection will be of interest to students, new researchers, and experienced researchers in these applied disciplines.

ALONG WITH FIELDWORK, analytic induction is the original methodology of the Chicago School of Sociology when it flourished in the first quarter of the twentieth century. Briefly, AI involves the use of theory, often loosely defined, in the conduct of research. Many of the research projects of both faculty and students during that time and later stated that the methodological approach was analytic induction (AI), when they named their approach at all. By the mid-twentieth century, AI had fallen into disrepute, partly because of misunderstandings related to causation and universality of findings but also because of unfounded claims that some researchers made about the reach of the approach. De-tails of the controversies are in some of the readings in this volume, such as chapters 10 and 18.

Grounded theory methodology arrived on the scene 50 or more years later and overshadowed AI. Grounded theory methodology (GTM) was cautious about the use of prior theory, warning about the imposition of theory on finding and advocating that researchers allow theory to "emerge" from the analysis. GTM also made no claims about causation and universality. It carried on some of the Chicago School traditions, such the importance of fieldwork, understanding meanings research par-ticipants attributed to their situations, the importance of understandings persons in contexts, the development of theory from data, and the im-portance of applied research to efforts for social change (chapters 11 and 20 and Gilgun, 2013, in press a & b).

Grounded theory methodologists never said not to begin research with theory but that became how many researchers understood its pro-cedures. The dominance of GTM and especially the idea that researchers must not begin with theory led to an underdevelopment of qualitative theory testing and theory-guided research. Furthermore, GT methodolo-gists have not addressed the question of what to do with grounded theories when we want to test them on new samples. Clues on the use of prior theory are scattered throughout the writings of researchers and methodologists who are part of the Chicago School of Sociology. To my knowledge, this collection of readings is the first attempt to bring these scattered clues together and to develop them further.

I COINED THE TERM *deductive qualitative analysis* after years of studying analytic induction and noticing how other researchers use theory in their research. As is shown in several readings in this volume, I use this term because analytic induction is not induction at all, but a moving back and forth between concepts and their indicators—or between theory and data. Dewey (1910) called this "complete thinking" which involves both induction and deduction. In deductive work, researchers begin with theory. "Complete thinking," also requires researchers to put aside their theory to identify aspects of the phenomena of interest that they did not anticipate. The latter is induction. They even purposely search for data that promise to undermine and thus flesh out their emerging findings. This is called negative case analysis, discussed in detail in several chapters in this volume, including chapters 6, 7, 10, 11, 13, and 19. There is a movement back and forth between deduction and induction. I also chose the term *deductive qualitative analysis* because of the spoiled identity of analytic induction. Anselm Strauss, one of the originators of GTM, wrote the first essay in this volume. He said GTM is a "way of thinking," which shows the connection of GTM to Dewey and the pragmatist philosophy that Dewey helped develop (Gilgun, 2005).

I want DQA to have more prominence for several reasons. First of all, many qualitative researchers begin their research with theory but don't have a name for what they do. They craft their research this way because it makes sense to them; they simply are theoretically oriented. I, for example, used life course theory as the conceptual framework for my dissertation research without self-consciousness. Theory guided me in both design and analysis. It seemed natural and normal. As I show in several essays in this volume, most if not all researchers today have training in logico-deductive methods, which means they learn to begin research with literature reviews and to test hypotheses and to use concepts. The procedures of DQA guide researchers in the use of theory from the beginning of a qualitative research project.

In addition, dissertation committees and funders are unlikely to give the okay to projects and to fund them if they don't know what the researchers intend to do and how they are going to do it. Conceptual frameworks, composed of literature reviews and reflexivity statements, are the sources of hypotheses and initial guiding concepts, as well as the foundation of design and analysis. The design and the concepts used in the analysis typically evolve over the course of the researchers, but gatekeepers such as funders and dissertation committees understandably want as much information as possible about the plans for the project.

3

Finally, policy, DQA can contribute to theories and findings that programs, policies and practitioners can use to guide them in their actions. Findings represent the perspectives of those for whom policies, programs, and interventions are crafted. Effectiveness depends on whether they meet people where they are.

In addition, findings often are composed of stories that may help policy makers, program planners, and direct practitioners understand the persons they are positioned to serve. Stories may break through the assumptions and biases that are built into many policies, programs, and interventions. In my own field of social work, I have seen practitioners and policy makers act on the basis of personal preferences and beliefs without challenging themselves to look for additional points of view and multiple sources of evidence. In addition to stories, DQA produces theory that are principles that can be used as guidelines for actions in a variety of situations. The guidelines are rooted in the stories of real people and so will have ready applicability to human situations.

COLLECTIONS OF RELATED ESSAYS often have repetitions across them. This is so in the present volume. Since some of the ideas go against contemporary trends, repetition may aide in assimilating the ideas and then in changing minds and beliefs about the conduct of qualitative research. Qualitative theory testing, for example, may be new to some researchers. The chapter in the appendix is an example. There are far too few of them, but prospect are bright.

Except for the article in the appendix, I arranged the essays in this volume in the order in which I wrote them. I did this to invite readers into the intellectual journey I took in order to understand how I came to see the roles DQA could have in social and human sciences research. The chronological order of the ideas shows the evolution of my understandings over time and through experience. I wrote all of the essays in the volume expect that first where Anselm Strauss is the author.

Jane F. Gilgun
Minneapolis, Minnesota, USA
15 May 2014

References

Angell, Robert A. *The family encounters the depression.* New York: Scribners.

Becker, Howard (1953). Becoming a marihuana user. *American Journal of Sociology, 59,* 235-242.

Becker, Howard (1999). The Chicago School, so-called. *Qualitative Sociology, 22(1),* 3-12.

Burr, Wesley, Reuben Hill, F. Ivan Nye, & Ira L. Reiss (Eds.) (1979a). *Contemporary theories about the family: Vol. 1: Research-based theories.* New York: Free Press.

Burr, Wesley, Reuben Hill, F. Ivan Nye, & Ira L. Reiss (Eds.) (1979b). *Contemporary theories about the family: Vol. 2: General theories/theoretical orientations.* New York: Free Press.

Cressey, Donald R. (1950). Criminal violation of financial trust, *American Sociological Review, 15,* 738-743.

Cressey, Donald (1953). *Other people's money.* Glencoe, IL: Free Press.

Dewey, J. (1910). *How we think.* Amherst, NY: Prometheus.

Fine, Gary Alan (Ed.) (1955). *A second Chicago School? The development of a postwar American sociology.* Chicago: University of Chicago Press.

Gilgun, Jane F. (2005). Qualitative research and family psychology. *Journal of Family Psychology,19(1),* 40-50.

Gilgun, Jane F. (2012). Enduring themes in qualitative family research. *Journal of Family Theory and Review, 4,* 80-95.

Gilgun, Jane F. (in press a). Social work-specific research and theory building. In William Nichols (Ed.), *Encyclopedia of Social and Behavioral Sciences* (2nd ed). New York: Elselvier.

Gilgun, Jane F. (in press b). Writing up qualitative research. In Patricia Leavy (Ed.). *The Oxford handbook of qualitative research methods.* New York: Oxford University Press.

Lindesmith, Alfred R. (1947). *Addictions and opiates.* Chicago: Aldine.

Znaniecki, Florian (1934). *The method of sociology.* New York: Farrar & Rinehart.

11

A PRIMER ON DEDUCTIVE
QUALITATIVE ANALYSIS

This article was first published in 2008 as an appendix to the book On Being a Shit: Unkind Deeds and Cover-ups in Everyday Life, *that is a humorous take on a serious topic. I developed and tested a theory of unkind deeds and cover-ups using DQA. My inspiration for the book was Harry Frankfurt's On Bullshit. When I read his book, I said to myself, "I can do that. Only I can write about being a shit." I had seen multiple instances of unkind deeds and cover-ups in my violence research. I gradually saw that many people use the same tactics to cover up their own unkind deeds that are far less grave but still hurtful. Frankfurt inspired me to test my theory on a new sample of cases that I drew from the mass media. Humor in social science research is rare. Frankfurt was a professor of philosophy at Princeton University, USA. When I read Frankfurt's book, I realized that my long-term research on violence had taught me a great deal about being a shit.*

DEDUCTIVE QUALITATIVE ANALYSIS is research that begins with theory. Researchers may test theory for the purpose of modifying it or use theory as sources of sensitizing concepts that are the basis of their interview questions, their preliminary codes, and their theoretical sensitivity. Theoretical sensitivity means that researchers already have knowledge of theory, research, and personal experience that contribute to implicit or explicit sets of ideas that helps them to notice certain things about their data and not notice others. These sets of ideas are conceptual frameworks. (See Glaser, 1978 for an extended discussion of theoretical sensitivity.)

In this brief paper, I discuss the theory testing and theory development strategies of deductive qualitative analysis (DQA). In this form of DQA, researchers begin with a preliminary theory. The initial theory can be composed of loosely formulated hunches based on personal or professional experience, formal hypotheses, or a set of that is a model of how things work (Gilgun, 2010, 2007, 2005c). The theory is tested on a series of cases. When the theory does not fit cases, the theory is changed. DQA is an updating of analytic induction, a form of qualitative inquiry that researchers at the University of Chicago, USA, developed in the early part of the twentieth century.

DQA and the Scientific Method

Researchers test preliminary theory on particular cases. Many do "natural experiments" in that they observe phenomena that they do not control, typically because they want to observe behaviors in natural settings or because it would be unethical to perform some social experiments. Post-hoc studies of trauma are examples. Sometimes researchers manipulate the actions observed, such as when researchers drop a wallet on the ground and watch what passers-by do when the see it lying there. Thus, DQA follows a scientific method, one that involves proposing a theory, testing it, and then revising it based on results of the test (Popper, 1969).

Another way to think about scientific method is the following. Science involves observation, the formulation of descriptions of what researchers see in their observations, and the testing of these descriptions, which may be called hypotheses. Researchers may—and probably should--purposefully seeking evidence that undermines or at least refines hypotheses and that promotes the production of new hypotheses when those that are tested are found lacking. Indeed, the production of new, more useful hypotheses is a goal of science. Science builds understandings based upon procedures of conjectures in the form of hypotheses, refutation through the process of testing hypotheses for their fit with observations, and reformulation when the hypotheses that are tested do not fit observations (Gilgun, 2005a; Popper, 1969).

In DQA as in the scientific method in general, researchers consider the initial theory to be preliminary. The purpose of DQA is to come up with a better theory than researchers had constructed at the outset (Gilgun, 2005c, 2007; 2010).

The Terminology of DQA

The terminology of DQA can be confusing. Researchers refer to the initial theoretical framework in various ways, such as a preliminary theory, an analytic framework, a theoretical model, a preliminary model, and the initial or preliminary hypothesis or hypotheses.

The final product of DQA also has more than one name, including tested and refined theory or model, the improved model, and the final model. Whatever terms researchers use, DQA is based on the idea that "final" theory is not final at all, but tentative and subject to revision when there is evidence to do so (Gilgun, 2005c, 2007, 2010).

The term *hypothesis* can also be a confusing term in DQA. In the present context, hypotheses are statements of relationships among concepts. Any hypothesis is composed of at least two concepts and a statement of the relationship between them, such as the hypothesis that Clever Foxes (a concept) know exactly what they are doing (a concept). Concepts in DQA serve sensitizing purposes, meaning they help researchers see aspects of phenomena that might not otherwise have noticed.

This is both their strength and weakness, strength precisely because they enlighten and thus serve as lenses with which to view the world. The sensitizing purposes of concepts also represent weakness because they may blind researchers to other significant aspects of phenomena (Blumer, 1954/1969). Thus researchers may only pay attention to data that support their assumptions and ignore other important data. It is easy enough to find material that upholds one's assumptions, but this is not science.

Negative Case Analysis

Researchers avoid finding what they intend to find through the conscious search for evidence that contradicts their emerging findings. This requires a form of sampling called negative case analysis, which involves the search for data that adds additional dimensions or even contradicts researchers' emerging understandings. Negative case analysis fits well with the ideas of conjectures, refutations, and reformulations (Gilgun, 2005c, 2007; 2010).

Another way to think of sampling in deductive qualitative analysis is the idea of maximum variability, where researchers attempt to sample a wide variety of cases in order to arrive at a comprehensive theory. The sampling is purposeful in that researchers intentionally select cases that represent a wide variety of types. The result is a set of cases that are representative of the many variations.

It is likely that other variations not accounted for in the sample actually do exist. Thus, any theory based on DQA is flexible, intended to be modifiable if a new situation or case calls for flexibility. Such are the challenges and pleasures of scientific endeavors.

DQA and Analytic Induction

Deductive qualitative analysis (DQA) is an updating of analytic induction (AI) which is a research method associated with the Chicago School of Sociology (Bulmer, 1984; Gilgun 2005c, 2007, 2010). Like DQA, AI starts with a preliminary theory, tests the theories on cases, selects sample based on negative case analysis, and continual revises the theory according to what researchers find through their analysis of cases.

Some researchers who used AI, stated that their findings were universal, meaning that they fit every case they investigated, not that they fit every specific instances of an entire class of phenomena. Those who originated AI recognized that their "final" theories are in fact tentative, subject to revision when new evidence comes to light (Cressey, 1953).

Analytic induction went through long period of disrepute because some methodologists misunderstood its premises. For instance, these methodologists thought by "universal," researchers using AI meant that their findings were general laws, applicable across time, place, and persons (Gilgun, 2005c). In fact, as stated, those who used AI saw findings as subject to revision (Gilgun, 2007).

Methodologists also misunderstood how to use the findings of AI. They correctly noted that findings are not applicable to an entire population. Those who developed AI also recognized this and expected findings to be tested for their fit with new situations.

Any findings from research, including findings based on true random samples cannot be assumed to fit any one individual, even someone who was part of the sample on which the findings were developed. What is true for a group may not be true of individuals who compose that group. Assuming that group findings fit individual situations has a name: the ecological fallacy. Any finding, no many how derived, must be tested for fit in applied settings (Cronbach, 1975).

Analytic induction, like DQA, has as its purpose theory-building and cannot answer questions about distribution of qualities within a population, such as how many people will vote Democratic, Republican, Green, Independent, otherwise, or not at all.

Many of the ideas connected to AI are also part of DQA, but DQA elaborates upon many of these ideas and adds new ones. For instance, those who have created AI gave scant attention to the various types of initial hypotheses with which researchers begin their studies, nor do they define such terms as theory, model, and hypotheses. They provided little guidance as to how to incorporate previous research and theory into the development of the initial hypotheses and into emerging findings. They appear not to have considered ideas related to the sensitizing nature of concepts that is so important in testing and revising hypotheses. They did not connect negative case analysis with Popper's ideas of conjectures and refutations nor with ideas of maximum variability. These are some of the elaborations that the present author did to create DQA and that are accounted for in the present investigation and in articles previously cited.

Deductive qualitative analysis (DQA) also states clearly how important it is for researchers to begin qualitative, case-based research with a preliminary theory that also services as a conceptual framework. If they do not, they have scant chance of having our proposals funded by sponsoring agencies or accepted by dissertation committees.

Some researchers fear that we will find what they expect to find if we begin our research with hypotheses (Glaser, 1973; Glaser & Strauss, 1967; Strauss & Corbin, 1998). These fears are well founded. In response, DQA offers the principles of conjectures, refutations, and reformulations to counteract these tendencies and, furthermore, shows how negative case analysis represents a means of refuting previous conjectures.

Induction and Deduction

Finally, analytic induction is not induction at all, but a combination of induction and deduction. For example, if a horse owner sees a gooey, yellow substance in the corner of her horse's eye, she uses both induction and deduction to conclude that her horse has an eye infection. She has prior understanding of pus as an indicator of infection. Prior knowledge is a source of deductive reasoning. She sees the yellow substance in her horse's eye and concludes the horse has an eye infection (induction).

The horse owner did not have a prior framework in mind when she looked at the horse's eye, but when she saw the yellow substance, she immediately thought of eye infection. In this instance, she began with no prior framework but immediately called one up when she saw the substance in the corner of the eye.

Had someone told her that her horse appears to have an eye infection, she would have looked at the eye with that hypothesis in mind. If she had seen the yellow, soft substance, she would have tentatively concluded that the hypothesis fit the situation. She would have sought further confirmation by calling a veterinarian and having the vet inspect the eye. If the hypothesis were to be confirmed, then action would follow. The vet would sell the horse owner medication and the horse owner would apply it to the horse's eye as directed. If the vet were correct in her conclusion, and if she prescribed the correct medication, and if the owner applied the medication as directed and in the correct dose, then the horse's eye would clear up. Results would confirm or disconfirm the hypothesis.

Deductive qualitative analysis (DQA) begins with a preliminary theory that is tested and hopefully refined as a result of an analysis. The theory also serves a sensitizing function, as discussed. When researchers seek evidence to disconfirm or to discover new dimensions of their emerging hypotheses, they often use induction as described above.

In other words, they may set aside their prior theory as much as they can and attempt to be open to new aspects of phenomena under investigation. They do not know exactly what they are looking for other than they want to find something different from what they already think they know.

Summary

To summarize, DQA is based on the scientific method and typically is used to test and refine hypotheses through observation of behaviors in their natural settings. Data can be created through researchers' own observations and interviews or through the examination of texts that others have constructed. As increasing numbers of social scientists see the merits of DQA for developing theory, theory development may take a more central place in social science in general and in the applied disciplines as well.

References & Further Reading

Blumer, Herbert. (1954/1969). What is wrong with social theory? In Herbert Blumer (1969/1986), *Symbolic interactionism. (pp* (pp. 140-152) Berkeley: University of California Press. Originally published in Vol. XIX in *The American Sociological Review.*

Bryant, Antony & Kathy Charmaz (Eds.) *(2007). The Sage handbook of grounded theory.* Thousand Oaks, CA: Sage.

Bulmer, Martin (1984). *The Chicago School of Sociology: Institutionalization, diversity, and the rise of sociological research.* Chicago: University of Chicago Press.

Corbin, Juliet & Anselm Strauss (2008). *Basics of qualitative research: Techniques and procedures for developing grounded theory* (3rd ed.). Thousand Oaks, CA: Sage.

Cressey, Donald (1953). *Other people's money*. Belmont, CA: Wadsworth.

Cronbach, Lee J. (1975). Beyond the two disciplines of scientific psychology. *American Psychologist, 30*, 116-127.

Daly, Kerry (2007) Qualitative methods for family studies & human development. Thousand Oaks, CA: Sage.

Gilgun, Jane F. (2005a). "Grab" and good science: Writing up the results of qualitative research. *Qualitative Health Research*, 15(2), 256-262.

Gilgun, Jane F. (2005b). Lighten up! The citation dilemma in qualitative research. *Qualitative Health Research, 15(5,) 721-725*.

Gilgun, Jane F. (2005c). Qualitative research and family psychology. *Journal of Family Psychology, 19(1)*, 40-50.

Gilgun, Jane F. (2010). Methods for enhancing theory and knowledge about problems, policies, and practice. In Katherine Briar, Joan Orme, Roy Ruckdeschel, & Ian Shaw, *The Sage handbook of social work research* (pp. 281-297). Thousand Oaks, CA: Sage.

Gilgun, Jane F. (2009). *On being a shit: Unkind deeds & cover-ups in everyday life*. Morrissville, NC: Lulu.

Gilgun, Jane F. (2006). The four cornerstones of qualitative research. *Qualitative Health Research, 16(3)*, 436-443.

Glaser, Barney. (1978). *Theoretical sensitivity*. Mill Valley, CA: Sociology Press.

Glaser, Barney & Anselm A. Strauss (1967). *The discovery of grounded theory*. Chicago: Aldine.

Popper, Karl (1969). *Conjectures and refutations: The growth of scientific knowledge*. London: Routledge and Kegan Paul.

Strauss, Anselm, & Juliet Corbin (1998). *Basics of qualitative research: Techniques and procedures for developing grounded theory* (2nd ed.). Thousand Oaks, CA: Sage.

12

DEDUCTIVE QUALITATIVE ANALYSIS AS MIDDLE GROUND: THEORY-GUIDED QUALITATIVE RESEARCH

The use of conceptual frameworks in the conduct of qualitative research was an approach of choice in the first two-thirds of the twentieth century for researchers linked to the Chicago School of Sociology, a research tradition in which much of contemporary qualitative research is rooted. With the publication of Glaser & Strauss's (1967) The Discovery of Grounded Theory, induction became associated with qualitative research and, for many researchers, prior conceptual frameworks, or deductive qualitative research, became suspect. The purpose of this paper is to review arguments for and against prior frameworks in qualitative research. I show that the procedures of analytic induction and grounded theory work well together and that theory-guided research has many advantages. I call this hybrid of the two approaches deductive qualitative analysis. *This is a slightly revised version of a paper presented at the Midwest Conference on Qualitative Research, St. Paul, MN, USA, April 18, 2008.*

THE USE OF PRIOR CONCEPTUAL frameworks was usual practice in the first two-thirds of the twentieth century for researchers linked to the Chicago School of Sociology. Researchers typically began with theory, sometimes hunches based on personal and professional experience and sometimes a bit more formal, composed of personal and professional experience and reviews of the literature. They also sought to identify new aspects of the phenomena of interest that their prior theory did not anticipate. From early on, then, qualitative research was broadly deductive as represented in prior frameworks and had a discovery-oriented approach.

The publication of Glaser and Strauss's (1967) *The Discovery of Grounded Theory in* the late 1960s cast serious doubts on the value of prior frameworks and advocated for the "discovery" of theory grounded in data, theory that emerged during the conduct of research. In combination with other criticisms, theory-guided qualitative research became suspect.

The purpose of this paper is to review the arguments for and against the use of conceptual frameworks in the conduct of qualitative research and to propose a middle ground that combines elements of both approaches. I call this combined approach *deductive qualitative analysis*.

In this paper, I define conceptual framework as a synthesis and integration of existing research and theory relevant to a topic. I assume that the personal and professional experience and values of researchers inform and shape conceptual frameworks. I also advocate for an explicit statement of researchers' experiences and values in order to be as clear as possible about the conceptual basis of the research.

Conceptual frameworks are the sources of hypotheses and sensitizing concepts. Sensitizing concepts are ideas that focus and guide research, or, in the words of Blumer (1969) that "suggest directions along which to look" (p. 148) as researchers engage in data collection, analysis, and interpretation. Sensitizing concepts and have no fixed meanings or benchmarks, as contrasted with "definitive" concepts that have clearly fixed meanings and attributes. Conceptual frameworks can also be the sources of hypotheses that researchers test and modify over the course of the research. Hypotheses are composed of sensitizing concepts. It follows that hypotheses also provide focus and guidance to research. Theory-guided research always uses sensitizing concepts but does not necessarily test hypotheses.

Analytic Induction

In analytic induction, researchers develop an initial conceptual framework prior to entry into the field. These hypotheses can be rough and approximate, based on hunches, based on a general theoretical orientation as broad as ecological theory, or based on professional and practice experience (Bodgan & Biklen, 2007; Cressey, 1953; Gilgun, 1995, 2009). Sometimes researchers do preliminary research in the form of interviews, observations, and document analysis to develop an initial framework that focuses and guides them in their research, as did Lindesmith (1947) in his study of opium addicts.

Negative Case Analysis

Researchers revise their findings throughout the research, whether they represent their findings as on-going revisions the initial hypotheses or as general statements of relationships that they also continually revise. Revisions are based upon the examination of negative cases, which involves looking for exceptions and contradictions to emerging findings within and across cases (Becker, 1953; Becker et al, 1961; Cressey, 1953;

Gilgun, 1995, 2005, 2009; Palmer, 1928, Znaniecki, 1934). This is how Becker and colleagues (Becker, Geer, Hughes, & Strauss, 1961) described the sampling approach they used for *Boys in White,* a participant observation of a medical school. The chapter on design in Becker et al highlight-highlighted negative cases as a basis for the development of theory. Here is one of their statements.

We thought extensive coverage of both students and situations important. If we were to carry on our analysis by successive refinements of our theoretical models necessitated by the discovery of negative cases, we wanted to work in a way that would maximize our changes of discovering those new and unexpected phenomena whose assimilation into such models would enrich them and make them more faithful to the reality we had observed (p. 24).

Through negative case analysis, the originators of analytic induction sought to ensure that their findings not only account for patterns and variations but that their findings fit all of the cases examined. Researchers assume that findings are open to modification and even rejection as new information contradicts present formulations (Cressey, 1953; Gilgun, 1995; Lindesmith, 1947; Thomas & Znaniecki, 1918-20/1927; Znaniecki, 1934). Most researchers--not just those who have done analytic induction--widely acknowledge the open-ended nature of research findings.

Analytic inductions has its roots in the early writings of contributors to the Chicago School. Often, as is the case with other practices associated with the School, researchers typically did not name their approaches to theory development. They either consciously chose not to label their approaches or they experienced them as so self-evident or taken-for-granted that they did not do so. When they did name their approach to theory-building, the name was analytic induction.

Znaniecki (1934)'s thinking about sociology is particularly relevant to analytic induction and adds depth to the above discussion. He argued that sociology "can be nothing but a strictly *inductive* science, meaning that its foundation is "empirical data." He recognized the interplay between induction and deduction. He noted that knowledge development is characterized by a "ceaseless pulsation" that involves "movement from concrete reality to abstract concepts and from abstract concepts back to concrete reality" (p. 25). He had no name that I know of for this overarching set of processes.

Znaniecki (1934) also gave a role to intuition. He said

Scientific induction in its best form may be said to combine deduction and intuition into a higher dynamic unity (pp. 220-221).

He may have discussed what he meant by intuition but I could not find it. By intuition, he could have meant hunches, insights, and what researchers learn from their education and from their professional and personal experiences, as well as the influences of personal and professional values. Sometimes what researchers know is so deeply embedded that some forms of knowledge become intuitive, but this is an informed and educated intuition, readily modifiable through experience. Intuition is a piece of how I and many other people do research, just as intuition is part of what makes any practice possible (cf., Schön, 1983).

Znaniecki (1934) also advocated for the inclusion of variations and patterns in theory, and the creation of theories that are bold, simple, and comprehensive and that classify, organize, and systematize "a large mass of reliable empirical knowledge" (p. 257). To arrive at classification, sociologists are to "abstract" defining or "essential" from each datum.

Znaniecki (1934) did not address what guides researchers in the processes of abstraction. Logically, to be able to abstract concepts from "concrete instances" requires some sort of prior conceptualization, which suggest that induction is not "pure," but requires prior knowledge. Perhaps this is the role that Znaniecki gave to intuition.

Znaniecki (1934) also said throughout the doing of science, hypotheses, or "relative truths," must be substituted for "absolute truths" (p. 221). This last statement established the principle that theoretical formulations are not absolute but open to modifications as researchers identify new evidence.

Finally, Znaniecki (1934) recognized the significance of "contradictory instances" (p. 281) and "exceptions" (p. 306) when researchers develop theory. Whenever such contradictory instances occur, sociologists (presumably other scientists, too) then have two positive conflicting theories to choose from and the choice can be decided only by introducing new evidence—previously unknown or neglected elements, characters, connects or processes. Thus, further research is made indispensable, and out of it emerge new hypotheses and new problems (p. 282).

These thoughts are similar to Popper's (1969) definition of how science proceeds: from conjectures, to refutations, to reformulations which become the new conjectures, in an on-going process.

Criticisms of Analytic Induction

By the mid-twentieth century, analytic induction fell into disrepute over questions of causality and universality of findings. Some commentators (Goldenberg, 1993; Manning, 1982; Robinson, 1951; Vidich & Lyman, 2000) have dismissed analytic induction as non-viable because some have made such claims.

Some researchers made such claims. Becker (1953), for instance, discussed his theory of marijuana use as if it were causal. Both Cressey (1953) in his study of embezzling and Lindesmith (1947) in his study of opium addiction assumed that their hypotheses are causal, though they never clearly stated what they meant by this term. Lindesmith questioned whether, in order to establish causal relationships, effects are "necessary" or simply "understandable" when they follow alleged causes in time (p. 98). Cressey (1953) also briefly discussed cause in terms of concomitant variation, a idea from Mill's (1843) method of logic. Once he cited Mill, he made no further claims about the causal nature of his hypotheses, although as he described evidence for his hypothesis, he arguably was implying that it is causal. Sutherland was so adamant about the causal nature of hypotheses related to origins of crime that he may provoked a backlash against analytic induction, for which he was a powerful advocate. (See Laub & Sampson [1991]for a review of controversies that Sutherland stirred.)

Other users of analytic induction did not seek to develop causal hypotheses. Thomas and Znaniecki (1918-20/1927), who used analytic induction, made clear statements disavowing the invariant nature of their theories. As they noted, their research does not provide "any definitive and universally valid sociological truths" (pp, 340-341). Rather, they stated clearly that their work is suggestive and may point the way to future research. In this statement and related others, these researchers also disavowed any claims for universality.

Although Thomas and Znaniecki (1918-20/1927) were clear about the non-universal, contingent--that is linked to persons, setting, and time--nature of their findings, other researchers who practiced analytic induction could have introduced some confusion about claims to universality. Their statements are often contradictory. For example, Cressey (1953) stated in the introduction to his book that reformulation of hypotheses "continues until a universal relationship is established" (p. 16). Yet, Cressey also stated in the last paragraph of his book, "The fact that our first hypothesis was revised several times before the final generalization could be formulated implies that the final generalization also must be revised if negative cases appear" (p. 157).

Practitioners of analytic induction argue that they must state their hypotheses in universal terms in order for them to be falsifiable. Lindesmith (1947) drew upon Braithwaite (1960), Lewin (1935), and

Znaniecki (1934) to make this argument. He pointed out that because an hypothesis stated in universal terms "claims much, it is easily disproved if it is indeed false" (p. 19). Within the spirit of falsifiability, both Becker (1953) and Bott (1957/1971) stated they wrote their hypotheses in universal language so as to permit testing. In other words, hypotheses stated in universal terms contain a challenge--is this hypothesis applicable in other situations with different people at different historical times?

Grounded Theory

An initial conceptual framework is not part of grounded theory. In their first book-length publications, Glaser and Straus (1967) and Glaser (1978) expressed concern that when researchers start with a "preconception," they will force data into the model rather than to construct concepts and hypotheses based on their observations or what research respondents tell them. They believed that research based on prior theory was a way of attaining "a grounded modifying of theory" (Glaser & Strauss, 1967, p. 2).

Emergence of theory is a key idea in grounded theory, whose purposes to "Build rather than test theory" and to "Identify, develop and relate the concepts that are the building blocks of theory." (Strauss & Corbin, 1998, p. 13). According to Glaser (1992), researchers enter the field with "an open mind to the emergence of the subjects' problem" (p. 23), trust that an important issue will emerge, and a commitment "not to know" until it does (p. 24). In Glaser's view, many influences "core out" the central problem, such as the researchers' training, the location of the study, the nature of the research subjects, funding, among others. Glaser (2007) clearly stated that researchers should not do prior literature reviews before beginning their research.

Glaser and Strauss (1967) proposed grounded theory in response to the kinds of theory that they said was prevalent at the time: highly abstract, disconnected from relevant social problems, non-modifiable, and whose sources were not always clear. Like many other social scientists of their era, Glaser and Strauss were concerned about the "embarrassing gap between theory and empirical research" (p. vii). They believed that theory generation requires empirical research and must distance itself from non-empirical grand theorizing and impressionistic use of theory in research. "Furthermore, they wanted to counter what they saw as an over-emphasis on theory verification and a neglect of theory generation. In their own words

Currently, students are trained to master great-man theories and to test them in small ways, but hardly to question the theory as a whole in terms of its position or manner of generation. As a result many potentially creative students have limited themselves to puzzling out small problems bequeathed to them in big theories (p. 10).

Their views fit with their contemporaries, such as Merton and Lazarsfeld and were consistent with the views of Znaniecki (1934) and Thomas and Znaniecki (1918-1920/1927).

In their focus on theorizing grounded in data, they overlooked the idea that what researchers identify as emergent theory is based upon what researchers already know. Glaser (1978) for example advocated for theoretical sensitivity, meaning that the more knowledgeable researchers are about relevant theories, the better grounded theorists they are. Both Glaser and Strauss (1967) recognized that researchers are not tabula rasa but bring their own ideas into research questions. Over time, Strauss softened his stance on the place of prior research and theory in the conduct of grounded theory (cf. Strauss & Corbin, 1998), while Glaser (1992, 2007) remained committed to the earlier idea. For example, (Strauss, 1987) stated that researchers must have a conceptual framework for research proposals submitted to funding agencies.

Theoretical Sampling

Sampling in grounded theory is theoretical, which means that sampling depends on what researchers want to know next, and this usually involves a principle of comparison within and across cases (Corbin & Strauss, 2008; Glaser & Strauss, 1967; Strauss & Corbin, 1998). In doing theoretical sampling, researchers select a homogeneous sample on which to focus. They continue interviewing and/or observing this sample until they find that they are learning little or nothing that adds to their emerging understanding. They are at the point of theoretical saturation. Researchers then reflect on what comparisons they need to make next to deepen their understanding. These reflections lead to a decision of which kinds of cases to select next.

The basic questions that theoretical sampling addresses are the following (emphasis in original):
what groups or subgroups does one turn to *next* in data collection? And for *what* theoretical purposes? In short, how does the sociologist select multiple comparison groups? The possibilities of multiple comparisons are infinite, and so groups must be chosen according to theoretical criteria (Glaser & Strauss, 1967, p. 47).

The theoretical criteria are the theories that are emerging in the field.

Glaser and Strauss's (1967) contrast theoretical sampling with negative case analysis. They believed that the procedures of how researchers chose and examine negative cases are inadequate because researchers specify their unit of analysis early in the research process and do not do adequate comparisons. They hold up theoretical sampling as superior because it is linked to constant comparison. Actually, as the earlier discussion shows, these statements are misrepresentations. By definition, negative case analysis is a flexible method of sample selection and is similar to theoretical sampling in its flexibility and the use of theoretical considerations in the selection of cases.

Confusions

I find the writings of Strauss and colleagues about the roles of prior theory confusing and even contradictory. On the one hand, researchers are supposed to "discover" concepts and categories in the data and to eschew *a priori* assumptions and theory. On the other hand, they state that researchers are not *tabula rasa,* and they cannot therefore leave behind everything they know or, presumably, intuit. Furthermore, they must be theoretically sensitive if they are to "discover" what is in the data. It is anathema, however, to begin research with theory, which they seem to define as theory that is developed independently of the empirical world.

There appears to be no place in their thinking for research that begins with theory, tests it, elaborates it, and even rejects it and formulates a new working theory, based on analysis of interviews, observations, and documents. But, then again, this might not be so. What, after all, are researchers supposed to do with all the grounded theory and formal theory that has been generated in the last 40 years or so? After reading their writings for more than 20 years, I realized that they see a place for *a priori* theory, as long as it is grounded in the empirical world. They said

When the vital job of testing a newly generated theory begins, the evidence from which it was generated is quite likely to be forgotten or ignored. Now, the focus is on the new evidence that will be used for verifying only part of the theory. Furthermore, sociologists will find it worthwhile to risk a period in their careers in order to test grounded theories, since these theories are certain to be highly applicable to areas under study (pp. 28-29).

Elsewhere they said

Substantive theory in turn helps to generate new grounded formal theories and to reformulate previously established ones (p. 34).

Glaser and Strauss (1967) believed that only theory that is "highly applicable to areas under study" should be used to start new studies. In fact, Glaser and Strauss actually believe that researchers can begin grounded theory studies with a conceptual framework as long as it is linked to a proposed field of study. Interestingly, Glaser and Strauss cite an early study that Strauss and other colleagues completed (Strauss et al, 1964) and noted that this study began with "a framework of idea known as 'the sociology of work' and 'symbolic interactionism' (p. 157). In other parts of the book, too, Glaser and Strauss mention studies that begin with "great-man theories."

Deductive Qualitative Analysis

Deductive qualitative analysis (DQA) is an updating of analytic induction. Like AI, in DQA, researchers begin with a preliminary theory that can be composed of loosely formulated hunches based on personal or professional experience, formal hypotheses, or a set of ideas that form a model of how things work (Gilgun, 2005, 2009). Researchers may simply use theory to focus and guide their research or they may develop hypotheses and test them. If doing theory development, researchers test the theory on cases. When the theory does not fit findings, the theory is changed. If using theory as focus and guide, researchers typically find new dimensions of the phenomena of interest that the theory did not predict.

Also like AI, DQA that involves theory-testing uses negative case analysis, but bases the rationale for negative case analysis on Popper's (1969) ideas of conjectures, refutations, and reformulations. scientific method, which involves proposing a theory, testing it, and then revising it based on results of the test (Popper, 1969). In DQA, the initial conceptual framework and hypotheses are preliminary. The purpose of DQA is to come up with a better theory than researchers had constructed at the outset (Gilgun, 2005, 2009). Indeed, the production of new, more useful hypotheses is the goal of DQA. Researchers avoid finding what they intend to find through the conscious search for evidence that contradicts their emerging findings. This of course is negative case analysis.

My first exposure to analytic induction was Cressey's (1953) description of how he developed his theory of embezzlement, or the violation of financial trust. I was fascinated and delighted. He showed how he continually changed his theory to include new dimensions of how embezzlers account for their theft over the course of interviewing hundreds of them. Inspired by Cressey (1953) and the potential I saw in analytic induction, I did my own study using the procedures of analytic induction, where I tested and modified hypotheses about the moral discourse of incest perpetrators (Gilgun, 1995). I found analytic induction to be focused way of doing qualitative research that also allowed me to "discover" aspects of incest that were new to me, such as a discourse of love that some incest perpetrators articulated.

Differences

Within a short time, however, I began to see problems with the term *analytic induction*. First of all, analytic induction is as much deduction as induction. Briefly, induction in a pure sense may be impossible because, as Glaser and Strauss (1967) and many others have pointed out, researchers perceptions are not *tabula rasa* but have many preconceptions, only some of which are in awareness. Perhaps this is what Znaniecki (1934) meant when he referred to intuition as having a role in induction and deduction. The term *induction* is a misnomer.

A more loose definition of induction, however, fits some of the procedures of analytic induction. This loose definition would encompass the idea that researchers try to the extent possible to put aside their own points of view and listen and hear and notice what informants' words and actions could mean within their own contexts. From my own experience and from working with other researchers, however, researcher intuition and assumptions influence what researchers notice and overlook, an idea that Blumer (1969) discussed at length. Attempting to connect to others "imaginatively," partially pulls researchers out of their own perspectives and opens up the possibility of understanding how other people construct and experience their lives. Researchers, then, approximate induction.

The term *deduction* as Glaser and Strauss (1967) and contributors to the first Chicago School define it does not fit the procedures of analytic induction. These definitions presuppose a rigidity of deductive processes that involves syllogisms: A general statement, an observation that a particular case fits within the scope of the general statement, and the conclusion that the particular case has the characteristics of the general case.

The kind of deduction that underlies analytic induction, GT, and DQA, is flexible. Theory-guided research uses research and theory as guides to focus a study and to help illuminate what might be important.

Researchers typically seek to modify the theory in the course of data collection and analysis. The findings add to or modify existing research and theory. They are also transportable in the sense that researchers and practitioners use findings in new settings by testing the findings for fit and see whether they help illuminate these new situations.

Another reason for considering another term is that, as previously discussed, analytic induction has gone through a period of disrepute because some of its practitioners stated or implied that the theory that analytic induction produces is universal and causal, a view rejected by many others who did not do analytic induction (cf., See Goldenberg, 1993; Manning, 1982; Robinson, 1951; Vidich & Lyman, 2000). Glaser and Strauss (1967) rejected analytic induction as a viable way of generating theory not only because of its emphasis on "pre-existing conceptualizations" (p. 15) but also because of its alleged claims about causality and universality. Whatever the multiplicity of views that practitioners held of causality and universality, the term *analytic induction* appears to have a spoiled identity.

Finally, some qualitative researchers do theory-guided research. As one example, Abrams, Anderson-Nathe, & Aguilar (2009) used masculinities theory as a framework to analyze how adolescent boys in juvenile correctional facilities construct masculinity. Their use of theory illuminates and guides their research, and their findings not only add to and modify existing theory, but also have powerful implications for prevention and treatment. Another example of theory-guided qualitative research is the work of Padgett et al (2008). They applied a "new paradigm of recovery" that emphasizes positive social relationships" (p. 333) in qualitative interviews with dual-diagnosed homeless persons with substance abuse issues and serious mental illnesses. They found that positive social relationships have complex implications for recovery, a finding important to theory, policy, intervention, and prevention.

For the above-stated reasons, I coined the term *deductive qualitative analysis* to indicate a form of qualitative research that begins with a structure and that guides research processes, data collection, analysis, interpretation, and the writing up of results. This clarity of structure is different from how practitioners had presented analytic induction in the past. Also, DQA does not have baggage related to the terms *causality* and *universality*. Instead, I link it to the idea of tentativeness and the social construction of human understanding, points of view that are both consistent with some contemporary viewpoints and that also connect to the earlier writings of contributors to the Chicago School.

DQA as an Approach of Choice

DQA solves many of the problems that the writings of Strauss and colleagues have raised. Imposing theory or "forcing" "empirical data" into preconceived categories are serious issues. Negative case analysis guards against this by guiding researchers to seek evidence that disconfirms their emerging understandings as well as to notice evidence that supports their understandings. Therefore, in DQA researchers may abandon initial hypotheses completely and construct new ones if they do not fit cases under investigation, or they can continually modify working hypotheses to fit their interpretations of findings.

Other procedures besides negative case analysis help guard against imposition and forcing. These include having more than one person conceptualize the research, do data collection and analysis, and write up findings. In other words, bring multiple perspectives to bear on the entire research enterprise so that those involve can challenge each other as well as come to agreement when there is evidence to do so. Team analysis of qualitative data is traditional in the Chicago style of research, including GT, and in most other kinds of research as well. Graduate students routinely meet regularly to mutually aid each other in the analysis of qualitative data. There are many ways to guard against the dangers that concerned Glaser and Strauss (1967) and other methodologists of their time concerned with theory development.

Having more than one person to analyze and interpret findings also challenges researchers' "intuitive" understandings and predispositions. It is unlikely that individual researchers duplicate each others' intuitions and perspectives. They have, as Thomas and Znaniecki (1918-1920/1928) stated, their own standpoints that shape what they notice and how they interpret what they notice. This helps to create theory that takes multiple perspectives into account, including the perspectives of researchers and informants.

Another dilemma that GT poses and that DQA addresses is the desire of dissertation committee members to have evidence that Ph.D. students have mastered a substantive area that also will be the focus of their research. This often includes suggestions that faculty members have for student researchers about existing research and theory that will assist them in conceptualizing their research project. It is unreasonable to expect faculty members to hold back on this. Since the days of the "master-theorists," social scientists have developed many middle range theories and research that substantiate these theories. For many faculty, it is self-evident to expect students to base their research on "preconceived" theories and research.

In addition, the procedures of DQA are familiar to them. With DQA, researchers follow similar procedures to those associated with logico-deductive researcher and that is to derive hypotheses from theory and research. The next step is to test them qualitatively, or use the theory to guide the general focus of the research. Theory as guide aids in the development of interview questions, observational guidelines, and guidelines for document analysis. In addition, as mentioned, theory and prior research serves sensitizing functions, an idea that is familiar to researchers from many different traditions.

In short, faculty members want to know what students are going to do, they want assurances that students understand the situations they wish to research, and that students have the expertise to carry out what they want to do.

These concerns are similar to concerns of funders who reject proposals whose conceptualizations are fuzzy and whose procedures lack detail. Funders may not have concerns about imposing theory or forcing data, but because they have many other requirements that force researchers into a logico-deductive mode. They hold the purse strings qualitative researchers have little choice in terms of how they present their proposals (Gilgun, 2002).

Using the structured approach that DQA offers is part of a possible solution to the problem of how qualitative researchers can get funding. Twenty years ago or more, Strauss (1987) recognized the necessity of structure in proposal writing. He wrote, "No proposal should be written without preliminary data collection and analysis" (p. 286). Therefore, the open-endedness of GT procedures could serve as preliminary research. Strauss (1987) also recommended that researchers identify the codes that will be the basis of their analysis. Doing so clarifies the focus of the research. This suggests that practical considerations gave way to Strauss's commitment to entering the field with an openness as to what researchers might find. He was well aware of funders' demands for clarity of focus and procedures and researchers' competence to do the research. In fact, what Strauss (1987) recommended is similar to what DQA offers researchers who seek funding. Strauss's views here suggest that he could consider a study to be GT even when it begins with a conceptual framework and tentative hypotheses.

I often suggest to Ph.D. students that they do informational interviewing and preliminary studies in order to find a focus for their research, which is a kind of preliminary research. Then they are positioned to do a literature review, write reflexivity statements, develop hypotheses, and define concepts provisionally. They then have a set of preliminary codes and some feasible ideas about how to organize findings. These will be refined and elaborated upon in the course of doing the study, but they work continually within a flexible framework that allows them to be focused and also to use their time efficiently.

There are other advantages to having literature reviews in preparation for theory-guided/theory-testing qualitative research. They are a source of sensitizing concepts, which also serve as part of the coding scheme. Having *a priori* codes guides researchers to look for particular aspects of phenomena. For example, in a recent paper on how girls and women interpret experiences of child sexual (Gilgun & Sharma, 2010), research and theory on gender socialization of girls and notions from critical discourse analysis enhanced and made more efficient our own theory testing and theory elaboration. Without the literature review, we might have missed important aspects of how girl and women survivors interpret sexual abuse. It would have taken us much longer to identity those aspects that are important to the theory as we conceptualized it initially and as we developed it over the course of testing it.

In addition, the use of *a priori* codes may also decrease the time researchers require to do a qualitative study. With a focus from the beginning, researchers do not have to immerse themselves in the field to find their focus. They already have one. They will, however, immerse themselves in order to refine and elaborate their focus, or even to find one that is more suitable.

In some ways, having prior codes increases researchers' theoretical sensitivity, while negative case analysis and the help of others in data collection, analysis, and interpretation can assure some degree of fit between conceptualizations and the material on which the conceptualizations are based. Such procedures also ensure that researchers challenge their *a priori* codes, find unanticipated dimensions of these codes, reject some, and formulate new ones.

Literature reviews and pre-established codes also provide the structure that some researchers want and may even require to keep them focused. Some researchers more than other thrive on structure. There is still some ambiguity in doing DQA, but far less than in doing GT, where the possibilities for focus could be endless and hard to pin down. Prior codes provide an early focus, while also guiding theory testing.

Finally, DQA enhances report writing. APA style is an outgrowth of logico-deductive research. The structure of an APA style report fits with the sequence of events in which researchers engage in the course of doing the research. The report can be a more or less faithful account of what researchers did in the order in which they did it.

Similarities and Differences

As I reflect upon my experiences as a researcher, I realize that in every study, even when I thought I was doing GT, I had some sort of conceptual framework. For example, when I began my research on violence more than 25 years ago, my conceptual framework was gender role socialization and theories of homogamy. I chose this framework for a couple of reasons. First, I wanted to understand the life histories of men who had perpetrated child sexual abuse. I chose men because they are much more likely than women to perpetrate.

Second, I wanted a comparison group that was similar to the men but that was composed of persons who had not perpetrated child sexual abuse. Research told me that most women married to men who perpetrate child sexual abuse divorce. I reasoned that if wives stayed with husbands who perpetrated they must have something in common with their husbands. Thus, I interviewed perpetrators and their wives who had stayed with them after the disclosure of child sexual abuse. As part of my conceptual framework, I chose the theory of homogamy, which in many marriages persons marry because they share personal qualities and experiences.

Therefore, I had a conceptual framework with which I began a decades-long research project that I thought was a grounded theory study. I have read and advised many other qualitative studies that begin with conceptual frameworks that state they are doing grounded theory. Some of them did not test theory but instead used theory to guide their research. Did these researchers do an end run around the precepts of grounded theory? Did I? Did they do a form of deductive analysis? Did I?

Both appear to be the case. We did deductive research in the loose sense, and we also did grounded theory as Strauss and colleagues conceptualize it. As I have only realized in the writing of this paper, Glaser and Strauss (1967) have two different points of view about prior frameworks. They do a poor job of linking their polemics (their word) about "great-man theories" to how researchers actually can test grounded theories, theories linked to the empirical world, and even "great-man theories." They have no difficulty with the use of *a priori* theory that is not grounded theory to generate theory when the theory is linked to findings. They wrote that researchers cannot apply theory to findings until they see that the emerging theory has clear links to prior theory.

Putting aside their now outmoded thinking that theory somehow emerges rather than is construction and interpretation (Charmaz, 2006), the defining feature of GT appears to be the injunction that theory fit findings and that finding theory that fits requires going into the field and seeing what emerges. As discussed already, what "emerges" is a construction and what is constructed already is linked to a priori intuition, subliminal theoretical sensitivity, or other mysterious sources of what researchers notice and overlook.

It seems much simpler to do preliminary studies, find a focus, do a literature review, compose the reflexivity statement, etc, and then do the research. After all the years I have done this kind of research, these procedures are logical to me and even self-evident. Strauss and colleagues may have viewed their own writings and how they did research in similar ways, but I find their work to be full of terrific ideas and also contradictory, confusing, and sometimes ignorant of the shoulders on which they have stood.

Discussion

Strauss and colleagues, who originated GT, wanted researchers to discover new theory and not simply test "great-man" theories that they believed were disconnected from the concrete instances of phenomena as they exist in the empirical world. They wanted to promote the discovery of theory that was grounded in the empirical world. In this quest, the originators of GT were well within the traditions of the Chicago School.

Ironically, analytic induction with its procedure for developing theory called negative case analysis was already established in the Chicago School Strauss and Glaser created what appeared to be a new way to do theory generation. Like many other methodologists of their time, they rejected negative case analysis and analytic induction, but they also incorporated many ideas from AI without acknowledgement.

Strauss and colleagues kept many ideas about qualitative research alive and introduced many creative and important ideas. The downside of the work of Strauss and colleagues is the wide-spread belief and actual practice that researchers cannot begin their studies with conceptual frameworks and initial theories and hypotheses. Strauss and colleagues appeared to have qualified this principle, but the overall impression is they forthrightly discouraged the use of initial conceptual frameworks. What they meant is difficult to ferret out because their statements about the role of prior theory are confusing, disconnected, and contradictory.

Their polemics (their word) against testing received theory has been the dominant interpretation of what grounded theory is.

This common understanding of the GT approach to theory-building is problematic for PhD students who have to have the approval of dissertation committees to procedure, for researchers who seek funding for qualitative research, and for the time needed to do the research, not to mention that state of ambiguity that can last for quite a while until researchers find their focus and then begin to elaborate and dimensionalize their core concepts.

I coined the term *deductive qualitative analysis*, not to introduce more confusion into theory-building in the Chicago tradition, but to respond to issues that grounded theory raised and to do an end run around the spoiled identity that has invalidated analytic induction. DQA structures and focuses research, builds upon many of the assumptions that are part of GT, and is consistent with the GT approach to data analysis and interpretation, particularly the coding scheme and the emphasis on the identification and dimensionalization of core concepts.

In the final analysis, it does not matter what researchers call studies that begin with conceptual frameworks and whose research goals are to use frameworks as sensitizing concepts and/or test hypotheses derived from the frameworks so as to elaborate upon—or trim—theories. What is important is that researchers have access to clear descriptions about how to do this kind of work. I have read the writings of Strauss and colleagues long enough to finally realize that they do not do this. They roared so hard against the way some people use prior theory, however, that the *term grounded* theory may never have meanings that suggest beginning studies with conceptual frameworks.

References

Abrams, Laura S. Ben Anderson-Nathe, & Jemel P Aguilar (2008). Constructing masculinities in juvenile corrections. *Men & Masculinities, 11(1),* 22-41.

Becker, Howard S. (1953). Becoming a marihuana user. *The American Journal of Sociology, 59,* 235-242.

Becker, Howard S., Blanche Geer, Everett C. Hughes, & Anselm L. Strauss, A. L. (1961). *Boys in white: Student culture in medical school.* Chicago: University of Chicago Press.

Blumer, Herbert (1969). What is wrong with social theory? *Symbolic interactionism: Theory and method* (pp. 140-152). Berkeley: University of California Press. First paperback printing, 1986. Originally published in the *American Sociological Review* in 1954.

Bodgan, Robert C. & Sari Knopp Biklen (2007). *Qualitative research for education: An introduction to theories and methods* (5th ed. Boston: Pearson.

Bott, Elizabeth (1957). *Family and social network.* New York: Free Press. Second edition published in 1971.

Bulmer, Martin (1984). *The Chicago School of Sociology: Institutionalization, diversity, and the rise of sociological research.* Chicago: University of Chicago Press.

Bryant, Antony & Kathy Charmaz (Eds). (2007). *The Sage Handbook of grounded theory.* Thousand Oaks, CA: Sage.

Charmaz, Kathy (2006). *Constructing grounded theory: A practical guide through qualitative analysis.* Thousand Oaks, CA: Sage.

Corbin, Juliet (1991). Anselm Strauss: An intellectual biography. In David R. Maines (Ed.). *Social organization and social process: Essays in honor of Anselm Strauss* (pp. 17-42). New York: Aldine.

Cressey, Donald R. (1953). *Other people's money.* Belmont, CA: Wadsworth.

Gilgun, J. F. (1999). Methodological pluralism and qualitative family research. In S. K. Steinmetz, M. B. Sussman, & G. W. Peterson (Eds.), *Handbook of marriage and the family* (2nd ed.)(pp. 219 –261). New York: Plenum.

Gilgun, Jane F. (1995). We shared something special: The moral discourse of incest perpetrators. *Journal of Marriage and the Family, 57*, 265-281.

Gilgun, Jane F. (2002). Conjectures and refutations: Governmental funding and qualitative research. *Qualitative Social Work, 1(3),* 359-375.

Gilgun, Jane F. (2005). Qualitative research and family psychology. *Journal of Family Psychology,19(1),* 40-50.

Gilgun, Jane F. (2009). Methods for enhancing theory and knowledge about problems, policies, and practice. In Katherine Briar, Joan Orme, Roy Ruckdeschel, & Ian Shaw, *The Sage handbook of social work research* (pp. 281-297). Thousand Oaks, CA: Sage.

Glaser, Barney (2007). Doing formal theory. In Antony Bryant, & Kathy Charmaz (Eds). The *Sage handbook of grounded theory* (pp. 97-113).Thousand Oaks, CA: Sage.

Glaser, Barney (1992). *Basics of grounded theory analysis: Emergence vs. forcing.* Mill Valley, CA: Sociology Press.

Glaser, Barney (1978). *Theoretical sensitivity.* Mill Valley, CA: Sociology Press.

Goldenberg, Sheldon (1993). Analytic induction revisited. *Canadian Journal of Sociology, 18(2)*, 161-176.

Laub, John H., & Robert J. Sampson (1991). The Sutherland-Glueck debate: On the sociology of criminological knowledge. *American Journal of Sociology, 96(6)*, 1402-1440.

Lewin, Kurt (1935). *A dynamic theory of personality*. New York: McGraw-Hill.

Lindesmith, Alfred (1947). *Opiate addictions*. Bloomington, IN: Principia.

Lindesmith, Alfred (1968). *Addiction and opiates*. Chicago: Aldine.

.Manning, Peter K. (1982). Analytic induction. In Robert B. Smith & Peter K. Manning (Eds.), *Qualitative methods, Vol. II, of Handbook of Social Sciences* (pp. 273-302). Cambridge, MA: Ballinger.

Mill, John Stuart (1843). *A system of logic*. New York: Harper.

Padgett, Deborah K., Been Henwood, Courtney Abrams, & Robert E. Drake (2008). Social relationships among persons who have experienced serious mental illness, substance abuse, and homelessness: Implications for Recovery *American Journal of Orthopsychiatry, 7(3)*, 333–339

Robinson, William S. (1951). The logical structure of analytic induction. *American Sociological Review, 16*, 812-818.

Strauss, Anselm L. (1987). *Qualitative analysis for social scientists*. New York: Cambridge University Press.

Strauss, Anselm L. (1991). A personal history of the development of grounded theory. *Qualitative Family Research, 5(2)*, 1-2.

Strauss, Anselm, & Juliet Corbin (1998). *Basics of qualitative research: Techniques and procedures for developing grounded theory* (2nd ed.). Thousand Oaks, CA: Sage.

Strauss, Anselm, & Juliet Corbin (Eds). (1997). *Grounded theory in practice*. Thousand Oaks, CA: Sage.

Strauss, Anselm, Leonard. Schatzman, Rue Bucher, Danuta Ehrlich, & Marvin Sabshin (l964). *Psychiatric ideologies and institutions*. New York: Free Press.

Sutherland, Edwin H. (1937). *The professional thief*. Chicago: University of Chicago Press.

Thomas, W. I., & Florian Znaniecki. (1918-1920/1927). *The Polish peasant in Europe and America*, Vol. 1-2. New York: Knopf. First published in 1918-1920.

Znaniecki, F. (1934). *The method of sociology*. New York: Farrar & Rinehart.

13

METHODS FOR ENHANCING THEORY AND KNOWLEDGE ABOUT PROBLEMS, POLICY, AND PRACTICE

First published as Gilgun, Jane F. (2010). Methods for enhancing theory and knowledge about problems, policies, and practice. In Katherine Briar, Joan Orme, Roy Ruckdeschel, & Ian Shaw, The Sage handbook of social work research *(pp. 281-297). Thousand Oaks, CA: Sage.*

ANYONE LOOKING for examples of methods that enhance theory and knowledge about problems and policies need look no further than the work of Selma Fraiberg, a US social worker who is the founding figure in the infant mental health movement (Shapiro, 2008), and John Bowlby, a British psychoanalyst, who is a prime figure in the development of attachment theory (Bretherton, 1992). Both did their seminal work in the mid to late twentieth century. Both translated their theory and knowledge into programs and policies. Their work is carried out today in a wide range of researcher projects, policy initiatives, and prevention and intervention programs (See Lederman, Osofsky, & Katz, 2007; Lieberman, 2007; Shirilla & Weatherson, 2002; Sroufe, Egeland, Carlson, & Collins, 2005).

Their methods were roughly similar, based primarily upon observations of infants and young children in interactions with their parents that they often filmed for further study, in conjunction with interviews with parents, creative thinking about their observations, thinking that they fostered through on-going reading and consultation with researchers, theorists, and practitioners from many different disciplines.

The theory and knowledge on which Fraiberg and Bowlby both drew included psychoanalytic theory, cognitive psychology, and the work of Renee Spitz (Bretherton, 1992; Shirilla & Weatherston, 2002; Sroufe, Egeland, Carlson, & Collins, 2005). In addition, Bowlby incorporated ideas from ethological theory and Fraiberg used attachment theory as Bowlby developed it and as others elaborated upon it.

John Roberston, a social worker, made an enormous contribution to attachment theory, when, as part of Bowlby's research team, he filmed his observations of parent-child interactions, a method that transformed understandings of the significance of early attachment relationships for human development (Bretherton, 1992). Observation remains the key method in infant mental health and attachment-based research and applied programs to this day (Shapiro, 2008; Shirilla & Weatherson, 2002; Sroufe, Egeland, Carlson, & Collins, 2005).

Purpose and Definitions

The purpose of this chapter is to describe and illustrate methods that generate theory and knowledge about problems, and policy and practice By "methods" I mean the actual procedures in which social workers and members of allied disciplines engage as they produce theory and knowledge. I will not discuss methodology to any degree. Methodologies are concerned with the epistemologies and ontologies of perspectives on social phenomena such as feminism, phenomenology, and constructivism. These perspectives fit social work well, but these topics are not part of the present chapter.

By "problems" I mean the multiple, complicated social issues that social workers encounter in their everyday practice, which can be direct practice, program development, administration, advocacy, and policy formulation and implementation. I use "social issues" interchangeably with "problems." By "policies" I mean strategies and principles that are applied to intervention programs, which can be structured formal protocols, a more loosely-defined set of interventions that particular programs implement, and the one-on-one interactions that occur between service providers, collaborators, and service users.

Theories are sets of transportable sets of ideas that social workers can apply to particular cases or situations, whether these situations involve individuals, families, groups, or advocacy efforts. Concepts and their relationship compose theory. Theories illuminate social processes and help observers notice aspects of phenomena they might otherwise have overlooked.

"Knowledge" in this chapter refers to information and understandings that researchers and practitioners develop from their professional practices as well as from their personal and professional values and personal experiences. This store of information from which social workers draw includes the contributions of advocates of various sorts, service user perspectives, and the personal testimonies and narratives of individuals throughout the world who also contribute to social work's base of information. These sources are inextricable parts of social work's store of information.

In my efforts to describe methods that generate theory and knowledge, I will present examples of methods that social workers apply to the multiple domains of social work. These examples will demonstrate methods that contribute to understanding social issues (problems), provides direction for social change (policy, programs, and interventions), and contributes to the process and outcome evaluations of interventions. I intend to highlight knowledge and theory that I believe direct practitioners, program developers, and policy makers find useful, and I will point out the characteristics of studies that make translation to the field difficult if not impossible. Occasionally I use examples from allied disciplines, but for the most part the examples are from social work.

In addition, I will address other methods that generate knowledge besides formal research methods. These methods include the collective wisdom of practitioners and the testimony and knowledge claims of person involved in social movements, including knowledge that the International Federation of Social Workers calls *indigenous* (IFSW, 2008). Such knowledge becomes part of practice and policy through oral transmission and narratives on practice. Some researchers and policy makers believe that these are not legitimate sources of knowledge because they do not adhere to their idea of what constitutes knowledge and science. From a pragmatic point of view, these sources of knowledge are a major and inextricable part of social work practice and therefore any review of methods for theory and knowledge building would be incomplete if they are ignored.

Besides common sense and pragmatism, the rationale for the inclusion of these diverse sources of knowledge as contributors to social work knowledge base is the view that the evidence base of practice is composed of four cornerstones. These cornerstones are research and theory, practice wisdom, service users' perspectives, and practitioners personal experiences and personal and professional values (Gilgun, 2005c). The ideas of reflective practice are infused in this understanding of evidence-based practice. The implications of this definition of evidence-based practice are only at their beginning stages of exploration. This present chapter is a step in that direction.

A Complicated Enterprise

The practice of social work is complicated, characterized not only by multiple domains in which social workers operate, but also by ecological perspectives that direct attention to persons, environments of all sorts, and the interactions between them. In addition, a set of core values and ethical principles guide social work and social work has a role in almost any setting where problematic human situations exist (IFSW, 2008). Because social work is an action-based discipline, social workers are supposed to do something to improve problematic situations through one-on-one work, program development, community development, advocacy, and policy formulation. Given these ecological perspectives and multiple roles, social workers must understand and intervene on a wide range of systems, from the individual level to families, groups, neighborhoods, states, counties, provinces, and countries.

Values that social work espouses include social and economic justice, autonomy or freedom of choice, and freedom to pursue personal goals without interference as long as actions meant to achieve these goals do not infringe on the rights of others. Social workers see a clear ethical, empowerment, and anti-oppression agenda in these values (cf., IFSW, 2008; Stier, 2006).

Research is one several practices in which social workers engage. If social work research is to be consistent with what social work claims to be, then social workers will create theory and knowledge that covers complex sets of domain, that is based on values, and that respects ethical dimensions of knowledge generation. No one research method and no one research project can respond to these complex knowledge demands. Instead, social work by its nature requires a division of tasks in its approaches to knowledge development. Methodological pluralism is key to social work's effective response to demands for many types of knowledge. This means that social work knowledge can come from many different sources that use a variety of methods.

Further complicating the social work theory and knowledge-building enterprise are competing perspectives on what constitutes acceptable knowledge about problems, policies, and programs. Controversies within the evidence-based practice movement color and shape what constitutes "evidence" and "best research evidence" and which methods contribute the best evidence for practice. Some researchers and funders appear to believe that randomized clinical trials (RCTs) are at the top of a research hierarchy and constitute a "gold standard," while qualitative research such as case studies are at the bottom (Soydan, 2008; Strauss, Richardson, Glasziou, & Haynes, 2005).

Those who place testing of interventions at the top of a hierarchy are focused only on intervention, and they are inattentive to the knowledge needed to understand social problems that include service users' situations, the knowledge required to build interventions in the first place, and the knowledge needed to understand how applied programs work. Descriptive research is an essential component of social work's knowledge base, in addition to results of controlled experiments that test the efficacy and effectiveness of intervention programs (Gilgun, 2005a). Knowledge of social issues is required to inform social action, whether these actions are interventions, programs, advocacy, or policies.

Signs of a thawing of adherence to the RCT as a "gold" standard research method has appeared in recent writings on evidence based practice. Some authors have expanded their understandings to include service provider expertise and the preferences, wants, and values of service users (APA Task Force, 2006; Marsh, Fisher, Mathers, & Fish, 2005; Soydan, 2008). Others add a fourth dimension, which is reflective practice, where personal and professional values and personal experience become part of the knowledge base that practitioners may apply to individual cases and to policy and program development and evaluation (Gilgun, 2005c). Service providers often have their own definition of evidence which is what they learn as they provide services; this knowledge is incorporated into the process of interacting with service users (Gilgun, 2005a).

Many believe that the situation to be understood suggests the appropriate research method. Situations to be researched in applied disciplines can include not only controlled interventions such as experiments and quasi-experiments that test the efficacy and effectiveness of interventions, but also the origins, development, and course of social issues and the perspectives of service users, social workers, policy makers, and other potential users of research (APA Task Force, 2006; Hawkins, 2006). Furthermore, some believe that social work practitioners contribute to the knowledge base on social issues and interventions through case notes, personal narratives, and oral transmission by way of supervision, case consultation, and workshops and other trainings (Gilgun, 2005a, 2005c; Shaw, 2005; Trevithick, 2008). This is consistent with the definition of EBP that includes service provider expertise, values, and personal experience as part of EBP.

Finally, social work researchers, practitioners, policy makers, and program developers use research and theory that other disciplines generate. Although some believe this undermines social work's status, identity, and mission, others find that multi-disciplinary perspectives enrich social work's knowledge base (Cnaan & Dichter, 2008). For example, research on resilience, attachment, cognitive science, and cognitive-behavioral therapy are examples of research and practice theory developed in other disciplines that social workers have adapted for our own use.

As applied research, social work research and the knowledge are meant to be used. In fact, some argue that the usefulness of research is one of the indicators of the quality of social work research (Gilgun, 2004). In order to produce such research, social worker researchers must know what kinds of research potential users find useful. This requires that researchers take potential users' perspectives into account when doing their work. These potential users include practitioners in the field, administrators, policy makers, and, at times, the general public.

A powerful argument for the usefulness of research as an indicator of quality is the long-standing finding that direct service providers do not have a coherent research and theory base for their practice. (See Emilsson, 2005 and Osmond & O'Connor, 2006, for reviews.) The goal of the evidence-based practice movement in social work is to educate direct practitioners to use the best research evidence in their practice (Gilgun, 2005c; Soydan, 2007). A serious task for social work researchers, therefore, is to discover what kinds of research social workers find useful and what facilitates or impedes their use of research. Social workers already draw upon many other sources of knowledge for their practice besides research.

Governmental agencies and private foundations fund much social work research and thus shape research agendas, including the methods researchers use to generate theory and knowledge. Some forms of knowledge production, however, are unfunded. Knowledge arising from unfunded research can be fundamental to the understanding of social problems, and knowledge from unfunded sources is an important part of the social work knowledge base.

Organizing Frameworks

The complexity of the kinds of theories and knowledge that social work requires leads to the necessity of developing organizing frameworks. One way to organize these knowledge requirements is to consider phases of social work practice and then to examine research? methods that can contribute knowledge and theory that will support social work's efforts. Although there are many ways to represent the phases of practice, I will use the most simple: assessment, program development, "street-level" interventions, evaluation of process, and evaluation of outcome.

I begin this discussion of methods with the presentation of conceptual framework that describes four general ways of generating and testing theory. I then discuss a series of methods and provide examples of how they operate in the generation of descriptive information and information for intervention effectiveness and efficacy. Finally, I give examples of methods for creating interventions and assessment and evaluation tools for practice. Such efforts require theory and knowledge on problems, policies, and effective interventions.

I will not spend much if any time on well-known methods, such as telephone surveys, but will focus on those methods that have great promise but are not widely used in social work. Some of these methods may be controversial.

The variety of research methods that social workers are used to generate theory and knowledge for social worker probably cannot be pinned down definitively. Knowledge requirements change depending upon individual and shared perspectives and the kinds of social issues that are prominent at any given time.

Methods for Theory Development

In the development of theory, social work researchersers have four broad choices. They can enter the field with no preformulated theories or hypotheses to test and the goal of developing them, they can enter the field with preformulated theories to test, they can do a combination of the first two (Gilgun, 2007), or they can engage in theory-guided research and direct practice that may result in descriptions or in theoretical statements and categories.

Glaser and Strauss (1967) named the first approach *grounded theory*, which in reality is a fundamental way of thinking that individuals have always done and will continue to do so. An example of grounded theory research in social work is Giles' and Cureen's (2007) research on phases of growth of New Zealand women who have experienced abuse. Researchers from the Chicago School of Sociology, named the second approach *analytic induction* (Becker, Geer, Hughes, & Strauss, 1961; Gilgun, 1995, 2005c, 2007). Like grounded theory, the term *analytic induction* simply names a process that is fundamental to human judgment and thinking. I, probably along with others of whom I am unaware, have named the third approach This has been named the *deductive qualitative analysis* (Gilgun, 2005b, 2007), yet another way of thinking about the world that human beings have always done and will continue to do.

Theory-guided research means that researchers and practitioners use theory to help them to focus and manage their inquiries, but their goals are not necessarily to develop theory further, but to develop deeper understandings of social issues and problems. Their products can be descriptions of social issues and/or interventions, as well as theoretical statements and categories.

In the first approach, individuals notice what their prior concepts help them to notice. Any conceptual thinking or theorizing that they do is based upon prior theory or other ideas. In research, direct practice, policy formulation, and program development, social workers may and usually do consult others to test their ideas as well as add to them, and they often consult relevant research and theory for the same reasons.

In the second approach, individuals have exerted effort to formulate hypotheses that can come from research, theory, and personal and professional experience. Typically, the hypotheses are relatively informal and the concepts that compose the hypotheses are defined in open-ended ways. Individuals test these hypotheses explicitly, whether in direct practice, in formal research projects, or in everyday life. If they are flexible thinkers, they use explicit prior theories to alert them to what is significant in their observations and thus the research is theory-guided, but they also look for data that contradict their initial theorizing. In fact, in analytic induction, researchers' purpose is to find contradictory evidence, or negative cases, in order to elaborate upon or even refute their initial hypotheses (Cressey, 1953; Gilgun, 2007).

The originators and users of this approach considered these procedures inductive. I did, too, for a long time (See Gilgun, 2005b.), but I have changed my mind for two reasons. First, research that begins with hypotheses is automatically deductive because deduction begins with a premise, which theory and hypotheses are. Second, I now believe that induction is impossible, simply because no one is a blank slate. We bring prior conceptions with us, whether or not we have formally states theories and assumptions. These prior understandings influence what we notice and how we interpret what we notice.

Thus, in the third approach, individuals construct hypotheses from multiple sources, including related research and theory and personal and professional experience and values. Like analytic induction, deductive qualitative analysis requires a continual effort to modify, undermine, and refute initial and emerging theoretical understandings.

In the fourth approach, researchers and practitioners develop research questions informed typically by research and theory and by personal and professional experience and values. The questions focus their research, and their goal, logically enough, is to answer the research questions. There are many examples of this kind of research, including Keeling's and Piercy's (2007) qualitative internet-based survey on the views of an international group of family therapists on power, gender, and culture in marriage. Keeling and Percy call their work analytic induction, as do a few other researchers, but since they do not have stated hypotheses to test, their studies do not qualify as analytic induction. They end with a set of conceptual categories and statements that qualify as theoretical statements or hypotheses that can be transported for use and tested for fit in other situations.

For all four approaches, individuals who are flexible thinkers change their theories when their interpretations warrant change. Inflexible thinkers do not change their ideas, and they are at risk to misinterpret phenomena, overlook important dimensions of the phenomena of interest, and force data into categories that are inappropriate rather than create new categories.

These four broad approaches are applicable to theorizing on data from direct practice, from formal research projects, and from informal everyday interactions. Individuals who theorize are not blank slates, but bring with them a whole host of ideas, assumptions, and biases based upon their personal and professional experience and their formal education. Glaser (1978) used the term *theoretical sensitivity* to describe capacities to use theory effectively in the interpretation of data. Whatever "theories" and other assumptions that we carry with us helps us to make sense of whatever data we consider. In this kind of theorizing then, theory is the formulation of ideas about what data connote.

At their best, all four approaches recognize that individuals have blind spots and biases that shape what they notice and how they interpret what they notice. It makes sense, then, that individuals who engage in theory development and test do a kind of reflective practice, which some researchers call reflexivity. Keeling and Piercy (2007) included a brief reflexivity statement in their research report. This may involve engagement in on-going discussions with others on their emerging interpretations and on personal meanings and emotions. Reflexivity or reflective practice can also involve journal keeping and memo writing that involves reflections on personal and professional meanings.

These three approaches are more typically used for the analysis of qualitative data (words and other texts), but individuals can base their theorizing on numerical, quantitative data as well. When doing hypothesis testing that depends upon quantitative results, researchers usually call their approach logico-deductive research or hypothesis-testing research.

I will use these three approaches to theory enhancement and development in the discussion to follow on methods that enhance theory and knowledge about problems and polices. I make copious use of examples to show how these researchers and practitioners use these methods.

Surveys and Questionnaires

Surveys are a form of questionnaire that may be administered in-person, by phone, or via the internet. Samples typically are selected through a random process. Surveys can provide information about the incidence, prevalence, and correlates of social problems. Questionnaires are used in direct practice in program development and evaluation. They are a relatively easy way to tap into perspectives of potential and actual service users and can, therefore, can contribute information that becomes important building blocks of assessments and interventions. They can be helpful in needs assessments and participatory action research (PAR) when researchers and advocates want to understand social issues from multiple points of view and possible ways to deal effectively with these issues (McTaggart, 1997; Sung-Chang & Yuen-Tsang, 2008). In evaluation of programs and direct practice interventions, questionnaires can provide information about effects and meanings of these interventions.

Surveys

Phone, internet, and in-person surveys provide information on social issues and interventions. Governmental agencies and local authorities often commission surveys that establish the prevalence of social issues. For example The Office of National Statistics in the United Kingdom commissioned a survey on the mental health issues of young people between the ages of five and 17 under the care of local authorizes. They found that 45% of these young people had mental disorders (Office of National Statistics, 2003). The federal government in the United States commissions many studies, such as the survey research of Straus and associates (Straus, Gelles, & Steinmetz, 1980, 2006) establish the incidence and correlates of family violence, research that major impact on the provision of social services in many countries.

Internationally, in a study of violence against children, the United Nations compiled administrative data, surveyed 138 countries on their approaches to violence against children, did field visits to 18 different countries, and convened nine regional conferences that included all parts of the world. An average of 350 people attended these conferences that heard testimony from a range of knowledgeable persons, including children, practitioners, and policy makers. This multi-method approach to establishing the prevalence, correlates, and responses to violence against children resulted in a report that has had wide-circulation (Penheiro, 2005) and has a world-wide influence on prevention programs and services to children and families.

Universities throughout the world provide internet survey software to faculty and increasing numbers of researchers rely upon internet-based surveys. An example is the work of Tower and Krasner (2006) who conducted an internet-based survey on more than 1,100 couples to study the relationship between marital closeness and symptoms of depression. Respondents were predominantly white and middle or upper middle class from all over the United States. Research using a translated version of the survey instrument was done in French and Vietnamese, and Spanish, Hebrew, and Korean versions are available.

Internet-based surveys are cost-effective, may cut down on response sets because respondents complete the survey privately, and allow respondents to fill out the survey at their own pace and at times convenient to them (Nikken, Jansz, & Schouwstra,2007). They also can be used to do cross-national studies, which has many advantages, including finding out whether social issues such as mental and physical health concerns have causes and correlates in common across settings and cultures. With such information, international bodies of researchers, advocates, and policy makers can fund international programs meant to have positive impacts on these conditions.

Many of the challenges of internet-based surveys are similar to those of telephone and in-person surveys, such as whether respondents are truthful, but others are unique to internet-based inquiry. Without appropriate safeguards, internet surveys run the risk of respondents filling out surveys more than once. Safeguards can be put in place by first identifying individuals willing to participate in the survey and doing a screening. Then researchers e-mail willing respondents with the location of the survey and the password to enter the site. Individual passwords are assigned to safeguard against the possibility of individuals filling out multiple surveys. More vexing are incompatibilities in software and servers that may make the surveys inaccessible to participants in international contexts (Keeling & Piercy, 2007).

Another challenge of internet-based surveys is sample bias. Participation in these surveys is restricted to persons who have access to the internet. Poor people in countries throughout the world, therefore, cannot participate. This is an issue similar to that of telephone interviews, where the poor may not have telephones and many no longer have land lines but mobile phones. The numbers for mobile phones are not available publicly.

Internet-based surveys are of recent vintage. Other innovations in survey research are in approaches to data analysis. Jenson (2008) pointed out what he considers to be advances in quantitative techniques for the analysis of complex data. He highlighted multi-level and hierarchical techniques as well as new approaches to handling missing data and for estimating statistical power. He stated that funding for research may depend upon the level of sophistication of researchers' proposed analysis plan. He does not discuss, however, how research using these complex analytic strategies are translated into findings that front-line service providers, program managers, and policy makers find useful. Since the usefulness of knowledge relevant to social work is of high concern, the benefits of quantitative advances could be weighed against how the findings can be used.

Survey Data and Theory Development

Surveys can also provide information about the workings of social policy and programs. Keeling's and Piercy's (2007) internet-based qualitative survey, for example, developed theories on how therapists in several different countries viewed and worked with issues related to gender, power, and culture. Edleson's (1999) review of 35 primarily survey research studies published in a recent 25-year period on the overlap between child maltreatment and woman battering is a highly influential piece of scholarship. He found that service providers from the two sectors have difficulties in collaboration. Child welfare agencies were not attending well to issues related to women battering, and services to women who were survivors of intimate partner violence often overlooked effects on children. This review article alerted policy makers, program developers, and direct practitioners about a serious defect in the provision of services to families where violence has occurred. This one review article has influenced policies and programs internationally.

Through his analysis of the survey research of others and his own research and professional knowledge, Edleson (1999) developed theory about gaps in services, although he did not call his conclusions theory. If theory can be defined as abstractions from more concrete indicators and also as abstract statements of relationships, then this finding qualifies as a theoretical statement. Furthermore, his work can be classified as theory-guided because he had extensive practice and research experience in the field of family violence and had already observed and documented the gaps in services he investigated in his review article. His conclusion that indeed the gap exists and has serious consequences qualifies as a theory because he extracted higher order concepts from lower order data.

Questionnaires

Questionnaires increase knowledge of social issues and can foster the development and evaluation of policies and programs and contribute to the evaluation of one-on-one interactions. Needs assessments, often done within a participatory action research (PAR) framework, are particularly helpful in policy formulation and program development. Participatory action research collects survey and questionnaire information—and observational and archival information typically--for the purpose of understanding social issues typically from the points of view of those affect and for advocacy and program development. This approach includes potential service users in the design, analysis, and interpretation of the survey, in advocacy efforts, and then in program development. By design, PAR integrates the perspectives of potential users of services into their efforts (McTaggart, 1997). As Denzin (1989) pointed out many years ago, applied programs are doomed to fail if the perspectives of potential services users are not taken into account.

In an action research project, Sung-Chang & Yeung-Tsang (2008) described a community survey participants conducted in order to identify a business the participants could establish that would meet the needs of the community. After extensive interviews, they chose to establish a summer camp for migrant children so as to provide a kind of child care for families where parents worked. Learning about community needs empowered and emboldened them and they managed the difficult tasks of finding funding for this service.

Questionnaires can be helpful in generating knowledge about direct practice, such as how services users experience the intervention and suggestions they have for improving services. The Criminal Justice Client Evaluation of Self and Treatment (CJ CEST) (Garner et al, 2007) is an example of a questionnaire that seeks to understand service users perceptions of their own treatment issues and of their own processes as they experience a prison-based treatment program. Questionnaires are important in the evaluation of interventions.

Mokuau et al (2008) used a variety of methods including questionnaires to do a formative evaluate a program for Hawaiian families of women with breast cancer. Other methods included informal interviews with service users and standardized instruments. Formative evaluations are done in order to understand how programs work and what might help them to work better.

The findings from such questionnaires become part of a knowledge base that documents what policies and programs might serve the social good, what can be done to improve them, and what new polices and programs are needed.

In-Depth, Open-Ended Interviews

In-depth, open-ended interviews can provide detailed information about the development, course, and present circumstances of problematic situations that human beings experience, as well as build knowledge about service users' and practitioners' experiences of policies, programs, and one-on-one interactions. Such information can provide a solid foundation for policy initiatives and for the development and re-design of intervention projects. Material from open-ended interviews provides a good basis for theorizing.

Coy (2008) conducted unstructured life history interviews with young women with a history of local authority care and who engaged in prostitution. Her review of available research showed that findings of surveys and ethnographies an association between young women being in care and engaging in prostitution. She had observed this association while in practice. She found that available research and theory did not provide knowledge on which to base day-to-day therapeutic social service activities with these young women. Services to these young women were largely ineffective.

Coy (2008) reasoned that in-depth interviews would provide information on why these young women are vulnerable to selling sex and how their involvement in this work might be prevented. The impetus for her research was her realization that she and her co-workers at a residential facility had very little knowledge on which to base their work with vulnerable girls.

Coy's (2008) work has many of the characteristics of an ideal social work research project because she used theory, previous research findings, and prior knowledge, including her own practice experience, to design her research and to interpret findings. She conducted the interviews in an open-ended way in order to allow the respondents to tell their stories in their own ways. They described their lives before going into care, their lives in care, and then their lives as sex workers. The theory she used to design her study and interpret findings included Bourdieu's notion of habitus and Goffman's notion of stigma.

Coy (2008) did not test hypotheses in her research, nor did she state that she was seeking to develop theory, but she did. She also used theory that others had formulated and her own theory based on her practice experience to both guide and interpret her findings. Her method fits into a loose definition of deductive research because of her use of prior theory. Because she did qualitative research, her method can be described as deductive qualitative analysis, as discussed earlier (See, Gilgun, 2005b).

The theory she produced was in the form of a conceptual framework that she grounded in the interview data, her own professional experience, and in theoretical concepts and that showed the transitions that the young women experienced as they moved from their families, to care, and then out of care into prostitution. Their self-concept and sense of self-worth while with their families was one of degradation and worthlessness because they felt unloved, discounted, and abandoned. Their descriptions showed that their time in care replicated their experiences in their families. The life of a prostitute fit with their self-concepts and sense of worthlessness and at times also provided a sense of belonging with their peers.

Studies such as Coy's (2008) not only theorize about a significant social issue, but also provide in-depth descriptions and show the effects of social policies and programs on service users. The implications for policy and practice are obvious. Policy makers and administrators entrusted with program development must build policies and programs that can transform stigmatized, degraded identities into identities of positive self-regard. Such interventions as far as I know have yet to be constructed. If they are, they would be subject to process and outcome evaluations that describe processes of change or lack of change as well as indicators of hoped-for outcomes.

Mancini's (2007) semi-structured interviews with persons with psychiatric illnesses is an excellent example of theory-building research. Through his analysis, Mancini developed a theory of recovery from serious psychiatric disability based on the notion of self-efficacy. The dimensions of this theory include supportive relationships that were collaborative partnerships, peer support from other persons with histories of psychiatric disabilities and who were in recovery, experiences of mastery of difficulty tasks and situations, and a variety of ways to maintain emotional equilibrium, including exercise, hobbies, and a healthy life style. Mancini showed how his findings are linked to Bandura's theory of self-efficacy and theory about informed choice and self-determination.

Mancini (2007) engaged in a long discussion about how this theory could be applied to work with persons with psychiatric disabilities. In its clarity and clear support not only in the stories of the persons he interviewed but also in the theory he applied to help interpret his findings, Mancini's theory of self-efficacy in work with psychiatric patients is a model for theory-building research.

A final note on open-ended interviews is their potential importance in randomized clinical trials. As Floersch (2003) points out, the subjective experiences and perspectives of youth must be taken into account when they take psychotropic medications. Of course, the perspectives and experiences of anyone participating in RTCs must be addressed. If not, practitioners and researchers not only violate values such as social justice, self-determination, and starting where clients are, but they also miss opportunities to understand what works with whom under what conditions. RCTs only provide information on groups of persons, and without open-ended interviews cannot provide information on the differing effects of medications on various within-group differences.

Focus Groups

Focus groups are an increasingly popular way of generating information. They are a form of interviewing. At their best, they delve deeply into social issues and contribute to a knowledge base that contributes to policy and programs. Examples are plentiful, but one that is particularly relevant to the purpose of this chapter is Kohli's (2005) review of the literature and focus group research on the experiences of unaccompanied refugee children. Kohli shows the complexity of issues that might be at play in children's silences, including silence as indicators of resilience, of attempts to manage trauma, of inability to cope with trauma, and mistrust of governmental officials and social workers. Stories they do tell may be rehearsed because parents and others have taught children what to say in order to increase the chances that officials will accept the children as refugees.

Knowledge of the personal circumstances of the children before they left their countries of origin and the nature of the catastrophes that led them to seek asylum are essential. Without in-depth knowledge of the circumstances of unaccompanied children, effective interventions are impossible.

Focus groups are also helpful in understanding policies and their effects. Clements and Rosenwald (2008), for example, conducted focused groups with foster parents in order to understand foster parents' experiences with and concerns about fostering gay, lesbian, or bisexual youth in their homes. They found that foster parents are fearful of caring for GLB children. They recommended that social workers help foster parents understand the uses of GLB children and that social workers themselves become better educated about the issues.

Crawford and Tilbury (2007) conducted focus groups with child welfare case managers using an interview guide in order to understand issues related to services for young people about to leave care. The researchers found that case managers were so preoccupied with finding and helping to stabilize placements that they had little time to work with youth on obtaining resources and otherwise helping them prepare to make the transition from foster care to the work force. They also found that there are few treatment options available for those youth with mental health issues or who had learning and behavioral issues that impeded their progress in school. These issues affected their capacities to find employment. School personnel were unprepared to deal with the learning and behavioral issues that youth in care often presented. Many also did not have knowledge of the vocation and educational options that young people have access to. Such findings have important implications for policy and also generated practice theory that practitioners can apply to their work with young people in other settings.

Personal and Professional Testimonies

Personal and professional experiences are part of social work's knowledge base and can contribute to the understanding of social problems. They also can inform policy and practice. Practitioners and policy makers often use their personal experience in their work. For example, besides exemplifying the use of questionnaires in formative program evaluation, as discussed earlier, the Mokuau et al (2007) study is also an example of how personal and professional knowledge contributes to program development. In this case, three of the four program developers were native Hawaiians who drew upon their own experience to ensure that program was culturally appropriate and sensitive. They could have gone even one step further and done a needs assessment or conducted informational interviews with potential service users to inquire about their preferences regarding cultural appropriate features of the program and suggestions regarding the services that the program might offer. Such a strategy might not have been feasible in terms of time and funding.

Personal Narratives, Stories, and Poetry

Personal narratives by both professionals and lay persons with compelling personal stories inform both policy and practice. A few social work researchers and practitioners have fictionalized cases with which they have worked in order to make social issues prominent in the minds of the general public. Some practitioners write poetry not only as a response to their work but also to share their experiences with the general public. In general, personal narratives not only facilitate self-understanding, but when they are shared they can enlighten others. The following brief discussion provides examples.

Personal Narratives

Personal narratives are oral (as in tape recordings, videotapes, and performances) or written accounts of individuals' life experiences that, at their best, involve minimal or no involvement of researchers in their construction. Within social work's knowledge base are narratives that survivors of harsh circumstances compose as well as narratives that service providers themselves compose. These narratives inform social policy and intervention. Without them, effectiveness of practice is impossible. Personal narratives can be thought of as forms of autoethnographies, whose goals are to invite audiences into the experiences of narrators and in so doing to deepen understanding and to bring about social change (Jones, 2005).

Kumsa's (2007) personal narrative about her relationship with her younger brother during the Ethiopian civil war dig deep into her heart and mind and deep into the hearts and minds of readers. She powerfully conveyed what it means to survive a national catastrophe and the loss of family, home, country, and the sense of identity and belonging that is bound up in these losses. Narratives such as these contribute enormously to social work's knowledge base. Understandings such as these truly start where clients are and are the foundations for effective policies, programs, and direct practice. They also can be the basis of theorizing. Practitioners and researchers can extract working hypotheses from this one narrative and use the hypotheses to illuminate other similar situation.

Personal narratives can be the foundation for participatory action research. Sung-Chang & Yeung-Tsang (2008) began their action research with unemployed women in China by having the women collect oral histories with other unemployed women. Oral histories are a form of narrative research where those who collect oral histories create situations where participants tell their stories in their own ways. They thus are minimally intrusive. The women also told their own stories and developed insight into their situations and the situations of other women.

From the insights they gained, the women worked in collaboration with the researchers to conduct a new practice framework based on the new understanding they had gained through processes the researchers stated were reflexive (Sung-Chang & Yeung-Tsang, 2008). They first developed a typology of unemployed women: obedient followers, ambivalent pathfinders, and the courageous risk-takers. Typologies serve as the starting points of theory-building.

Through this work, the women developed new theories of unemployed women that rejected the dominant discourse and that involved seeing other women as active agents who can bring about changes in their own lives through collective action. They applied this new theory of unemployed women to themselves that gave them a framework for new actions and the development of an income-generating business.

Oral histories, a form of narrative, were the foundation of Sung-Chang's & Yeung-Tsang's (2008) action research that empowered participants to engage in advocacy on behalf of themselves and an unmet community need. Similarly, personal narratives about social work practice itself have great promise as an advocacy tool (Craig, 2007; Weick, 2000) that can educate the general public about social work's day to day work. As a profession that women largely shaped, social work does its daily task out of view of the public. Weick noted that the status of social work parallels the status of women in society. The private domain of social work replicates the work women have traditionally done in the private domains of families, also out of public sight. This results in large-scale misunderstandings about the nature of social work, including the nature of social problems, policies required to address these problems, and the money needed to run them. In the United States, myths of "the welfare Queen" stand for such misunderstandings and have had long-standing crippling effects on knowledge and theory development about policies and programs.

Weick (2000) recommended that social workers speak publicly about their work, and that is what Craig did in her narrative about a day in her life as a hospital social worker. She described a session with a man dying from cancer he believes was contracted from toxic waste from a nearby airbase, a man with diabetes who had had his leg amputated from the knee down, and a man dying from cancer and his wife. Each of their stories is poignant and to lighten things, Craig described how the wife took off her sweater to put on a back brace without skipping a beat. Craig (2007) noted that when social workers tell our stories, they can be difficult to hear. We therefore have to develop approaches that include the hope, humor, and inspiration we find in our work.

Creative Non-Fiction and Poetry

Sometimes social workers experience powerful stories that they want to convey to a wider audience, and they write the stories as creative non-fiction. This means that they use the techniques of fiction and change some of the facts so that the privacy of the service users is protected. Ungar (2003) wrote a short story called Stale that won a large amount of money in the Toronto Star short story contest. Ungar Stale based his story on his experiences as a child and family social worker.

I was so taken by a story that one of my research informants told me and so much wanted the real-life story to have a different ending that I wrote a novel where the informant lived up to his potential and turned his life around instead of becoming a person who beats his wife and molests boys. I published an excerpt from the novel (Gilgun, 2004a) where I described the sexual assault of the informant as a boy and its immediate aftermath. Both Ungar and I decided that the stories needed to be told in the most full manner possible. The techniques of fiction-writing helped us to accomplish their goals.

Such stories add to social work's knowledge base on problematic human situations. Like personal narratives, they also reach a broad audience and have promise of influencing public opinion, which can in turn influence policy and programs. They therefore can be tools of advocacy.

Some practitioners are so moved by stories they hear and the persons whose lives they witness that they respond by writing poetry. Sometimes the poetry is autoethnographic, meaning it conveys personal experiences that are nonetheless relevant to social work. Furman (2005), for example, used three different poetic forms to convey his experience of being an emergency room patient with what he thought was a heart attack. His poetry was a form of self-therapy, or a way of helping him process his experience, and as a means of expressing his affective state He situated his poetry within a tradition of social science writing whose purpose is to "evoke deep and powerful emotional reactions in the consumer of research" (p. 561). Such expressive uses of language allow audiaudiences to participate in the experience and perhaps enlarge their own understandings. Rather than reducing research findings to numbers, Furman said arts-based representations can portray the richness and complexity of "the human condition" more completely than data reduced to numbers (p. 565).

I have written poetry in response to both my direct social work practice and to my practice as a researcher (Gilgun, 2009). My goals were similar to those of Furman (2005). I was deeply and powerfully affected by what I witnessed and experienced vicariously. I wanted to share my experiences with others. At time, I may also have sought to cope with such powerful emotions.

Critical Discourse Analysis

Critical discourse analysis (CDA) can provide an in-depth view of issues with which client contend and by definition involves person-environment interactions, making it suitable for social work policy, programs, and interventions. CDA examines language and other texts for its implications for power, privilege and prestige as well as resistance to them (Fairclough, 2001; Wodak, 2001). Language and text are full of meanings on both the individual levels and the cultural levels. Indeed, individual gestures and speech acts only have meaning as they connect to shared meanings within particular cultural groups. A critical discourse analysis can reveal what otherwise may have been hidden meanings in language, gestures, clothing, and other texts.

For example, the discourse of "cool pose" (Majors & Billson, 1992) for young African American men involves clothing, hair style, body language, speech acts, attitudes toward women, and a multitude of other qualities that creates spaces can identities that may in fact be a form of resistance to a larger culture that continually threatens to marginalize them.

Valandra, Gilgun, and Sharma (2008) used CDA and critical race theory (CRT), which highlights the contemporary and historical contexts of race relations and racist practices (Decuir & Dixson, 2004; Dunbar, 2008), to analyze the discourse of a young black man on the brink of puberty and his white upper class case manager. Dueling discourses ensued when the young man expressed sexual interests in girls. The young man drew upon gendered and racialized discourses of cool pose to construct his version of how he wanted to relate to girls and the white case manager drew on a very different discourse to reprimand him. This analysis showed the importance of understanding the discourses of clients—in other words, to first understand where service users are coming from before making decisions about how to respond.

Another example of critical discourse analysis is the work of Sung-Chang & Yeung-Tsang (2008) who embedded a critical discourse analysis in their interpretations of the oral histories of unemployed women in China. Within the women's oral histories, they identified the voices or discourses of the government that not only has a deficit model of unemployment but paternalistic solutions. In response, the researchers took a more active role and invited the participants to reflect on the implications of these discourses and engaged them in a search for alternatives that empowered them to take actions based on their own competencies and agency.

Critical discourse analysis is under-used in social work research, but has great potential for identifying issues that disempower service users and that also can render social interventions ineffective because of unexamined assumptions. Critical discourse analysis provides a set of procedures for uncovering hidden assumptions. Furthermore, social workers can extract theoretical statements from discourse analyses and transport these ideas to other situations, thus contributing to the enhancement of theory and knowledge on problems and policies.

Ethnographies

Ethnographies are of two general types: a more traditional written ethnography and a performance ethnography. Ethnographies describe or portray persons in their environments that result from researchers' prolonged engagements in these environments. They are particularly useful for highlighting aspects of culture that persons who create and live the culture take for granted. There are many issues related to how researchers represent the persons and cultures they observe, and researchers therefore have to monitor their own assumptions and reactivity to the situations and person they observed.

In developing ethnographic representations, researchers can be strictly observers or they may participate in various degrees in the lives of the people they seek to understand. Ethnographies also involve interviews with key informants and often reviews of written documents such as governmental records, maps, histories, other ethnographies and personal documents such as diaries and letter. .

The tasks of ethnographers are similar to those of service providers, who observe service users in various contexts, including in homes, group residential settings, and in the office. Those who make home visits observe the communities and neighborhoods in which service users live. They make case notes of their interactions and may review reports and other documents that are relevant to their work. When applied to social work practice, ethnographies can result in many different products, such as descriptions of social phenomena, descriptions of program activities, descriptions of what works for whom under what conditions, and assessment and evaluation tools.

Findings from ethnographic approaches are immediately useful to direct practitioners. The rich and complex details of ethnographies match the rich and complex detail of social work direct practice. For example, Britton's (2008) street-level ethnography of race relations on a Chicago, USA, street, would make a lot of sense to service providers and policy makers alike because what Britton reported is an in-depth look at a readily identifiable pattern on use of public places based on race and social class.

One of the startling findings of this research is the observation that race relations are more cordial and less segregated in a nearby soup kitchen than in the racially-segregated group interactions on the street. It is as if the rules of conduct change with the characteristics of settings, a useful finding for practice theory building, for constructing programs, and for one-on-one interactions. This is an example of how persons and environments interact.

Performance Ethnographies

Sometimes researchers chose to present their ethnographies as performances, borrowing from the humanities, such as cultural studies, theatre, and creative writing, to do so. Performance ethnographies can be intensely personal or they can represent a significant event in the life of a culture. It can be difficult to distinguish between ethnographies that are performances of personal experiences and autoethnography and personal narratives as discussed earlier.

Performance ethnographies can involve an ensemble of actors who use the words of informants to portray in as full a manner as possible the lived experienced of the informants. The goal is to raise the audience's critical awareness of significant social issues. Five students in Alexander's

(2005) undergraduate course in performance studies did ethnographic interviews and participant observation with immigrant Mexican street vendors in Los Angeles. The students presented the results of their research as a re-enactment of how the street vendors hawk their goods, such as cherries, oranges, flowers, and clothing. They walked around the classroom hawking their items in rhythmic voices using both Spanish and English. Periodically, the action stopped, and one of the students told a personal story they had gathered from the informants. By performance's end, the students had conveyed the multiple meanings and issues that Mexican immigrant street vending represents.

The potential of performance ethnography for social work advocacy is huge. Not only can various groups tap into their own experiences and creativity to inform audiences in their communities, but they could videotape these performances and put them on YouTube or other internet sites. Such information would be an important tool for informing the general public world-wide about the everyday issues that service users confront. As stated earlier, an informed public is required in order for social policies to be responsive to social needs.

Practice Theory

How applied programs actually work is one of the "black boxes" in social work, meaning that there is little information about what goes on day to day in social service agencies. Such information is of high importance because it provides a front-row view of "street-level bureaucracy (Ellis, 2007; Lipsky, 1980)," or how social policies are implemented in one-on-one interactions. With such knowledge, policy makers, administrators, program planners, and direct service providers can reflect on what is going on and make judgments about what is working and what is not, what resources are available and which are lacking, among many other policy and program issues.

Floersch (2002) did an ethnographic study of strengths-based case management in a mental health center in the Midwestern United States. His purpose was to understand how case managers used strength-base practice theory to respond to the policy of deinstitutionalization of mental health patients from hospitals to the community. For more than seven months, Floersch, as a researcher, joined one of four treatment teams and was given entrée into all of the settings in which team members did their work. This included daily team meetings, regularly scheduled clinical and business meetings, visits to the homes of service users, and trips to the many venues that encompass community mental health services.

Floersch (2002) kept detailed field notes of these observations, interviewed key service providers, and analyzed many documents, such as policies, reports, letters, case records, and personal communications. Through case studies he created vivid portraits of the settings, services, and interactions that are involved in community mental health practice. He also created diagrams that described how case managers implemented strengths-base practice theory and various charts, such as summaries of information on types of drugs used and their various combinations and case managers' educational backgrounds.

In terms of method, he concluded that the interviews were essential to his understanding of how case management works in this setting. Reviews of written documents do not portray many important aspects of practice. His findings included an analysis of the strengths and shortcomings of the strengths-based practice model and made suggestions for how to develop a more comprehension model. In particular, he recommended that strengths-based case management develop a theory of the self that could account for self-monitoring, self-observing, and self-regulation. His observations, interviews, and case record reviews revealed repeated instances where service users were unable to perform these essential human functions and that strengths-base theory did not account for these issues.

Theories of Change

One of the enduring questions in social work is what works with whom under what conditions. Such a question can be answered by researcher immersion in the field and multiple research methods, which can be thought of as an ethnographic approach. Theories of change provide a kind of "road map" that describes the operations of applied programs and is one of many types of program evaluations (Patton, 2002). These operations take place within specific types of situations, persons, and impinging conditions. Typically, theories of change identify the antecedents, processes, and conditions associated with problematic situations, the activities and interventions that programs initiate in order to ameliorate the problematic situations, and the persons, the activities, the conditions, and the interactions among them associated with favorable and unfavorable outcomes. Approaches to theories of change vary according to the perspectives of those who develop them.

An example of theories of change with these ambitious goals is my work with EXCEL (not the real name of the agency), a program that provides services to children under ten who commit acts that could be charged as felonies. The purpose of the program is to promote child and family well-being and to divert children from the juvenile justice system. The intended product is a detailed description of the program in terms of activities, the environments in which the activities take place, the clients and their historical and present circumstances, and the case managers and their practice theories.

My co-researchers and I are in the process of describing many aspects of the program, such as the conditions and processes that occur when children do well in the program and when they do not (Gilgun, Sharma, & Valandra, 2008a), the uses of case manager humor at case consultations (Gilgun, Sharma, & Valandra, 2008), issues of race and discourse in case manager-client interactions (Valandra, Gilgun, & Sharma, 2008b), and a framework for assessing children and their families based on neuroscience, executive function attachment, trauma, and self-regulation (NEATS) (Gilgun, 2008; Gilgun, Sharma, & Valandra, 2008c).

The methods are participant observations, interviews, and case record reviews. Participation is minimal, but at times, I and my co-researchers are part of group-based programs that the agency conducts. As the senior researcher on the team, I sometimes provide my analyses at case conferences. We keep detailed field notes and my perspectives are phenomenological and constructivist, and we have taken a grounded theory approach where I had no hypotheses to test but simply "waded" into the field and observed what was going on (See Gilgun, 2007 for details on this method.).

Longitudinal Multi-Method Studies

The 30-year longitudinal study of Alan Sroufe and Byron Egeland (Sroufe, Egeland, Carlson, & Collins, 2005) is an example of a longitudinal research that has provided an enormous amount of information to policy makers, program developers and direct service providers in social work, early childhood education, family education, children's mental health, and child welfare services. Designed to explore aspects of attachment theory, the researchers used multiple methods that involved assessments for attachment relationships over time, interviews with parents and teachers, paper and pencil questionnaires, and observations at in a child development laboratory, and at home, school, and at summer camps. The researchers believe that this combination of methods allows for cross-validation of findings because what parents and teachers say can be assessment through observations, while the interviews can provide insights into behaviors.

Intervention Research
and the Development of Evaluation Tools

The kinds of research discussed above provide the theory and knowledge about policies and program that are required for the development of interventions and of assessment and evaluation tools.

Intervention Research

Intervention research is a central task of social work (Fraser, 2004). The Mokua et al (2008) program not only drew upon the practice and personal experiences of the program developers but also incorporated relevant research and theory as well as the various evaluation approaches discussed. Furthermore, true to the tenets of intervention research, the developers also did a careful evaluation of process and outcome for the purposes of improving their program (cf., Rothman & Thomas, 1994).

Assessment and Evaluation Tools

With a solid research base, social workers are positioned to develop assessment tools that alert practitioners to areas of service user functioning and contexts that research and theory suggest are important. Clinical assessment tools have been used in psychology for decades. Within the last several years, social work researchers have devoted considerable effort in creating assessment tools specific to social work practice.

Some hope that the tools they produce have a strong enough knowledge base so they also become guidelines for practice. Examples of these types of assessment tools are the CASPARS (Gilgun, 1999a; Gilgun, Keskinen, Marti, & Rice, 1999) and the 4-D (Gilgun, 2004b). The CASPARS, for example, directs service providers to assess for five areas that research and theory have shown are important for optimal child and family development. The emotional expressiveness tool contains such items as "Child expresses a range of emotions" and "Child's expression of emotions is appropriate to the situation." Even when service providers are not knowledgeable about emotional development, the instrument cues them to important dimensions of emotion expression and may indeed provide some guidance for their intervention efforts, such as educating themselves about approaches to educating children and their parents about emotions and making referrals to specialists in emotional development and expression.

A solid knowledge base of research and theory can result in assessment approaches that are not instruments per se but are summaries of important areas of human function. The RSGB (resilience-schema-gender-brain) (Gilgun, 2005a) assessment summarizes a great deal of knowledge in order to educate practitioners, program developers, and policy makers to these important aspects of human development. Likewise the NEATS (neurobiology, executive function, attachment, trauma, and self-regulation) (Gilgun, 2008) has similar goals.

Evaluation Tools

Ethnographic methods can help develop evaluation tools. One of my first research projects was an ethnographic study of a family incest treatment program where my task was to identify indicators that incest perpetrators were ready to graduate from the program (Gilgun, 1988). After 18 months of observing the treatment team discuss cases, I interviewed each treatment team member to test my developing ideas and to solicit feedback on what I had found. When I presented the assessment tools to the team, they were clear that I had identified the practice guidelines that they had used. What I had added was to put their more implicit knowledge into words that make their own practice thinking more explicit. The agency adopted the tools and used them successful for many years.

Grounded theory can take a great deal of time and may not be suited to most forms of social work research. Social work researchers typically require funding to do their research, and funders require reviews of the literature and often testable hypotheses before they would sponsor research projects. While doing preliminary work prior to proposal writing to identify core concepts and then to do a literature review is possible—indeed Strauss (1987) encouraged this—even this may be too time-consuming for many researchers.

Another way to develop theory is deductive qualitative analysis (DQA), which is an updating of analytic induction (AI) (Gilgun, 2005b). Deductive qualitative analysis—and analytic induction—are methods of testing theory with the goal of refining the theory and even discarding it if the theory does not hold up when tested. DQA is an updating of AI, which is the original approach to analysis that originated in the Chicago School of Sociology (Gilgun, 1999b; 2007). DQA makes no claims to producing findings that are universal, which some analytic inductionists claimed, and typically DQA begins with a conceptual framework and the testing of hypotheses. The conceptual framework builds from a literature review and, when applicable, from a description of researchers' personal and professional experience as well as results of any preliminary research. Examples of studies that label themselves DQA and AI are rare, but increasingly qualitative researchers begin their studies with a review of the literature and use concepts from the literature as sensitizing concepts, which are ideas that guide them in the development of research questions, in the analysis, and in the write-up of results.

Discussion

Social work is a complicated endeavor that requires a wide range of methods that generate knowledge about policies, problems, and practices. I premised this chapter on the principle that effective programs, policies, and practices are built upon 1) understanding the social problems into which we want to intervene and 2) the specification of what works, for whom, under what conditions. The scope of social work is vast, covering different types of efforts whose goal, in general, is to ameliorate personal and social conditions and problems in the name of social justice. Many of the areas in which social workers practice are underresearched and therefore not well understood. Furthermore, as is widely recognized, social work is in great need of tested, reliable interventions that can be tailored to fit particular situations. The present chapter is an attempt to outline some of the methods that can be responsive to these issues.

Social work practice takes place over time, with a beginning, middle, and end. Practice begins with the recognition of the existence of a social justice issue or problem, continues with a decision to respond to the issue, which in turn leads to assembling and developing theory and knowledge about the issue, followed by the development, testing, and implementation of the intervention, and concludes with evaluations of the effectiveness of the intervention. These time-ordered segments can be thought of as phases of practice. In the real world of policy and practice, there are varying degrees of fidelity in each of these phases and sometimes biases and even suspect sources of theory and knowledge, but overall these phases are quite stable across fields of practice.

Each phase of practice requires its own type of knowledge and requires research methods best suited to generate this knowledge. When social work researchers design their studies, they could specify the phase or phases of practice to which they hope their findings contribute. When they write up their results, they could show how what they found contributes to which phases of practice.

In the end, the core of any research method, meant to ameliorate social problems, that contributes to policy, programs, and practices must add to understandings of populations to be served, must describe interventions and the change processes involved, and must evaluate both processes and outcomes. How researchers do this varies as functions of their assumptions and worldviews. Such variations are consistent with the wide scope of social work, which accommodates and requires this pluralism.

References

APA Taskforce on Evidence-Based Practice (2006). Evidence-Based Practice in Psychology. *American Psychologist, 61(4)*, 271-185.

Australian Institute of Health and Welfare 2008. Child protection Australia 2006–07 (2008). Child Welfare series no. 43. Cat. no. CWS 31. Canberra: AIHW.http://www.aihw.gov.au/publications/cws/cpa06-07/cpa06-07.pdf. Downloaded 22 November 2008.

Aber, J.L., Bishop-Josef, S. J., Jones, S. M., McLearn, K. T., & Phillips, D. A. (2006). *Child development and social policy: Knowledge for action.* Washington, D.C.: American Psychological Association.

Alexander, Bryant Keith (2005). Performance ethnography: The reenacting and inciting of culture. . In *Sage handbook of qualitative research* (3rd ed.)Norman K. Denzin & Yvonna S. Lincoln (Eds.)(pp. 411-441). Thousand Oaks, CA: Sage.

Becker, Howard S., Blanche Geer, Everett C. Hughes, & Anselm L. Strauss (1961). *Boys in white: Student culture in medical school.* Chicago: University of Chicago Press.

Boruch, R. (2007). Encouraging the flight of error: Ethical standards, evidence standards, and randomized trials. *New Directions in Evaluation, 113*, 55-73.

Britton, Marcus (2008). "My regular spot:" Race and territory in urban public space. *Journal of Contemporary Ethnography, 37(4)*, 442-468.

Budd, K.S., Eyeberg, S.M. (2005). Child and adolescent advocacy through research: Introduction to the special issues. *Journal of Clinical Child and Adolescent Psychology, 34*, 602-605.

Campbell Library. http://www.compbellcollaboration.org/doc-pdf/ssr.pdf

Cnaan, Ram A. & Melissa E. Dichter(2008). Thoughts on the use of knowledge in social work practice. *Research on Social Work Practice, 18(4)*, 278-284

Coy, Maddy (2008). Young women, local authority care, and selling sex: Findings from research. *British Journal of Social Work*, *38*, 1404-1428.

Craig, Rita Wilder (2007). A day in the life of a hospital social worker: presenting our role through the personal narrative. *Qualitative Social Work*, *6(4)*, 431-446.

Crawford, Crawford & Clare Tilbury (2007). Child protection workers' perspectives on the school-to-work transition for young people in care. *Australian Social Work*, *60(3)*, 308-320

Cressey, Donald (1953) The criminal violation of financial trust. *American Sociological Review*, *15(6)*, 738-743.

Decuir, J. T., & Dixson, A.D. (2004) "So when it comes out, they aren't that surprised that it is there": Using critical race theory as a tool of analysis of race and racism in education. *Educational Researcher 33(5)*, 26-31.

Denzin, Norman (1989*). Interpretive interactionism.* Newbury Park, CA: Sage.

Dobash, R. Emerson & Russel Dobash (1992). *Women, violence and s0cial change.* London: Routledge

D'Cruz, Heather, Philip Gillingham and Sebastian Melendez (2007). Reflexivity, its meanings and relevance for social work: A critical review of the literature. *British Journal of Social Work (2007)* 37, 73–90

Dominelli, Lena (2007). Contemporary challenges to social work education in the United Kingdom. *Australian Social Work*, *60(1)*, 29-45.

Dubowitz , Howard & Diane DePanfilis (2000). *Handbook for child protection practice.* Thousand Oaks, CA: Sage.

Dunbar, C. Jr. (2008). Critical race theory and indigenous methodologies. In Norman K.Denzin Yvonna S. Lincoln (Eds.). *Critical race theories and indigenous methodologies* (pp. 85-100). Thousand Oaks, CA: Sage.

Eaton, W.W. (1998). Epidemiologic methods: In A. S. Bellack & M. Hersen (Eds.). *Comprehensive clinical psychology: Vol. 3. Research methods* (pp. 91-116). New York: Pergamon.

Edleson, Jeffrey L. (1999). The overlap between child maltreatment and woman battering. Violence Against Women, 5(2), 134-154.

Elliott, D. S., & Mihalic, S. (2004). Issues in disseminating and replicating effective prevention programs. *Prevention Science, 5*, 47-53.

Ellis, Kathryn (2007). Direct payments and social work practice: The significance of "street-level bureaucracy" in determining eligibility. *British Journal of Social Work, 37*, 405-422.

Emilsson, Ulla Melin (2005). Recognizing but not acknowledging: On using research information in social work with elderly people suffering from dementia. *British Journal of Social Work (35)*, 1393-1409.

Evaluating the definition of social work practice [Special issue]. (2003). *Research on Social Work Practice, 13(3)*.

Fairclough, N. (2001). *Language and power* (2ⁿᵈ ed.). Essex, UK: Pearson.

Floersch, Jerry (2003). The subjective experience of youth psychotropic treatment. *Social Work in Mental Health, 1(4)*, 51-69.

Floersch, Jerry (2002). *Meds, money, and manners*. New York: Columbia University Press.

Fisher, M. (2002) 'The social care institute for excellence: The role of a national institute in developing knowledge and practice in social care', *Social Work and Social Sciences Review*, **10**(2), pp. 6–31.

Fragueula, J. A., Martin, A. L., & Trianes, E. A. (2003). Drug-abuse prevention in the school: Four-year follow-up of a program. *Psychology in Spain, 7*, 29-38.

Fraiberg, Selma (1981). The muse in the kitchen (Part A). In H. Wechsler, H.A. Reinherz, & D.D., Dobbin. (Eds.), *Social work research in the human services* (2nd ed.) (pp. 28-42). New York: Human Sciences Press.

Fraser, Mark W. (2004). Intervention research in social work: Recent advances and continuing challenges. *Research on Social Work Practice, 14(3)*, 210-222.

Freedberg, Sharon (2007). Re-examining empathy: A relational-feminist point of view. *Social Work, 52(3)*, 251-259.

Furman, Rich (2006) 'Poetic forms and structures in qualitative health research', *Qualitative Health Research* 16(4), 560–6.

Garner, Bryan R., Kevin Knight, Patrick M. Flynn, Janis T. Morey, & D. Dwayne Simpson (2007). Measuring offender attributes and engagement in treatment using the client evaluation of self and treatment. *Criminal Justice and Behavior, 34(9)*, 1113-1130.

Gambrill, Eileen (1999). Evidence-based practice: An alternative to authority-based practice. *Families in Society, 80*, 341-350.

Gambrill, Eileen (2001). Social work: An authority-based profession. *Research on Social Work Practice, 11(2)*, 166-175.

Gellis, Zvi D., Jean McGinty, Lynda Tierney, Cindy Jordan, Jean Burton, and Elizabeth Misener (2008). Randomized controlled trial of problem-solving therapy for minor depression in home care. *Research on Social Work Practice, 18(6)*, 596-606.

Giles, Janice & Helen Curreen (2007). Phases of growth for abused New Zealand Women. *Affilia: Journal of Women and Social Work, 22(4)*, 371-384.

Gilgun, Jane F. (2009). *I want to show you: A memoir in poems*. Morrissville, NC: Lulu.

Gilgun, Jane F. (2008). *The NEATS: A child and family assessment.* Morrissville, N.C.: Lulu.

Gilgun, Jane F. (2007). "The Legacy of the Chicago School of Sociology for Family Theory-Building," (2007, November). Pre-Conference Workshop on Theory Construction and Research Methodology, National Council on Family Relation, Pittsburgh, PA, November.

Gilgun, Jane F. (2005a). Evidence-based practice, descriptive research, and the resilience-schema-gender-brain (RSGB) assessment. *British Journal of Social Work. 35 (6),* 843-862.

Gilgun, Jane F. (2005b). Qualitative research and family psychology. *Journal of Family Psychology,19(1),* 40-50.

Gilgun, Jane F. (2005c). The four cornerstones of evidence-based practice in social work. *Research on Social Work Practice,* 15(1), 52-61.

Gilgun,

Gilgun, Jane F. (2004a). Fictionalizing life stories: Yukee the wine thief. *Qualitative Inquiry, 10 (5),* 691-705.

Gilgun, Jane F. (2004b). The 4-D: Strengths-based assessments for youth who've experienced adversities. *Journal of Human Behavior in the Social Environment, 10 (4), 51-73.*

Gilgun, Jane F. (2002). Completing the circle: American Indian Medicine Wheels and the promotion of resilience in children and youth in care. *Journal of Human Behavior and the Social Environment, 6(2),* 65-84.

Gilgun, Jane F. (1999a). CASPARS: New tools for assessing client risks and strengths. *Families in Society, 80,* 450-459.

Gilgun, Jane F. (1999b). Methodological pluralism and qualitative family research. In Suzanne K. Steinmetz, Marvin B. Sussman, and Gary W. Peterson (Eds.), *Handbook of Marriage and the Family* (2nd ed.) (pp. 219-261). New York: Plenum.

Gilgun, Jane F. (1995). We shared something special: The moral discourse of incest perpetrators. *Journal of Marriage and the Family, 57,* 265-281.

Gilgun, Jane F. (1988). Decision-making in interdisciplinary treatment teams. *Child Abuse & Neglect, 12,* 231-239.

Gilgun, Jane F., Alankaar Sharma, & Valandra (2008,a May). Developmental trajectories of children at risk for chronic, serious delinquency" Paper presented at a symposium on children in Conflict with the Law. Fourth International Congress on Qualitative Research, Urbana, Il. May 17.

Gilgun, Jane F., Alankaar Sharma, & Valandra (2008d, May). Humor in social Work." Paper presented at a symposium on children in Conflict with the Law. Fourth International Congress on Qualitative Research, Urbana, Il. May 17.

Gilgun, Jane F., Alankaar Sharma, & Valandra (2008c, May). The NEATS: Assessment and practice guidelines for work with children and families. Paper presented at a symposium on children in Conflict with the Law. Fourth International Congress on Qualitative Research, May 17, 2008. Urbana, IL.

Gilgun, Jane F., Susan Keskinen, Danette Jones Marti, & Kay Rice. (1999). Clinical applications of the CASPARS instruments: Boys who act out sexually. *Families in Society, 80,* 629-641.

Glaser, Barney (1978). *Theoretical sensitivity.* Mill Valley, CA: Sociology Press.

Glaser, Barney & Anselm Strauss (1967). *The discovery of grounded theory.* Chicago: Aldine.

Greene, Roberta R. (2006). *Social work practice: A risk and resilience approach.* Florence, KY: Cengage.

Hawkins, J. David (2006). Science, social work, prevention: Finding the intersections. *Social Work Research, 30(3),* 137-152.

Hoe, Maanse & John S. Brekke (2008). Cross-ethnic measurement invariance of the Brief Symptom Inventory for individuals with severe and persistent mental illness. *Social Work Research, 32(2),* 71-78.

International Federation of Social Workers (IFSW) (2008). *Definition of social work.* http://www.ifsw.org/en/f38000138.html Retrieved 1 December 2008

Jenson, Jeffrey M. (2008). Editorial: Keeping pace with methodological and analytic advances in social research. *Social Work Research, 32(2),* 67-69.

Jenson, Jeffrey M. (2007). Editorial: Research, advocacy, and social policy: Lesson from the risk and resilience model. *Social Work Research, 31(1),* 3-5.

Jenson, Jeffrey M. & Mark W. Fraser (2006). *Social policy for children and families: A risk and resilience perspective.* Thousand Oaks, CA: Sage.

Jones, Stacy Holman (2005). Autoethnography: Making the personal political. In *Sage handbook of qualitative research* (3rd ed.)Norman K. Denzin & Yvonna S. Lincoln (Eds.)(pp. 763-791). Thousand Oaks, CA: Sage.

Margaret L. Keeling, Margaret L., & Fred P. Piercy (2007). A careful balance: Multinational perspectives on culture, gender, and power in marriage and family therapy practice. *Journal of Marital and Family Therapy, 33(34),* 443-463.

Kindler, Heinz (2008). Developing evidence-based child protection practice: A view from Germany. *Research on Social Work Practice, 18(4),* 319-324.

Kindler, Heinz, Lillig, S. Blüml, H., Meysen, T., & Werner, A. (2006). *Handbuch Kindeswohlgef ährdung nach § 166 BGB und Allgemeiner Sozialer Dienst (ASD).* Munich: Germany: DJI. Available from www.dji.de/asd.

Kohli, Ravi K.S. (2005) The sound of silence: Listening to what unaccompanied asylum-seeking children say and do not say. *British Journal of Social Work, 36(5),* 707-721.

Kufeldt, K. & B. McKenzie (Eds.) (2003). Child welfare: Connecting research, policy, and practice.

Kumsa, Martha Kuwee (2007). Home and exile. *Qualitative Social Work,* 6(4), 483–487.

Lederman, Cindy S., Joy D. Osofsky, & Lynne Katz z(2007). When the bough breaks the cradle will fall: Promoting the health and well-being of infants and toddlers in juvenile court. *Infant Mental Health Journal, 28(4),* 440-448.

Lieberman, Alicia F. (2007). Ghosts and angels: Intergenerational patterns in the transmission and treatment of the traumatic sequelae of domestic violence. *Infant Mental Health Journal, 28(4),* 422-439.

Lipsky, M. (1980). *Street-level bureaucracy: Dilemmas of the individual in public services.* New York: Russell Sage.

Lord Laming (2003). Inquiry into the death of Victoria Climbie. London: HMSO. Retrieved January 4, 2006, from http://www.victoria-climbieinquiry.org.uk.

Macmillian, H.L., Jamieson, E., Wathen, C.N., Boyle, M.H., Walsh, C.A, Omoura, J.M., & Lodenquai, G. (2007). Development of a policy-relevant maltreatment research strategy. *Milbank Quarterly, 85,* 337-374.

McTaggart, Robin (1997). *Participatory action research: International contexts and consequences.* Albany, NY: SUNY.

Maglajli, Reima Ana & Jennifer Tiffany (2006). Participatory action research with youth in Bosnia and Herzegovina (2006). Co-published simultaneously in *Journal of Community Practice* (The Haworth Press, Inc.) Vol. 14, No. 1/2, 2006, pp. 163-181; and in Barry N. Checkoway, and Lorraine M. Gutiérrez (Eds.), *Youth participation and community change* (pp. 163-181).

Majors, R. & Billson, J.M. (1992). *Cool pose: The dilemmas of black manhood in America.* New York: Simon & Schuster.

Mancini, Michael A. (2007) The role of self-efficacy in the recovery from serious psychiatric disability. *Qualitative Social Work, 6(10),* 49-74.

Marsh, J. C. (1983) Research and innovation in social work practice: Avoiding the headless machine, *Social Service Review, 57,* 584-598.

Marsh, Peter, Mike Fisher, Nigel Mathers, & Sheila Fish (2005).*Developing the evidence base for social work and social care Practice.* Using Knowledge in social care report 10. London, UK: Social Care Institute for Excellence. www.scie.org.uk. Downloaded 1 December 2008.

Mokuau, Noreen et al (2008). Development of a family intervention for native Hawaiian women with cancer: A pilot study. *Social Work, 53(1),* 9-19.

Mrazek, Patricia J. & Haggerty, R.J. (Eds.). (1994). *Reducing risks for mental disorders: Frontiers for prevention intervention research.* Washington, D.C.: National Academy Press.

Nikken, Peter, Jansz, Jeroen, & Schouwstra (2006). Parents' interest in videogame ratings and content descriptors in relation to game mediation. *European Journal of Communication, 22(3),* 315-336.

Office of National Statistics (2003). The mental health of young people looked after by local authorities. http://www.statistics.gov.uk/pdfdir/hel0603.pdf. Retrieved 22 November 2008.

Patton, Michael Quinn (2002). *Qualitative research and evaluation methods.* Thousand Oaks, CA: Sage.

Parton, Nigel (2008).Changes in the form of knowledge in social work: From the "social" to the "informational." *British Journal of Social Work, 38,* 253-269.

Pawson, R. (2006). *Evidence-based policy: A realist perspective.* Thousand Oaks, CA: Sage.

Penhiero, Paulo Sergio (2005). An end to violence against children, New York, New York: United Nation's Secretary General's Study on Violence Against Children. http://www.violencestudy.org/IMG/pdf/I._World_Report_on_Violenc e_against_Children.pdf. Downloaded 22 November 2008.

Petrosino, A., Petrosino-Turpin, C., & Buehler, J. (2002). Scared Straight and other juvenile awareness programs for preventing juvenile delinquency. Available from the Campbell Library. http://www.compbellcollaboration.org/doc-pdf/ssr.pdf

Rosen, A., Proctor, E.K.,& Staudt, M. M. (1999). Social work research and the quest for effective practice. *Social Work Research, 23,* 4-15.

Rothman and Thomas, Edwin John (1994). *Intervention research: Design and development for human services.* Binghamton, N.Y: Haworth.

Saleebey, Dennis (2008). *The strengths perspective in social work practice* (5th ed.). Boston: Allyn & Bacon.

Schön, Donald A. (1983). *The reflective practitioner: How professionals think in action.* New York: Basic.

Shadish, W. R., Cook, T.D., & Campbell, D. T. (2002). *Experimental and quasi-experimental designs for generalized causal inference.* Boston: Houghton-Mifflin.

Shapiro, Vivian (2009). Reflections on the work of Professor Selma Fraiberg: A pioneer in the field of social work and infant mental health. *Clinical Social Work Journal,* published on-line at http://www.springerlink.com.floyd.lib.umn.edu/content/700862721301x j51/fulltext.pdf

Sheldon, B. (2003). Brief summary of the ideas behind the Centre for Evidence-based Social Services. Retrieved August 16, 2006 from http://www. ex.ac.uk/cebss/introduction.html. Economic and Social Research Council, UK.

Sheppard, M. (1998) Practice validity, reflexivity and knowledge for social work, *British Journal of Social Work* 28(5): 763–81.

Shirilla, Joan J. & Deborah J. Weatherson (Eds.) (2002). *Case studies in infant mental health: Risk, resiliency, and relationships* (pp. 1-13). Washington, D.C.: Zero to Three.

Soydan, Haluk (2008). Applying randomized controlled trials and systematic reviews in social work research. *Research on Social Work Practice, 18(4),* 311-318.

Soydan, Haluk (2007). Improving the teaching of evidence-based practice: Challenges and priorities. *Research on Social Work Practice, 17(5),* 612-618.

Sroufe, L. Alan, Byron Egeland, Elizabeth Carlson, & Andrew Collins (2005). *The development of the person: The Minnesota study of risk and adaptation from birth to adulthood.* New York: Guilford.

Straus, Murray A., Richard J. Gelles, & Suzanne K. Steinmetz (2006*). Behind closed doors: Violence in the American family.* Edison, NJ: Transaction Publishers (First published in 1980).

Sue, Derald Wing, Christina M. Capodilupo, Gina C. Torino, Jennifer M. Bucceri, Aisha M. B. Holder, Kevin L. Nadal, & Marta Esquilin (2007). Racial Microaggressions in everyday life: Implications for clinical practice. *American Psychologist, 62(4)*, 271-286.

Rothman, Jack & Edwin J. Thomas (1994). An integrative perspective on intervention research. In Jack Rothman & Edwin J. Thomas (Eds*.) Intervention research: Design and development for human service* (pp. 3-23). New York: Haworth.

Ruch, Gillian (2005). Relationship practice and reflective practice: Holistic approaches to contemporary child care social work. *Child and Family Social Work, 10*, 111-123.

Saggese, Michael (2005). Maximizing treatment effectiveness in clinical practice: An outcome informed, collaborative approach. Families in Society, 86(4), 558-564.

Samuel, M. (2005). Social care professionals overwhelmed by paperwork. *Community Care*, 14 December, p. 8.

Shaw, Ian (2005). British Journal of Social Work

Stier, F (Ed.) (1991). *Research and reflexivity*. London: Sage.

Strauss, Anselm L. (1987). *Qualitative analysis for social scientists*. New York: Cambridge University Press.

Strauss, Anselm & Juliet Corbin. (1998). *Basics of qualitative research: Techniques and procedures for developing grounded theory* (2nd ed.). Thousand Oaks, CA: Sage.

Strauss, S. E., Richardson,W. S., Glasziou, P.,& Haynes, R. B. (2005). *Evidence-based medicine: How to practice and teach EBM* (3rd ed.). Edinburgh, UK: Elsevier.

Sung-Chang, Pauline & Angelina Yeung-Tsang (2008). Our journey nurturing the voices of unemployed women in China through collaborative-action research. *Qualitative Social Work, 7(1)*, 61-80.

Upshur, R. E. G. (2001). The status of qualitative research as evidence

Taylor, Carolyn (2006). Narrating significant experience: Reflective accounts and the production of (self) knowledge. *British Journal of Social Work, 3(2)*, 189-206.

Hunter, D.E.K. (2006) Using a theory of change approach to build organizational strength, capacity and sustainability with not-for-profit organizations in the human services sector. *Evaluation and Program Planning, 29*, 193-200.

Thyer, Bruce A. (2001). What is the role of theory in research on social work practice. Journal of Social Work Education, 37(1), 9-25.

Thyer, Bruce A. (2008). The quest for evidence-based practice?: We are all positivists! *Research on Social Work Practice, 18(4)*, 339-345.

Tower, Roni B. & Mirel Krasner (2006). Marital closeness, autonomy, mastery, and depressive symptoms in a U.S. internet survey. *Personal Relationships, 13*, 429-449.

Trevithick, Pamela (2008). Revisiting the knowledge base of social w0rk: A framework for practice *British Journal of Social Work, 38*, 1212–1237.

Ungar, Michael (2003). *Stale*. Toronto Star (Canada), July 29, p. D15.

Vinnerljung, B., Sundell, K. Löfholm, C.A., & Humlesjö, E. (2006). Former Stockholm child protection cases as young adults: Do outcomes differ between those that received services and those that did not? *Children and Youth Services Review, 28,* 59-77.

Walsh, Froma (2006). *Strengthening family resilience* (2nd ed.). New York: Guilford.

Weatherson, Deborah J. (2002). Introduction to the children's mental health program. In Joan J. Shirilla & Deborah J. Weatherson (Eds.), *Case studies in infant mental health: Risk, resiliency, and relationships* (pp. 1-13). Washington, D.C.: Zero to Three.

Webb, S. (2003). Local orders and global chaos in social work. *European Journal of Social Work, 6,* 191-204.

Weick, Ann. (2000). Hidden voices. *Social Work, 5(5),* 395-402.

Wodak, R. (2001). What CDA is about. In R. Wodak & M. Myers (Eds.), *Methods of critical discourse analysis* (pp. 1-13). London: Sage.

14

THE INTELLECTUAL ROOTS
OF GROUNDED THEORY

This article shows that grounded theory is not about technicalities but is about a open, adaptable approach to understanding human beings in their own terms in their own contexts. Researcher immersion and reflexivity are hallmarks not only of grounded theory but in the Chicago School traditions in which grounded theory originated.

This article was first published in Report, *a magazine of the National Council on Family Relations, 55.2, Summer 2010. I republished it in volume 9, issue 1 of* Current Issues in Qualitative Research. *Portions of this article appeared in Gilgun, Jane F. (1999), Methodological pluralism and qualitative family research. In Suzanne K. Steinmetz, Marvin B. Sussman, and Gary W. Peterson (Eds.),* Handbook of Marriage and the Family *(2nd ed.) (pp. 219-261). New York: Plenum.*

WHEN NORMAN DENZIN (2010) changes his mind about grounded theory (GT), you know something important has happened. More than 40 years ago, Denzin (1997) tried GT at the urging of Anselm Strauss. "Pretty soon, I had more GT than fieldnotes," he said. He found that his efforts distanced him from the children in daycare who were the focus of his participant observations.

Denzin (2010) said, "I had failed at grounded theory." Soon after he "became a critic of grounded theory" (p. 1). His failure did not affect his relationships with Strauss. For instance, he worked with Strauss and Alfred Lindesmith on several editions of *Social Psychology* (1999).

In 2010, Denzin came out as an enthusiastic promoter of a particular form of GT: collaborative, constructivist, and critical. Forty years earlier, during his first attempts to use GT, Denzin appears to have been caught up in the "trees" of GT; in other words, the technicalities of GT swamped him. He followed instructions that Strauss delivered in person about the constant comparative method, comparisons across field sites, and the search for emerging concepts, indicators of concepts, and links to theory (Denzin, 1997).

By 2010, Denzin saw that GT does not have to be about technicalities, but researchers can use it as an adaptable and open-ended approach to developing understandings of human situations. When researchers view GT this way, the goal is to listen, hear, and understand what others are saying and doing, in their own terms as much as possible. Its open-endedness permits researchers to adapt it to their own particular methodologies and conscious and unconscious biases. In short, there are many ways to do GT. Recently, Denzin adapted GT to serve his commitment to social justice issues in research that includes researcher collaborations with participants, the importance of local knowledge, and, once the research is completed, advocacy for social change.

The Roots of GT

This view of GT is consistent with its roots in the Chicago School of Sociology, where professors such as W.I. Thomas, Florian Znaniecki, & Robert Park urged their students to immerse themselves in the lives and situations of the persons whom they wished to study in order to develop deep understandings (*verstehen*) that resulted in descriptions of *erlebnis*, or lived experience. Many Chicago professors studied philosophers such as Kant, Dilthey, and Simmel when they were students at German universities (Bulmer, 1984; Gilgun, 1999, 2013). These perspectives were embedded in their views about how to do research.

Robert Park's famous words summarize this aspect of the Chicago School methodology. Park talked to his students about the necessity of "getting your hands dirty in research." He didn't stop here, however. He also said

> But one more thing is needful: first hand observation. Go and sit in the lounges of the luxury hotels and on the doorsteps of the flophouses; sit on the Gold Coast settees and on the slum shakedowns; sit in the Orchestra Hall and in the Star and Garter Burlesk. In short, gentlemen [sic], go get the seat of your pants dirty" (McKinney, 1966, p. 71; also quoted in Gilgun, 1999 and elsewhere).

As a clear statement of immersion and the importance of multiple perspectives, this quote has few equals.

Theory development was also part of the Chicago School, although different professors had different perspectives on its centrality in research processes (Gilgun, 1999). Thomas and Znaniecki (1918-1920/1927), prominent in the Chicago School, believed that the purpose of science was to reach "generally applicable conclusions." This could be done through studying "each datum" "in its concrete particularity." Such strategies, from their view, is the basis of science. They emphasized induction, or the drawing general statements from careful analysis of particular situations (Gilgun, 1999). They said

> The original subject matter of every science is constituted by particular data existing in a certain place, at a certain time, in certain special conditions, and it is the very task of science to reach, by a proper analysis of these data, generally applicable conclusions. And the degree of reliability of these general conclusions is directly dependent on the carefulness with which each datum has been studied in its concrete particularity (p. 1191).

This is no less true for the study of the individual who must be understood "in connection with his [sic] particular social milieu before we try to find in him [sic] features of a general human interest" (Thomas & Znaniecki, 1927, Vol. 2. p. 1911). Although, as the above excerpt suggests, they valued scientific generalization, they stated that they do not consider their work as giving "any definitive and universally valid sociological truths" (pp, 340-341). Rather, their work is suggestive and prepares the ground for further research (Gilgun, 1999).

These are early statements about the importance of theory development through building upon concrete particularities, which today we call case studies. These statements also show connections to the ideas of Strauss and colleagues (Corbin & Strauss, 2008; Glaser, 1978, 1992; Glaser & Strauss, 1967; Strauss, 1987; Strauss & Corbin, 1998) who advise researchers to connect concepts to particularities in their efforts to construct grounded theories.

Although there were variations among researchers, Chicago faculty also had a commitment to social reform (Bulmer, 1984; Deegan, 1990; Gilgun, 1999). John Dewey, for example, set up a series of laboratory elementary schools, where he could try out the ideas being developed in the philosophy department as well as develop new ideas based on his interactions with of observations of teachers, students, and other personnel involved in the schools (Bulmer, 1984).

Jane Addams linked poverty and exploitation of workers with oppressive social and economic conditions, and she was a key figure in such reform movements as standards for occupational safety, the establishment of unions and the support of strikes, and various federal legislation on child labor and family social welfare (Bulmer, 1984; Deegan, 1990).

Robert Park and others studied social problems for the purposes of reform, but believed that an educated public would bring about social change. They did not directly advocate for change as did Addams and others associated with the Chicago School (Bulmer, 1984).

Denzin's commitment to social justice and his stance on advocacy, then, is consistent with the roots of GT. His view of GT as constructivist, emancipatory, and action-oriented research has deep intellectual roots.

What's New?

What's new about GT is the name and some of its explanations of procedures of qualitative analysis, such as theoretical sampling, theoretical sensitivity, and elaboration analysis. Unfortunately, Glaser, Strauss, and Corbin did not explore or explain the intellectual roots of GT. The brief discussions they had of the Chicago tradition typically were dismissive, such as disparaging negative case analysis while giving a superficial account of it (cf., Glaser & Strauss, 1967).

What Denzin now calls GT is a good old-fashioned Chicago School of Sociology methodology. Members of the Chicago School did not name this approach to research except to call it fieldwork. *Grounded theory* is a suitable name, unless researchers are looking to describe experiences. Then they may call their research interpretive phenomenology, which is a descriptive approach to *verstehen* and *erlebnis*. (See Benner, 2002; Polkinghorne, 1983). Even critical theory has some of its intellectual roots in these philosophies, consistent with Denzin's current perspectives on critical GT.

50 Years of Confusion

If Norman Denzin can experience confusion about what GT is, it is not surprising that legions of other researchers have, too. From the beginning, Anslem Strauss and Barney Glaser (1967), the originators of GT, laid the groundwork for almost 50 years of subsequent confusion, as well, of course, of protecting and promoting a rich intellectual heritage of qualitative research (Gilgun, 1999, 2005).

On the one hand, GT as originally formulated was a set of procedures for generating theory through prolonged immersion in the field. They were responding to concerns that many sociologist had about "grand theories;" that is, theories that were abstract and disconnected from more concrete descriptions of human, social phenomena (Glaser & Strauss, 1967).

This was arm-chair theorizing that Robert Merton (1968), among others, wanted to redress through the concept of "middle-range theories." In fact, Merton's (1968) description of middle range theories sounds like descriptions of GT. This is what Merton said

> theories of the middle range…lie between the minor but necessary working hypotheses that evolve…in day-to-day research and the all-inclusive efforts to develop a unified theory (p. 39).

On the other hand, GT was a set of generic procedures that researchers could use on many different types of qualitative research. Even the subtitles of their main texts show the confusion. The original book, that Strauss and Glaser co-authored, is called *The Discovery of Grounded Theory: Strategies for Qualitative Research*. The most recent iteration, *Basics of Qualitative Research: Techniques and Procedures for Developing Grounded Theory* (Corbin & Strauss, 2008), continues the tradition of confusion.

Examples of generic procedures abound. For example, group analysis of data, which they highly recommend, was part of earliest research efforts, including Booth's studies of the London poor (Webb & Webb, 1932). Grounded theory has no claim to this procedure. Even theoretical sensitivity (Glaser, 1978) may not be original because it is similar to Blumer's (1954/1969) notion of sensitizing concepts, which, like theoretical sensitivity, are concerned with researchers' capacities to identify social processes and construct theoretical statements about them.

It has become a cliché that researchers are not really doing GT if they don't come up with a theory (Bryant & Charmaz, 2007). Maybe so, but the originators of GT made claims that their procedures were for doing qualitative research in general. Many of the procedures the originators discussed are useful for generic qualitative research and not necessarily for theory development. Open, axial, and selective coding are generic coding procedures that are not limited to theory-building.

Bryant and Charmaz recognize this confusion. They distinguish between grounded theory as methodology (GTM) and grounded theory (GT) as a product that is theory. They and several authors of chapters in their edited volume attempt to clarify the confusions that have arisen from Strauss' and colleagues' mixing of grounded theory as generic procedures and grounded theory as a product. They discussed such terms as "grounded," "data," "induction," "deduction," "abduction," "theoretical sensitivity," and how to do some of the tasks associated with grounded theory, such as group analysis of data and when and how to include related research and theory.

The Split

As this discussions shows, Strauss, Glaser, and Corbin split off a part of the Chicago School legacy to emphasize theory development. They also made original and enduring contributions to qualitative analysis. Important, too, they kept a significant research tradition alive—this is, the open-ended, flexible approach to understanding of human phenomena.

Other researchers besides Denzin rejected GT and aligned themselves with the interpretive research. One of Strauss's own students, Patricia Benner (1992), is one of them. Benner developed a form of interpretive phenomenology, which she taught to generations of students at the University of California, San Francisco, the same institution where Strauss, Glaser, & Corbin also taught for many years.

Benner's interpretive phenomenology seeks to convey lived experience and what it means to be human, presented in straightforward categories and theoretical statements that are inductively derived. She sees interpretive phenomenology as a scholarly discipline that provides perspectives that can promote understanding of everyday practices and meanings. As a professor of nursing, Benner, like Denzin, is within the Chicago tradition of research to be used to promote the social good.

Discussion

The spirit of GT is open-ended and flexible, a form of research that seeks to understand individuals involved in social interactions of various types within contexts that range from the micro to the macro. Which aspects of contexts researchers chose to address depend upon a variety of factors, but primarily their own biases and perspectives.

Thirty years after his initial failure, Denzin has come back to grounded theory with a deeper understanding of its spirit. He now promotes reformist, interpretive grounded theory. Benner has spent about 30 years doing interpretive phenomenological research, partially in reaction to the distancing she too experienced when she tried to do grounded theory in the mode that Strauss and colleagues promoted (Gilgun, 1999).

Strauss and colleagues seized upon a significant idea and promoted it through many iterations. Their efforts, however, were imperfect. Researchers have spent and will continue to spend time and effort figuring out what they meant and forging their own paths. Strauss encouraged researchers to do this. In his writing, he advised other researchers to be creative, to decide what they want from their research, and to stick with it no matter what others may do to undermine them (Strauss, 1991). As prescriptive as the originators of GT appear to be, Strauss remained until the end a researcher and methodologist within the style of the Chicago School: flexible, open-minded, and committed to the social good.

References

Benner, Patricia. (Ed.) (1994). *Interpretive phenomenology*. Thousand Oaks, CA: Sage.

Booth, Charles (1903). *Life and labour of the people in London*. Final volume. London and New York: Macmillan.

Blumer, H. (1954/1969). What is wrong with social theory? In Herbert Blumer (1969/1986), *Symbolic interactionism. (pp* (pp. 140-152) Berkeley: University of California Press. Originally published in Vol. XIX in *The American Sociological Review*.

Bryant, Antony & Kathy Charmaz (Eds.) (2007). *The Sage Handbook of Grounded Theory*. Thousand Oaks, CA: Sage.

Bulmer, M. (1984). *The Chicago School of Sociology: Institutionalization, diversity, and the rise of sociological research*. Chicago: University of Chicago Press.

Corbin, Juliet & Anselm Strauss (2008). *Basics of qualitative research: Techniques and procedures for developing grounded theory* (3rd ed.). Thousand Oaks, CA: Sage.

Deegan, M. J. (1990). *Jane Addams and the men of the Chicago School, 1892-1918*. New Brunswick, N. J.: Transaction.

Denzin, Norman K. (2010). Grounded and indigenous theories and the politics of pragmatism. *Sociological Inquiry, 80(2)*, 286-312.

Denzin, Norman (1997). Coffee with Anselm. *Qualitative Family Research 11(2)*, 1-4. Gilgun, Jane F. (2013). Qualitative family research: Enduring themes and contemporary variations. In Gary F. Peterson & Kevin Bush (Eds.), *Handbook of Marriage and the Family* (3rd ed.) (pp. 219-261). New York: Plenum.

Gilgun, Jane F. (2005). Qualitative research and family psychology. *Journal of Family Psychology, 19(1)*, 40-50.

Gilgun, Jane F. (1999). Methodological pluralism and qualitative family research. In Suzanne K. Steinmetz, Marvin B. Sussman, and Gary W. Peterson (Eds.), *Handbook of Marriage and the Family* (2nd ed.) (pp. 219-261). New York: Plenum.

Glaser, Barney. (1992). *Basics of grounded theory analysis.* Mill Valley, CA: Sociology Press.

Glaser, Barney. (1978). *Theoretical sensitivity.* Mill Valley, CA: Sociology Press.

Lindesmith, Alfred R., Anselm Strauss, & Norman K. Denzin (1999). *Social psychology* (8th ed.). Thousand Oaks, CA: Sage.

Merton, Robert K. (1968). *Social theory and social structure.* New York: Free Press.

Polkinghorne, Donald. (1983). *Methodology for the human sciences: Systems of inquiry.* Albany: State University of New York at Albany.

Smith, Linda Tuhiwai. 2005. "On Tricky Ground: Researching the Native in the Age of Uncertainty." Pp. 85–108 in Handbook of Qualitative Research. 3rd ed., edited by N. K. Denzin and Y. S. Lincoln. Thousand Oaks, CA: Sage.

Strauss, A. (1991). A personal history of the development of grounded theory. *Qualitative Family Research, 5(2)*, 1-2.

Strauss, Anselm. 1987. *Qualitative Analysis for Social Scientists.* New York: Cambridge University Press.

Strauss, Anselm & Juliet Corbin (1998). Basics of qualitative research: Techniques and procedures for developing grounded theory (2nd ed. Thousand Oaks, CA: Sage.

Thomas, W. I. & Florian Znaniecki. (1918-1920/1927). *The Polish peasant in Europe and America*, Vol. 1-2. New York: Knopf. First published in 1918-1920

Webb, Sidney & Beatrice Webb. (1932). *Methods of social study.* London: Longman, Green.

15

THE QUALITATIVE BASIS
OF QUANTITATIVE MODELS

This article is concerned with the nature of science and the importance of trustworthy conceptual models. A trustworthy model is one of the products of the Chicago School traditions. Other first-order products are theories and descriptive research that are based on lived experience. I wrote this article in 2010 for Current Issues in Qualitative Research.

"THE QUANTS ARE REELING" reads a headline in today's *New York Times.* They're reeling because quantitative models did not predict the loss of billions of investor dollars. Investors by the hundreds of thousands are bailing out of hedge funds based on quant models. Once called the Wizards of Wall Street for the huge profits they racked up, managers of quant hedge funds now look like dunces, absurdly rich dunces, but dunces all the same.

Self-proclaimed geniuses when their models fit the economic bubble, many now blame market forces for their failures. The problem is with their models. They had inadequate models. These managers did not take into account important factors that influence how markets behave.

It is a truism that quantitative models are only as good as their underlying concepts. Managers did not understand this, or if they did, they persuaded themselves of the goodness of fit of their models and how markets behave. They were wrong.

Science and Qualitative Thinking

As Campbell and Stanley (1979) pointed out, science is based on qualitative thinking. Advocates touted the scientific bases of quant models, but they did not understand what science is, which continually tests and revises models of how things work.

Adequate conceptual models are based upon qualitative thinking and attempts to revise them to make them more adequate to solving problems and promoting the social good.

Model developers identify relevant factors that comprise their model. They test the model under a variety of situations. The purposefully seek exceptions to their developing model. They want to find situations where the model does not work. They then can change the model to fit these situations.

Models are always tentative. Model developers are continually on the outlook for situations that do not fit their developing models or that can add to them. Excellent model developers look just about everywhere, such as historical records and analyses, theories backed up with plausible data, and observations of various sorts. They specify conditions under which their models work. They recognize that various conditions have various effects on their models.

Familiar Strategies

These strategies are familiar to qualitative researchers. We want to build theories and models in order to improve human situations, such as crime and poverty. We continually seek exceptions to our emerging understandings. We take seriously the idea that model building is part of an experimenting society committed to social justice and care.

We are impelled to seek exceptions to our models because of the values we hold—such as justice and care.

Justice and Care

Values could be at the root of the failures of quant models. Managers may have been committed to the value of making profits and being kings of the hill. "My hedge fund is bigger than yours" kind of thinking. They were not uneasy that perhaps they were missing something. They were making too much money. They were adored.

Social researchers often have doubt. They often are uneasy. They have concern that they may be missing something. They know that the quality of human lives is at stake if they misspecify their models.

People driven by greed and blind pride apparently have no doubts and are not concerned that a misspecification of their models could hurt others.

It's time for those with blind faith in their quant models not only to re-specify their models but also to examine the values that are the basis of their blindness, blindness that is both conceptual and moral.

Reflexivity

Researchers call this examination of values "reflexivity." Wall street managers could use a lot more reflexivity. What they do in their joy in making money and being bigger than the other guy affects untold millions of others. It's about time they took reflexivity seriously.

Conclusions

It's time for Wall Street managers to adopt strategies that social scientists use—doubt, reflexivity, values based on care and justice, and continually seeking to improve their models of how things work.

References & Further Reading

Blumer, Herbert. (1954/1969). What is wrong with social theory? In Herbert Blumer (1969/1986), *Symbolic interactionism. (pp* (pp. 140-152) Berkeley: University of California Press. Originally published in Vol. XIX in *The American Sociological Review.*

Campbell, Donald T. (1979). "Degrees of freedom" and the case study. In Thomas D. Cook & Charles S. Reichardt (Eds.), Qualitative and quantitative methods in evaluation research. (pp.49-67). Beverly Hills, CA: Sage.

Cook, Thomas D., & Donald T. Campbell (1979). *Quasi-experimentation: Design & analysis for field settings.* Boston: Houghton Mifflin.

Creswell, Julie (2010). The quants are reeling. *New York Times*, August 20, p. B1, B6.

Cronbach, Lee J. (1975). Beyond the two disciplines of scientific psychology. *American Psychologist, 30,* 116-127.

Gilgun, Jane F. (in press). Qualitative research: Enduring themes and contemporary variations. In Gary F. Peterson & Kevin Bush (Eds.). *Handbook of Marriage and the Family* (3rd ed.). New York: Plenum.

Gilgun, Jane F. (2005). Qualitative research and family psychology. *Journal of Family Psychology, 19(1),* 40-50.

Gilgun, Jane F. (1994). A case for case studies in social work research. *Social Work, 39(4),* 371-389.

Popper, Karl (1969). *Conjectures and refutations: The growth of scientific knowledge.* London: Routledge and Kegan Paul

16

THE RISE OF ELIZABETH WARREN:
LESSONS FOR QUALITATIVE RESEARCHERS

Elizabeth Warren's research is well within Chicago traditions. When she was a professor at the Harvard Business School, she sought to understand the views of consumers who had been hurt by unfair banking practices. Her work showed immersion, an understanding of consumers" and bankers' experiences, and concerns for economic justice. What she learned from her research and her values led her to become an advocate. In 2012, she became a U.S. Senator from Massachusetts. President Obama did not appoint her as head of the new consumer protection agency that she had proposed because of political opposition. I wrote this article in 2010 for Current Issues in Qualitative Research, *6(1).*

THE RISE OF ELIZABETH WARREN to become a leading candidate for head of the recently created Federal Consumer Protection Agency has lessons for qualitative researchers who want to make a difference. Rational-technical models of research tell researchers to be objective, separate themselves from their values, and not to become advocates, as advocacy would interfere with objectivity. Rational-technical models also advise researchers to use specialized language that is hard for outsiders to understand.

Human sciences traditions suggest that researchers focus on subjectivity, to be clear about their own values, and to do research that is based on values, including becoming advocates themselves. They write their research in plain English to make it accessible to a lot of people. Some researchers believe that their research should be written so as to draw audiences in (Gilgun, 1999, in press).

Elizabeth Warren's research and actions are within human sciences traditions. Her story has many lessons for qualitative researchers in human sciences traditions.

The Story

The career of Elizabeth Warren, a Harvard Law professor, provides an example of what can happen when researchers apply principles from the human sciences. Warren has specialized in research on middle class families who have experienced bankruptcies. Bankers had been saying that bankruptcy is the "easy way out." Warren and two colleagues found that people who filed for bankruptcy had lost their jobs or had some other major life event that made it impossible for them to pay their bills. They were desperate. The research resulted in a well-received book called *As We Forgive Our Debtors* (Sullivan, Warren, &, 1999. Warren later co-wrote another influential book (Warren & Tyagi, 2004) called *The Two-Income Trap*.

One of Warren's colleagues on the bankruptcy research project said that looking through bankruptcy filings gave "a sense of human beings in real trouble. All of us were very much affected by what we found in those files" (Nocera, 2010, p. B6).

Like many researchers before her, Warren found the research led her to take an advocacy stance (Gilgun, 1999, in press). In 2007, she wrote an article in *Democracy: A Journal of ideas* (Warren, 2007), reprinted in *Harvard Magazine* (Warren, 2008), where she discussed deceptive bank practices and laid out her case for regulation. She proposed a regulatory agency for financial products. She called the proposed agency The Financial Product Safety Commission (FPSC). She wrote

Consumers entering the market to buy financial products should enjoy the same protection as those buying household appliances. Just as the Consumer Product Safety Commission (CPSC) protects buyers of goods and supports a competitive market, a new regulatory agency is needed to protect consumers who use financial products. The time has come to recognize that regulation can often support and advance efficient and more dynamic markets (Warren, 2008).

The Consumer Financial Protection Agency came into being early in 2010 through federal legislation. People across the country want President Obama to appoint Warren to be the agency's new director. There is even a popular youtube rap video that depicts her as a sheriff who will take down bankers who deceive and harm consumers (http://www.youtube.com/watch?v=6W0vCgMRX0o). In fact, there are many youtube videos showing Warren in action, with such titles as "Warren Makes Timmy Geithner Squirm Over AIG." The sheriff idea is from a *Time* magazine article highlighting the roles of women in financial reform, calling the women "the new sheriffs of Wall Street" (Scherer, 2010).

President Obama is considering another candidate, a man who is already part of the Obama administration and the apparent pick of Timothy Geithner, secretary of the treasury (Nocera, 2010).

The *Democracy* article propelled Warren to national prominence. In December 2008, the U.S. Senate appointed her head of the Congressional oversight panel for the $700 billion bank bailout fund (TARP). She said that the job of the panel is to make sure that banks are using taxpayer's money for the benefit of taxpayers. One of her many public statements about the panels findings was that taxpayers had subsidized ten of billions of dollars of shareholder profits while the money had little or no effect on bank lending.

Such clear and forthright language has resulted in the tidal waves of support for her to head the protection agency she proposed. One commentator summed up what legions of people believe:

> I'm convinced that no one grasps the true nature of our hard times better than Elizabeth Warren, the Harvard Law School professor….(Scurlock, 2009).

Evocative Language

Warren (2008) coined the term "tricks and traps" to depict how banks fooled people into signing credit agreements that had terms they did not know existed. She wrote in the *Democracy* article

> Lenders have deliberately built tricks and traps into some credit products so they can ensnare families in a cycle of high-cost debt.

She began the article with a comparison.

> It is impossible to buy a toaster that has a one-in-five change of bursting into flames and burning down your house, but it is possible to refinance an existing home with a mortgage that has the same one-in-five chance of putting the family out on the street."

In this article, she uses words such as "fleece," "tricks," and "bribes" to describe actions of bankers. She showed a flair for words in an article in *The Wall Street Journal*, Warren (2010) wrote

> Banks and brokers have sold deceptive mortgages for more than a decade. Financial wizards made billions by packaging and repackaging those loans into securities. And federal regulators played the role of lookout at a bank robbery, holding back anyone who tried to stop the massive looting from middle-class families. When they

weren't selling deceptive mortgages, Wall Street invented new credit card tricks and clever overdraft fees.

Warren wants the new consumer protection agency to make a rule that banks have to write their contracts in language a 10th-grader would understand. This, she said, would help stop "cheating by contract."

This is evocative language and bold thinking. Neutrality does not mean that researchers should depict deception in terms that drain away the actualities of the dishonesty and harm their actions cause. To get people's attention, researchers would do well to use evocative language along the lines of the language that Warren uses.

Her Words Convey Understanding

As Joe Nocera of *The New York Times* stated, Warren writes about consumer issues "precisely in ways that most Americans have experienced them." He continued, "She conveys a powerful sense that she understands what we've been through this last decade." Nocera is part of the legions of people who want Warren to be appointed head of the new consumer financial protection agency.

To convey understanding requires a deep appreciation of subjectivity—that is, other people's experiences. In order to understand others, researchers must be comfortable with their own subjectivity. Thus, researchers have to become comfortable with their own inner lives and the inner experiences of others, if they want to convey human experience and if they want other people to pay attention to what they say.

Values

Warren's values are clear in her statements. She said about her job as head of the oversight commitment on the bailout funds, "I'm not hanging on to this job. I'm here at the pleasure of the Senate that appointed me. But having said that, I'm not looking over my shoulder. I'm here to do what I think is right."

In her mind, what's right is a matter of fairness, of social justice. Similar values drive many researchers. This does not mean that we twist our research to fit our values, but we must be clear to ourselves and others that we do hold values and values are important to us. We must ensure that we remain fair and even-handed ourselves, even as we seek to identify, understand, and challenge social injustice and unfairness. To do less will render us ineffective and unfair.

Values and Courage

Warren's convictions about the value of fairness have given her courage. Even as she presents a soft-spoken demeanor, she said, "Don't let my politeness fool you. I can't think of anyone I'm afraid of, certainly not someone who may have had a hand in bringing this country to the brink of disaster" (Nocera, 2010, p. B6). This is courage based on values.

Researchers may need this same kind of value-based courage. Once we have solid research on which to base our claims, we, like Elizabeth Warren, must share them in whatever forums we can find, not only in journal articles, but also in internet postings, YouTube, appearances in the mass media, in classrooms, and at conferences. Research projects do not stop with publication in scholarly journals, but must be widely disseminated.

Values, Powerful Language, & Excellence of Thought

Bankers and financiers have complained that Warren's proposed policies would threaten the soundness, safety, and profits of banks. Warren answered, if banks depend upon deception and taking advantage of consumers, then there is something wrong with the banking system. Banks must change (Nocera, 2010). This is a turning of the tables, not backing down with scare tactics based on self-interest.

Patterns and Exceptions

A hallmark of human sciences research is to acknowledge variations in human phenomena. It is rare that any generalization fits all cases. Warren's thinking and writing shows this. While critiquing current banking practices for deception in the *Democracy* article, Warren (2007) acknowledged how important credit is.

Sometimes consumer trust in a creditor is well placed. Credit has provided real value for millions of households, permitting the purchase of homes that can add to family wealth accumulation and cars that can expand job opportunities. Credit can also provide a critical safety net, a chance for a family to borrow against a better tomorrow when they confront layoffs or medical problems today. Life insurance and annuities also can greatly enhance a family's security. Consumers may not spend hours poring over the details of their credit-card terms or understand every paper they sign at a real-estate closing, but many of those financial products are offered on fair terms that benefit both seller and customer.

In making these statements, Warren presented variations on her main point of how harmful deceptive practices are. She did not paint all credit practices as deceptive. It's important for researchers to make their points in a similar fashion: to make their main points clear, but also to document exceptions and variations (Gilgun, 1999, 2005, in press).

Conclusion

Human sciences traditions give researchers guidance on how to conduct research that focuses on subjectivity, honor patterns and exceptions to general statements, allow for researcher values, and encourage emancipatory research; that is, research that examines and documents human situations where justice and care at are issue. Warren's work and career show what can happen when researchers follow the guidelines of human sciences research.

Few researchers may want the national prominence and media attention that Warren has garnered, but we do want our research to be noticed, used, and effective. Following human sciences traditions and the example of Elizabeth Warren can foster these goals.

References & Further Reading

Blumer, Herbert (1986), *Symbolic interactionism*. Berkeley: University of California Press.

Elizabeth Warren, TARP overseer (2008). *Huff Post*. December 16. http://www.huffingtonpost.com/2008/12/16/elizabeth-warren-tarp-ove_n_151418.html/.

Gilgun, Jane F. (2013). Qualitative research: Enduring themes and contemporary variations. In Gary F. Peterson & Kevin Bush (Eds.). *Handbook of Marriage and the Family* (3rd ed.). New York: Plenum.

Gilgun, Jane F. (2005). Qualitative research and family psychology. *Journal of Family Psychology, ,19(1),* 40-50.

Gilgun, Jane F. (1999). Methodological pluralism and qualitative family research. In Suzanne K. Steinmetz, Marvin B. Sussman, and Gary W. Peterson (Eds.), *Handbook of Marriage and the Family* (2nd ed.) (pp. 219-261). New York: Plenum.

Kolhatkar, Sheelah (2009). Elizabeth Warren: Riding Herd on the Bailout. Time, June 22. http://www.time.com/time/magazine/article/0,9171,1904151,00.html/.

Scherer, Michael (2010). The new sheriffs of Wall Street. *Time,* May 13.
http://www.time.com/time/nation/article/0,8599,1988953,00.html/.

Scurlock, James (2009). The TARP queen: Why we should all bow before Elizabeth Warren (even if you've never heard of her). The Big Money, April 23.
http://www.thebigmoney.com/articles/judgments/2009/04/23/elizabeth-warren-my-hero

Sullivan, Teresa A., Elizabeth Warren, & Jay Lawrence Westbrook (1989). *As we forgive our debtors: Bankruptcy and consumer credit in America.* New York: Oxford.

Warren, Elizabeth (2007). Unsafe at any rate. *Democracy: A journal of ideas* (5), Summer.
http://www.democracyjournal.org/article.php?ID=6528

Warren, Elizabeth (2008). Making credit safer: The case for regulation. *Harvard Magazine.* May-June.
http://harvardmagazine.com/2008/05/making-credit-safer-html

Warren, Elizabeth & Elizabeth Warren Tyagi (2004). *The two-income trap.* New York: Basic.

Warren, Elizabeth (2010). Wall Street's race to the bottom. *Wall Street Journal,* February 8.
http://online.wsj.com/article/NA_WSJ_PUB:SB10001424052748703630404575053514188773400.html

17

Theory and Case Study Research

First published in Current Issues
in Qualitative Research, 2(3) *in 2011.*

CASE STUDY RESEARCH is important because of its contributions to theory. A case study is an intensive look at an individual unit. The unit can be composed of a single entity, such as one person, or it can be composed of multiple entities, such as marital partners or parents and children in one family unit. The study of a single unit includes studies of businesses, social service agencies, hospitals, court cases, and state and national governments. These latter kinds of cases are called complex case studies because the single unit has multiple entities within it and researchers have focused their investigations on these multiple entities. The sample size of case study research can range from one to hundreds.

A single case study of an individual is as viable as a complex case study or multiple case studies when the analysis is of high quality, is well documented, and contributes to theoretical understandings. A single well-analyzed and well-documented case study can upend existing theory, or at least begin the process of undermining existing theory. For example, a recent study of medical cases provided enough evidence to suggest that some patients long diagnosed as having Lou Gehrig's disease may actually have died from the effects of concussion. The study involved the comparison of the brain proteins of three athletes with a history of concussion and thought to have died of Lou Gehrig's disease with the brain proteins of 12 persons thought to have died of Lou Gehrig's disease.

The researchers found that the brain proteins of the three athletes differed from those of the persons in the comparison group. A single case casts doubt on existing theory and opens the door for studies to replicate the case. Successive replications of single cases build stronger evidence for alternative explanations; that is, for new theories.

Definition of Theory

In case study research, theory is defined as statements of relationship between two or more variables, which are also sometimes called concepts. Concepts are the building blocks of theory. An example of a theory is the following: concussions can lead to brain degeneration whose symptoms are similar to those of Lou Gehrig's disease. Statements that represent theory are based upon evidence for the viability of the concepts of the theory and of the relationships between them. Thus, the researchers investigating Lou Gehrig's disease based their conclusions on copious case material.

Working theories are statements of relationships among two or more concepts where researchers have not presented evidence for the viability of the concepts and of the relationships between them. Researchers typically use working theories in the course of developing theory as they select their samples, collect data, and analyze data. Something has to guide the decisions they make as they do sample selection and collect and analyze data. What guides these decisions are working theories. Medical researchers had a working hypothesis about Lou Gehrig's disease that involved relationships between a history of concussion, brain degeneration, and symptoms of Lou Gehrig's disease. In order to test this working hypothesis, they had to select comparison groups in order to test their working hypothesis.

Sometimes researchers use the term *hypothesis* or *working hypothesis* as synonyms for working theory. They use *working hypotheses* the same way they use the term *working theories*. Researchers also may call working hypotheses *empirical generalizations*. To complicate matters even further, the terms *hypothesis* is used to name the statements of relationships that researchers derive from their initial conceptual frameworks and that they test in the course of doing the research. As soon as they use these hypotheses in the conduct of research, they become working hypotheses. These are complicated ideas that require researchers to be able to think flexibly and expansively.

Conceptual Frameworks

Researchers sooner or later link their theories, hypotheses, working theories, and working hypotheses to related research and theory. Some case study research begins with conceptual frameworks based on pervious research and theory and sometimes also on professional and personal knowledge. Researchers develop hypotheses from conceptual frameworks. They further develop and test these hypotheses in the conduct of the research.

In some instances where researchers begin with conceptual frameworks, researchers might not derive hypotheses from the conceptual framework. Instead, researchers develop working hypotheses after they have begun their research. To do this, they take open-ended approaches in their efforts to understand individual cases. Eventually, they develop working hypotheses.

Finally, some case study research does not begin with conceptual frameworks at all, but instead researchers develop working hypotheses through open-ended research. Once they have working hypotheses, they then relate the working hypotheses to existing research and theory.

No matter when researchers derive their hypotheses, they must show how findings contribute to existing research and theory, challenge existing research and theory, and/or provide evidence for the modification of existing theory. The medical researchers studying Lou Gehrig's disease did just that. Their findings consisted of the theories they have developed, the evidence that supports their theories, and the links between the theories, the evidence, and previous research and theory.

In applied fields, researchers must also show the implications of their findings for practice. In the study of Lou Gehrig's disease, for example, the researchers recommended that, when athletes show symptoms of Lou Gehrig's disease, that physicians also explore the hypothesis that the athletes may have other degenerative diseases besides Lou Gehrig's. It makes sense that when patients present with symptoms of Lou Gehrig's disease that medical personnel take a detailed history that includes history of head trauma.

More Detail

As the previous discussion shows, case study research is theory-guided research and theory development research. The three ways that researchers develop working hypotheses have names. When researchers begin their research with a working hypothesis/theory derived from their conceptual framework, this is called analytic induction (AI) or deductive qualitative analysis (DQA), which is an updating of AI. Case studies that begin with theory go back for at least 100 years to the procedures used at the Chicago School of Sociology.

These initial hypotheses help focus the research and thus guide the conduct of the research, as in selecting samples, guiding the questions and the focus of observations, and in interpreting findings. The researchers who studied Lou Gehrig's disease used working hypotheses to guide their studies in this way.

Researchers continually revise their working hypotheses to fit their interpretations of the findings. Revisions occur as researchers look for cases and instances within cases that might contradict or add new dimensions to their working hypotheses. This is called negative case analysis. Researchers typically do AI/DQA when their goal is to test and develop already existing theory or when they want a clear focus at the onset of their investigations.

Beginning with a clear focus has many advantages, including making use of the literature review that most researchers conduct before they begin their research and also to test any ideas researchers developed from professional and personal experience. Dissertation committees and funders require literature reviews and clear foci. Therefore, researchers and students who want to do case study research typically do literature reviews and begin their studies with working hypotheses.

When researchers develop their working hypotheses in the course of doing the research, this procedure has the name *grounded theory*. The uses of theory in grounded theory are almost identical to the procedures of AI/DQA. Once researchers doing grounded theory have developed working hypotheses that guide their research, they seek to test and develop them further. Grounded theorists typically use theoretical sampling, which is a way of selecting the next case to study based upon what directions the researchers want to go in the development of their working theories/hypotheses. When researchers do not use theoretical sampling in the conduct of grounded theory, they have to explain how their method of sample selection served the purpose of further developing their theory.

Researchers who do an initial review of the literature and then being their research with no hypotheses to test are doing a viable kind of study. Once they develop their working hypotheses, their procedures are similar to those of GT and IA/DQA.

As researchers develop and test working hypotheses, they must be aware that their general store of knowledge and the literature review primes them so that certain theories and ideas are more salient in their minds than others. Thus, while grounded theorists want to be open-ended in identifying working hypotheses, they also are more likely to notice phenomena that are already salient. Researchers are never blank slates. Grounded theorists have a name for priming, which is theoretical sensitivity. In doing grounded theory, the assumption is that researchers have a wide repertoire of knowledge of theories and expertise based on professional and sometimes personal experience on which to draw. While this may be so for seasoned researchers, it is not the case for most new researchers. Thus, the more focused approached of AI/DQA may work better for new researchers.

Writing Up Case Study Research

When researchers write up case study research, they describe the procedures they used for developing, testing, and revising working hypotheses. They then document the evidence on which they base the final versions of their working hypotheses. In their analysis, they document each case carefully, developing an empirical generalization or working hypothesis for each case. Depending on the amount of space they have for research reports, they share varying amounts of the documentation for each working hypothesis. Next, they show how their working hypotheses are similar to, add to, contradict, and force modification of existing theory. Strong conceptual skills and capacities for abstract reasoning are required for this kind of analysis.

If researchers begin with a conceptual framework, they show how the findings led any modifications in the initial framework. If they did not begin with a conceptual framework, they build one based on findings.

In short, the findings of case study research include the theory researchers have developed, the evidence that supports the viability of the theory, and what the theory contributes to existing knowledge. In applied fields, researchers also make suggestions for how findings can be useful in practice, policies, and programs. As is true for any reports, researchers also make recommendations about types of further research that can continue to advance knowledge.

Classic Case Study Research

The theories of Freud, Piaget, and Erickson are based on case studies. They did intensive investigations of individual units, who were persons. They extracted from these case studies abstract concepts and principles. They showed the grounding of these abstractions through the presentation of case material. They described their reasoning and the logic of their thought. Through these efforts, they produced theory that revolutionized understandings of human development.

Case studies are the foundation of many disciplines. Laboratory experiments are case studies. Much of medical, legal, social work, and clinical psychology education is based on case studies. Students, with the guidance of professors, take intensive looks at individual units in order to derive lessons or working hypotheses about these cases. They then use these working hypotheses to help them understand subsequent cases. They study the characteristics of the subsequent cases and do the best job they can to see how their working hypotheses help them to understand and to make decisions about these subsequent cases. Professionals built their expertise when they extract general principles from case studies, test these principles on subsequent cases, and when the principles fit, use these principles to guide their practice. Throughout their practice with individual cases, professionals continually monitor whether their thinking and judgments fit the particularities of the cases.

A Note on Language

The language of social research can be confusing to newcomers. For example, the term *concept* is a synonyms for *variables*. Grounded theorists seek core concepts, which are the building blocks of hypotheses and theories. As shown in the previous discussion, the terms *hypothesis* and *theory* may be used interchangeably and which term to used depends upon context. The notion of conceptual framework is confusing, too. Typically *conceptual framework* refers to the entire first section of a proposal or research report, ending at the methods section. Some researchers, however, use the term *conceptual framework* to stand for initial hypotheses and sometimes for working hypotheses and working theory, and even for the final version of a theory that is part of the results of the research. Again, the contexts in which the term is used provide some clues as the meanings users intend.

Some other useful terms are *concept-indicator model* and first and *second order concepts*. Concepts in the concept-indicator model are abstractions from indicators. Indicators are descriptions of particular concrete social processes. First order concepts are defined in the same way as indicators. Second-order concepts are defined the same way as concepts in the concept-indicator model. The ideas of concept-indicator and first and second-order concepts are important in case study research. In reporting findings, researchers must present their theories, which are based on concepts, and the evidence for their theories, which are indicators or first-order concepts. Situating findings within existing research and theory is the next step in building case study findings. The final step is composed of recommendations for further research and applications.

Discussion

Case study research is valuable because of its contribution to theory. Without reference to theory, case studies provide anecdotal information. In other words, case studies only have value in relationship to currently held understandings and practices.

Case study research is difficult. Researchers must have superior conceptual skills. They must be able to apply concepts and hypotheses to particular situations, to extract concepts and hypotheses from particular situations, to use evidence to modify working hypotheses and to develop new working hypotheses, to explain how they developed the theory, to write theory clearly, to present the evidence that supports their contention that their theory is viable and credible, and relate the theory they develop to what is already known.

If researchers begin with a conceptual framework, they must be able to identify the range of research and theory that is relevant to their topic, understand, categorize, and synthesize this information, and, in AI/DQA, derive hypotheses from the conceptual framework. They then must further develop and test their initial hypotheses, seek disconfirming evidence, keep track of the changes they make in their working hypotheses and the data that led them to make changes. They then have to situate their findings in what is already known. In choosing not to develop initial working hypotheses while engaged in the research, in the style of grounded theory, researchers must have skills that are similar to those of researchers who begin their studies with hypotheses.

References & Further Reading

Bryant, Antony & Kathy Charmaz (Eds.) (2007). *The Sage handbook of grounded theory.* Thousand Oaks, CA: Sage.

Corbin, Juliet & Anselm Strauss. (2008). *Basics of qualitative research: Techniques and procedures for developing grounded theory* (3rd ed.). Thousand Oaks, CA: Sage.

Covan, Eleanor Krassen (2007). The discovery of grounded theory in practice: The legacy of multiple methods In Antony Bryant & Kathy Charmaz (Eds.), *The Sage handbook of grounded theory* (pp. 58-93). Thousand Oaks, CA: Sage.

Denzin, Norman (1997). Coffee with Anselm. *Qualitative Family Research, 11 (1 & 2),* 1-3. http://www.scribd.com/doc/27352636/Coffee-with-Anselm

Ellet, William. (2007). *The case study handbook: How to read, discuss and write persuasively about case studies.* Harvard, MA: Harvard Business School.

Espino, Michelle M., Susana M. Muñoz, & Judy Marquez Kiyama (2010). Transitioning from doctoral study to the academy: Theorizing trenzas of identity for Latina sister scholars. *Qualitative Inquiry, 16(10),* 804-818.

Glaser, Barney & Anselm Strauss (1967). *The discovery of grounded theory.* Chicago: Aldine.

Gilgun, Jane F. (1992). Hypothesis generation in social work research. *Journal of Social Service Research, 15,* 113-135.
http://www.scribd.com/doc/45000017/Hypothesis-Generation-in-Social-Work-Research

Gilgun, Jane F. (1993). Erik Erikson and case study research. Current Issues in Qualitative Research, 8(1), 1-2.
http://www.scribd.com/doc/38414815/Erik-Erikson-Case-Study-Research

Gilgun, Jane F. (1994). A case for case studies in social work research. *Social Work,*
39, 371-380.

Gilgun, Jane F. (2011). Coding in deductive qualitative analysis.
http://www.scribd.com/doc/47331325/Coding-in-Deductive-Qualitative-Analysis

Gilgun, Jane F. (2010). A primer on deductive qualitative analysis as theory testing and theory development.
http://www.scribd.com/doc/35886233/A-Primer-on-Deductive-Qualitative-Analysis-as-Theory-Testing-Theory-Development

Gilgun, Jane F. (2010). Methods for enhancing theory and knowledge about problems, policies, and practice. In Katherine Briar, Joan Orme, Roy Ruckdeschel, & Ian Shaw, *The Sage handbook of social work research* (pp. 281-297).

Gilgun, Jane F. (2010). The power of the case.
http://www.scribd.com/doc/36079001/The-Power-of-the-Case

Gilgun, Jane F. (2005). Qualitative research and family psychology. *Journal of Family* Psychology,19(1), 40-50.

McKee, Ann C., & Brandon E. Gavett, et al (2010). TDP-43 proteinopathy and motor neuron disease in chronic traumatic encephalopathy. *Journal of Neuropathology & Experimental Neurology, 69(9),* 918-299.

Sternberg, Robert J. (2009). *Cognitive psychology* (5th ed.). Belmont, CA: Wadsworth.

Strauss, Anselm (1992). A personal history of grounded theory. Qualtiative Family Research, 5 (2), 1-2.

http://www.scribd.com/doc/44659994/Anselm-Strauss-Writes-A-Personal-History-of-Grounded-Theory-Other-Articles

Tracy, Sarah J. (2010). Qualitative quality: Eight "big-tent" criteria for excellent qualitative research. *Qualitative Inquiry, 16 (8)*, 837-851.

Yin, Robert K. (2010). *Case study research: Design and methods* (4th ed.). Thousand Oaks, CA: Sage.

18

HAND INTO GLOVE: GROUNDED THEORY, DEDUCTIVE QUALITATIVE ANALYSIS, AND SOCIAL WORK RESEARCH AND PRACTICE

This paper updates an earlier version published more than 18 years ago (Gilgun, 1994c). I kept an emphasis on grounded theory research, and I added information on deductive qualitative analysis, which involves hypothesis-testing and theory-guided research in the conduct of qualitative research. These additions are responsive to funders and dissertation committees who are more likely to support research that begins with conceptual models and testable hypotheses. Grounded theory and deductive qualitative analysis have common roots within the Chicago School of Sociology and work well for knowledge-building in social work. Social work academics and activists made contributions to the Chicago School and thus can claim to be part of the original formulations of analytic induction, on which grounded theory is based. Deductive qualitative analysis is an updated version of analytic induction.

This chapter was first published as Gilgun, Jane F. (2012) Hand into glove: Grounded theory, deductive qualitative analysis and social work research and practice. In Anne E. Fortune, William Reid, & Robert Miller (Eds.). Qualitative Methods in Social Work *(2nd ed.) (pp. 107-134). New York: Columbia University Press.*

GROUNDED THEORY and deductive qualitative analysis are important ways to do social work research. They can contribute to knowledge-building not only in the three main areas of social work direct practice--assessment, intervention, and evaluation--but also in other domains where social workers practice, such as policy research, program development and evaluation, community organizing, social development, advocacy, and studies of program implementation. The findings of grounded theory (GT) and deductive qualitative analysis (DQA) are a good fit with the research agenda of social work because they arise out of the interaction of researchers with research participants, show multiple meanings and multiple dimensions of human phenomena, and, at their best, show connections between concepts and theories and their concrete indicators in the natural world. Social work's emphasis on social justice comes to life when researchers seek the meanings that research participants attribute to social issues that are part of their lived experience. The emphasis of GT and DQA on multiple meanings and perspectives sensitizes researchers to the worlds of direct practitioners, which typically are complicated, untidy, sometimes confusing, and often and sometimes traumatizing (Gilgun, 2008; 2010b, 2013).

In addition, the procedures of GT and DQA are similar to many of the procedures of direct practice and practice in other domains as well, including processes of interviewing and observing, developing and testing hypotheses in response to complex, situated phenomena, skills in organizing massive amounts of data, and emphasis on values such self-determination and doing no harm. Learning how to do these types of research and using the findings may feel natural to social work practitioners who seek research training in graduate programs, like sliding a hand into a well-made glove. In fact, some claim that the procedures of this style of research are similar to excellent everyday thinking (Corbin & Strauss, 2008).

The purpose of this chapter is to demonstrate the relevance of GT and DQA to the development of knowledge relevant to social work direct practice. Although the focus is limited to direct practice, the ideas may be tested for fit with other domains of practice. The chapter begins with a discussion of the procedures for doing these two forms of qualitative analysis, moves on to a demonstration of parallels between these procedures and the assumptions of direct practice, and then provides an overview of the kinds of products that researchers can develop from these two approaches. While there are many ways to do qualitative research, I chose to focus on two approaches, both of which have roots in the Chicago School of Sociology, that, in turn, have connections to social work research in the first part of the twentieth century (Bulmer, 1984; Deegan, 1990; Gilgun, 1999c, 2012, 2013).

Definitions

For the purposes of this discussion, hypotheses are statements of relationships between concepts or variables. Concepts are the components of hypotheses and are abstractions from concrete descriptions of processes and other phenomena. Theories are composed of inter-related hypotheses. They are provisional and subject to further testing and modification. A set of related theories become models when they are thought to account for how something works. Models may be theoretical; that is, researchers have not tested them. They typically are based on multiple sources of information, such as research, theory, practitioner expertise, personal experience, and personal and professional values.

Direct practice is any form of social work that involves face-to-face contact and interaction with service users. This includes child welfare, children's mental health, medical social work, work in shelters, group homes, and residential treatment programs, therapy with families, couples, and individuals, group work, community organizing, and in the many other domains in which social workers do their practice.

Deductive Qualitative Analysis

Many researchers assume that to do qualitative studies, they have to begin their research with no hypotheses to test and, in so doing, by-pass hypothesis testing and theory-guided research (Gilgun, 2005b, 2010b). This wide-spread impression stems at least in part from the idea of "emergence," linked to procedures of GT (Glaser & Strauss, 1967; Glaser 2007; Corbin & Strauss, 2008) where researchers assume that researchable questions and valuable findings will arise through immersion in the worlds of informants (e.g., research participants). Yet, researchers interested in particular bodies of research and theoretical models cannot nor should they be expected to start anew, or act as if they don't already know something about their areas of interest. There is no reason why they cannot test their theories and models qualitatively or do theory-guided research. Furthermore, dissertation committees are unlikely to approve studies that don't build on what is already known, nor are funders inclined to commit money to such studies (Gilgun, 2005b, 2010a).

Deductive qualitative analysis recognizes these issues and provides guidelines for doing research that begins with an initial conceptualization that can range from a parsimonious model or theory to a rather loose set of ideas. I use term *deductive qualitative analysis*, after trying out many others, because my experience had led me to conclude that having a prior conceptual framework is an important way to do qualitative research. I pieced together the procedures of DQA from earlier work on analytic induction (Cressey, 1953; Lindesmith, 1947; Znaniecki, 1934) and the thinking of philosophers John Dewey (1910) and Karl Popper (1969).

The unit of analysis of DQA is the case. Cases are individual units. The cases themselves can be simple or complex. Simple cases are composed of a single person or other individual phenomenon of interest. Complex cases are composed of two or more entities of interest, such as case studies of couples, families, agencies, counties, provinces, countries, and regions of the world.

In DQA, coding, analysis, and interpretation can be done any number of ways, such as the generic three-level codes described in works on GT (Corbin & Strauss, 2008; Strauss, 1987; Strauss & Corbin, 1998) or the kinds of analysis associated with interpretive phenomenology (Benner, 1994; Crist & Tanner, 2003) that include several levels of analysis such as the identification of themes and the construction of exemplars and paradigm cases. Group analysis of data is effective because researchers can discuss emerging understandings with other people who have different life experiences, training, knowledge, and perspectives (Olesen, Droes, et al, 1994). In this way, it is more likely that the findings will account for the complexity and variations of social phenomena. Group analysis of data originates at least with Charles Booth's studies of the London poor in the latter part of the nineteenth century (Webb & Webb, 1932).

Typically, analysis includes three levels of writing. The first level is writing up individual cases in their complexities. The second level is making comparisons between and across cases. The third-level is comparing the conclusions of the first two levels of analysis with existing research and theory and any personal and professional experiences that might be relevant. Researchers then change their hypotheses to fit these findings and ground these revisions in data. The procedures are similar for each successive case. The final product is a hypothesis or a set of hypotheses that fit the cases on which researchers developed them.

Induction and Deduction

My use of the term *deduction* in this paper is modeled after Dewey (1910) who provided a discussion of what he calls "complete thinking" which involves both deduction and induction. Deduction is a process of testing working hypotheses, for the purposes of "confirming, refuting, and modifying" (p. 82) them. Hypotheses are working hypotheses when researchers do not think of them as final conclusions, but as emerging understandings that are open to further testing and change. Induction is the processes of creating abstractions from concrete data, which is probably impossible to do independently of deductive thinking because we notice and overlook phenomena depending upon the prior ideas we carry with us (Blumer, 1986; Gilgun, 1999c, 2010a; 2013). Nonetheless, inductive thinking represents an attempt to put aside researchers' own views and do active listening and open-minded observations in research interviewing, observations, and document analysis. Glaser (1978) has offered the concept of theoretical sensitivity and Blumer (1986) the idea of sensitizing concepts to help us understand how prior ideas are part of processes that some consider to be inductive.

Dewey's pragmatist philosophy influenced the Chicago School of Sociology (Bulmer, 1984; Deegan, 1990) whose faculty and students developed the procedures of analytic induction (AI). It's important to note that some Chicago School faculty members were social workers, such as Hull House residents Sophonisba Breckinridge and Edith Abbott (Abbott, 1910; Abbott and Breckinridge, 1916; Deegan, 1990). In addition, the Chicago School faculty, including Dewey, were in on-going dialogue for years with Jane Addams and other residents of Hull House about the conduct of urban research and on the pragmatist philosophy of experience and action (Bulmer, 1984; Deegan, 1990, 2006; Gilgun, 1999c, 2013).

Analytic induction recognizes the movement between induction and deduction and the importance of modifying theory to fit available evidence. To ensure that theories are adequately tested, transformed, refined, and even refuted, researchers who do analytic induction engage in negative case analysis (Cressey, 1953), a sampling method that involves the selection of cases that have promise of undermining the emerging understandings that researchers construct over the course of data collection and analysis. When researchers see that some findings contradict their hypotheses, they change their hypotheses to fit these new findings. Thus, hypotheses may show patterns and variations within the phenomena of interest. This method fits with Popper's (1969) idea of conjectures, refutations, and reformulations that he believes is the fundamental process of science. This method also has the potential to account for multiple possible variations in human phenomena, such as how persons cope with adversities or how people from non-Western cultures respond to Western medical procedures. One size, one pattern does not fit all.

In earlier writings, I used the term *analytic induction* to describe what I am now calling DQA (e.g., Gilgun, 2001a, 2001b, 1995). Analytic induction is the procedure that researchers used on now classic studies, such as the work of Becker, Geer, Hughes, and Strauss (1961), Cressey (1953), and Lindesmith (1947). The primary reason I prefer the term *deduction* is my belief that induction is not possible as an initial step in the doing of research. In order to sort particular observations from innumerable possible observations, researchers do not begin as blank slates, as noted earlier. Something helps them notice particular phenomena and not others. I view this something as prior knowledge, sensitizing concepts, conceptual frameworks, or cognitive schemas, call them what you will, that orients researchers as to what to notice and what to overlook. Even Glaser and Strauss (1967), widely considered premier and pioneering inductive qualitative researchers, acknowledge the impossibility of researchers being blank slates in a footnote in their well-known text. Induction, then, is a misnomer in this type of research.

A second reason I decided to put together procedures that I call deductive qualitative analysis was to invite researchers trained in logico-deductive methods to do qualitative research. For too long, the idea that qualitative research does not begin with a conceptual model has been dominant. Social work researchers have a wealth of theory-, research-, and practice-based knowledge that can be put to use in qualitative studies whose purpose is to document and understand the complexities of person-environment interactions. Even personal experience and values have their places in knowledge building. None of these models, no matter how constructed, can be taken for granted. They must be tested not only for fit but for lack of fit with particular persons in particular places, at particular times. In this way, results that researchers develop will be closely linked to experiences of service users and thus will be useful to policy, programs, prevention, and intervention.

A third reason I encourage DQA in my teaching and writing is the wide-spread perception that AI is based on obsolete philosophies of science that promote the idea that researchers should seek causal and universal hypotheses that are invariant and that researchers can construct such hypotheses on as few as one or two cases (Gilgun, 2001a, 2010a). Because of these claims, the term has a "spoiled identity." Some commentators (Goldenberg, 1993; Manning, 1982; Robinson, 1951; Vidich & Lyman, 2000) dismissed AI because of the claims of universality and invariance. As a result, the term *analytic induction* has rarely been used for about 50 years. Glaser and Strauss (1967) mention the procedure but dismiss it with little commentary.

Types of Initial Conceptual Models

In DQA, the initial conceptual model with which researchers begin their studies may range from tightly defined to rough and unfocused, as mentioned earlier. One possible type of initial conceptual model is highly abstract and parsimonious, based on previous research and theory and from which researchers construct hypotheses to be tested qualitatively.

This type of hypothesis testing appears not to have been done in social work as of yet, but it is a viable approach.

A second type of conceptual model is composed of a loose set of ideas and concepts derived from one or more sources such as previous research and theory, professional experience, and personal experience. Researchers can put this model to many different uses, such as to develop open-ended hypotheses that bring some focus to the study, use the model to do pattern matching, or use the theory as a guide in exploring new areas of understanding. In pattern matching, researchers use the conceptual model as a screen that they place over their findings (Campbell, 1979). They then compare the patterns of the conceptual model with the patterns of the findings they construct from data.

An example of hypothesis-testing based on a loose framework is my analysis of the moral discourse of incest perpetrators where I began with hypotheses I developed from theories of feminist moral development and ended with revised hypotheses that I constructed from my analysis (Gilgun, 1995). An example of pattern matching is my work with Brommel on emotion display rules and the accounts prison inmates gave of their violent behaviors in families and communities (Gilgun and Brommel, 2004). We first developed a framework that delineated possible ways that men display their emotions and then we compared this framework to how the men actually expressed their emotions. An example of theory-guided research is the analysis of Abrams (2003) on young women's gender identity negotiations. Abrams used a loose conceptual framework to illuminate and interpret her analysis. This use of prior theory is common in qualitative research, as perusals of journals show.

A third type of DQA begins with roughly formulated ideas and hunches, sometimes based on professional and/or personal experience. The guidance that this type of DQA provides is that of a general orientation or framework. Elizabeth Bott's (1957) work on family social networks is a classic example, where she used Lewin's ecology theory as her initial general framework, had no hypotheses to test, and ended with a richly described social network theory, where she shared her processes of theorizing in some detail. Undoubtedly, there are many other ways to use conceptual models at the onset of qualitative research, and there are probably more to be developed.

Researchers have to be on the alert to ensure they are not fitting their findings into pre-established categories, or imposing theory onto findings (Glaser & Strauss, 1967). Negative case analysis and group analysis of data, discussed earlier, guard against this. The final product of theory-testing efforts in qualitative research is a set of concepts and inter-related hypotheses that have been subjected to rigorous analysis. During the course of testing and analysis, researchers typically fold into the model additional related research and theory that enhance and clarify the meanings and significance of the components of the model that are under development, which is the third level of analysis mentioned earlier. Such a well-documented and well-tested model can be developed for assessments, interventions, policy and programs. They can also be subjected to statistical analysis. As Lenzenweger (2004) stated in his discussion of taxometric analysis, a salient issue in statistical analysis is the adequacy of the underlying model. Deductive qualitative analysis is a significant way to construct conceptual models. As researchers explore the potential of this approach, relevant, generative theories about phenomena relevant to social work will continue to grow.

Grounded Theory Approaches

The purposes of GT, according to Strauss and Corbin (1998), are "to "Build rather than test theory" and to "Identify, develop and relate the concepts that are the building blocks of theory." (p. 13). A key idea is the identification of research problems, or basic social processes, as a result of immersion in the field. Strauss, who earned a PhD in sociology from the University of Chicago in the mid-1950s, carried on many of the traditions of the Chicago School of Sociology. Thus, DQA and GT have some research traditions in common (Gilgun, 2001b, 2005b).

To generate grounded theory, researchers enter the field, according to Glaser (1992), with "an open mind to the emergence of the subjects' problem" (p. 23), with a trust that the central problem will emerge, and with a commitment "not to know" until it does (p. 24). Many influences "core out" the central problem, such as the researchers' training, the location of the study, the nature of the research subjects, funding, among others. Both Strauss and Glaser maintained a career-long interest in basic social processes, derived from Lazarfeld's elaboration analysis and symbolic interaction theory (Glaser, 1978, 1992; Glaser and Strauss, 1967; Strauss, 1987; Strauss & Corbin, 1998). Thus, "emergence" might not be an accurate term because we see in texts what we've already been sensitized to see; our own favored theories and other "coring out" influences shape our interpretations of texts. Nonetheless, the point here is to make every effort to understand and theorize informants' (research participants) points of views and attempt to refute and reformulate them.

The Original Formulation

In its original formulation, an initial conceptual model was not part of GT. The originators considered such models preconceptions and a way of attaining "a grounded modifying of theory" (Glaser and Strauss, 1967, p. 2). In their first book-length publications, Glaser and Straus (1967) and Glaser (1978) expressed concern that when researchers start with a "preconception," they will force data into the model rather than to construct concepts and hypotheses based on their observations or what research respondents tell them. My experience as a researcher has shown that negative case analysis, discussed earlier and based on the ideas of conjectures, refutations, and reformulations, and group analysis of data, help researchers to avoid such forcing.

Glaser and Strauss (1967) proposed GT in response to the kinds of theory that they said was prevalent at the time: highly abstract, disconnected from relevant social problems, non-modifiable, and whose sources were not always clear. They also had concerns about the imposition of theory onto observations and the tacking on of theory at the end of a report based on atheoretical research.

Later Formulations

Over time, Strauss softened his stance on the place of prior research and theory in the conduct of GT (cf., Corbin & Strauss, 2008; Strauss & Corbin, 1998), while Glaser (1992) remained committed to the earlier idea. In his last formulation, published after his death in 1995, Strauss and his co-author Juliet Corbin (Strauss & Corbin, 1998), offered several different uses of research and theory before entering the field and while engaged in analysis and interpretation. I will highlight some of them.

One use is as sources of research questions and problems to be studied, although the focus of the study should eventually be on the concerns of respondents as identified through fieldwork. They also acknowledged that prior knowledge may sensitize researchers to particular questions and concerns, which is akin to Blumer's (1986) idea of sensitizing concepts that help researchers to identify patterns and meanings in data.

Another use of preconceived theory is what I've called deductive qualitative analysis (DQA). For Strauss and Corbin (1998), researchers use preconceptions when they want to "elaborate and extend an existing theory" (p. 12). In the later edition of their co-authored book, Corbin and Strauss (2008) wrote with approval about the work of a researcher who used a prior framework, namely one of Strauss's grounded theories, to structure her own research. She used Strauss's grounded theory throughout her research, from the initial conceptualization to the choice of measurement instruments. Citing discussions with me about the use of prior frameworks, Corbin in Corbin and Strauss, said that "Though it is these authors' preference not to begin our research with a predefined theoretical framework or set of concepts, we acknowledge in some instances theoretical frameworks can be useful" (p. 39).

My preferences depend upon my research issue. In my long-term research on the development of violent behaviors and the meanings of violence to perpetrators, I immersed myself in the field with no "predefined theoretical frameworks or sets of concepts." I did have a value-based framework based on social justice and care and a conviction that violence is wrong. The purpose of my research is primary prevention, which is an emancipatory, social justice and care stance (Gilgun, 2010c). Over the course of many years, I have developed what appears to be a complex theory that involved the procedures that Corbin and Strauss (2008) prefer. The full scope of the theory is yet unpublished, although I have published many pieces over the years. I developed DQA because of its efficiency and its common sense for researchers who want to do and sometimes must do focused qualitative research, "must do" because of external constraints from gatekeepers, such as funders and dissertation committees. (Gilgun, 2005b).

Another use of related research and theory that Strauss and Corbin endorse is its use in data analysis and interpretation. They said that a commitment to a particular theoretical model can blind researchers to other possible interpretations of their data. They gave as an example the experience of a student researcher "who had difficulty *not* seeing exchange theory" (Strauss & Corbin, 1998, p. 69) in his interviews with African-American adolescent boys about their negotiations for sex with their female peers. In class discussions, other students shared their interpretations, including ideas of negotiation and manipulation, gender role expectations, and consumerism. The student left the class with new ideas about how to interpret his interview material. This analysis shows the commitment of grounded theorists to group analysis of data so as to broaden and sharpen their interpretations.

Data Collection

Methods of data collection typical in GT and in other forms of qualitative research as well, including DQA, are interviews, observations, and document analysis. Videotapes and transcripts of audiotapes, can provide some of the documents that compose the texts that are analyzed as well as archived narrative material such as oral histories, photographs and other graphic materials, and case records.

Many researchers use a combination of methods. Open-ended interviewing is particularly amenable to soliciting the points of view of informants. Observation and interviewing often brings researchers into the social world of informants. For this reason, GT and DQA research commonly are naturalistic, that is, taking place in everyday settings where people live their lives. Writing fieldnotes either during or immediately after interviewing or observations and mechanical recording through audio or videotapes are typical methods of capturing data. Researchers often embed observer comments and memos within fieldnotes. Observer comments are spontaneous reactions in the forms of thoughts, emotions, or insights that come to them as they write their fieldnotes or that they recall they had in the process of data collection. Memos usually come at the end of fieldnotes and are analytic attempts at interpretation, including making connections between the emerging findings and related research and theory. Bogdan and Biklen (2007) have an excellent discussion of fieldnotes, observer comments, and memos. In some instances, informants themselves provide written data, as for example, when they write out their own life histories (Taylor & Bogdan, 1998).

Theoretical Sampling

Sampling in GT is theoretical, which means that sampling depends on what researchers want to know next, and they guide their choice of next case by what they find in their comparisons within and across cases (Glaser and Strauss, 1967; Strauss and Corbin, 1998). Rarely is there reason to do random or convenience sampling in GT, although descriptive qualitative researchers may make use of these methods. In doing theoretical sampling, researchers select a homogeneous sample on which to focus. They continue interviewing and/or observing and/or analyzing textual and graphic records until they find that they are learning little or nothing that adds to their emerging understandings. They are at the point of theoretical saturation. Researchers then reflect on what comparisons they need to make next to deepen their understanding. These reflections lead to a decision of which kind of sample to recruit next. An example is in a study I did on incest perpetrators and the women who were married to them (Gilgun, 1992) where I wanted to isolate qualities what differentiated incest perpetrators from persons with similar social histories.

Coding

Strauss and colleagues' coding scheme is a set of generic procedures that can be used in research other than GT, such as oral histories and other narrative approaches. For example, they originated a coding scheme that at first accounted for two levels of analysis (Glaser and Strauss, 1967; Glaser, 1978) and then added selective coding as the third (Strauss & Corbin, 1998). The first level is open coding, where researchers search transcripts, fieldnotes, and other texts for meaning units, which they label. These labels are the codes. The second level consists of axial coding where researchers decide whether a concept is substantial enough to become a core concept, where a core concept is code around which researchers can develop an analysis (Strauss, 1987; Strauss &Corbin, 1998). An example of a core concept is emotion regulation, where it is likely that in any given text that focuses on emotion, emotion regulation will tie together many aspects of emotion and its expression. The third level of coding is selective, which researchers do after they have chosen the core concepts and want to dimensionalize them. Selective coding involves fleshing out of the core concepts by finding in the texts as many relevant instances of the phenomena that the concepts represent.

Research Questions and Hypotheses

Another point that the originators of GT made is their understandings of qualitative research questions and hypotheses. From their points of view, the purposes of research questions are to provide a general focus to the research, a focus that will sharpen as researchers engage with respondents, listen to their stories, and observe them in interaction with others. The idea of independent and dependent variables is rare in qualitative research. Instead, researchers want to know how respondents experience something, think about something, or respond to something, and researchers look for the processes involved. Hypotheses can be written in any number of ways. The hypotheses that Strauss and Corbin and other qualitative researchers use are statements of relationships that link two or more concepts, as stated earlier. For example, a hypothesis I tested in my research on the moral discourse of incest perpetrators (Gilgun, 1995) was "Incest perpetrators have special regard for themselves and do not have regard for the impact of incest on their victims" (p. 268). I used the language I did because I developed this hypotheses from writings on justice and care, which used the term "special regard." Persons unfamiliar with qualitative methods might not recognize this as a hypothesis at all.

Summary. Although widely thought of as an approach that eschews the formulation of conceptual frameworks prior to entering the field, contemporary grounded theorists at least entertain this as a possibility. Deductive qualitative analysis is my attempt to encourage researchers to test, refine, reformulate, refute, and replace theoretical models qualitatively. This approach acknowledges the importance of logico-deductive methods, although I depart in many ways from traditional ways of doing this kind of research. Qualitative thinking underlies all science (Cook & Campbell, 1979). Qualitative analysis is a way of thinking, whether or not the research begins with a conceptual model or develops what appears to be a new one in the process of doing the research.

Finally, GT is a far more detailed set of procedures for doing qualitative research than is DQA. What DQA adds is an invitation to do deductive research, suggestions for several different types of deductive qualitative research, guidelines for ensuring that researchers do not impose preconceptions onto their findings (search for negative evidence/conjectures and refutations), and guidelines for ensuring that findings account for diversities (negative case analysis). Many of the notions and procedures of GT fit well with DQA, including the coding scheme that GT encourages, the notions of core concepts and their dimensions, definitions of hypotheses, commitment to identifying and representing the points of view of informants, and open-mindedness as to how researchers present their findings, among many others. The notions of processes, contexts, and consequences are embedded within GT, and, although researchers may not use these terms, much of qualitative research involves these ideas.

Links to Direct Practice

The following characteristics are typical within GT and DQA. Other forms of qualitative research, such as narrative analysis (Riessman, 1993, 2008) and oral histories (Martin, 1995), frequently have some of these qualities as well. Many of these characteristics are also procedures that are present within direct practice.

Connections

Qualitative approaches allow researchers to connect with other people in deeply personal ways. The two main types of qualitative methods, in-depth interviewing and observation, bring researchers into close contact with lived experiences of the persons with whom we do research. These interactions often involve personal and sometimes painful topics that can evoke powerful emotions in researchers and informants. In such evocative situations, researchers have opportunities to explore deep meanings of the phenomena of interest and thus develop new theories and understandings that have rich and nuanced dimensions (Gilgun, 2008, 2010b; 2012, 2013).

The knowledge we gain, therefore, is not information that simply passes through the central processors of our brains. It also arises from our hearts and often our deeply-held emotions. Understandings gained through an engagement of heart and mind have an immediacy that potentially connects to the hearts and minds of audiences. Giesela Konopka (1958, 1963, 1966, 1988), who died in December 2003 at the age of 93, practiced this kind of social work research. She said, "Get to know people. Live there with them. Let them talk" (personal communication, September 2001).

The persons who are social work's constituencies--children who have been maltreated, poor minorities of color, homeless families, persons with mental illness, and frail elderly, among many others—are typically disenfranchised and excluded from the political system. Their voices are routinely suppressed within the many arenas in which their fates are debated and shaped--public opinion, the mass media, legislatures, and sometimes even social service agencies.

Researchers share a professional and cultural authority that permits us, if we so choose, to bring these voices to the forefront of public decisions and debates (Weick, 2000). This power to speak for others is by nature a problematic and unequal power arrangement and a subject of discussion by many within and outside the discipline of social work. Witkin (1999), editor of *Social Work* during the end of the 20th century and the beginning of the 21st, recognized the urgency of including the voices of clients within the arenas in which their interests are at stake.

There are at least three potential pitfalls to the closeness of contact, however, with safeguards for all three. One pitfall is the risk of a loss of an analytic stance. Researchers need to stay in tune with informants while at the same time maintaining a focus on concepts and hypotheses that are to be explored and tested. Sometimes the material informants provide is compelling to the point where researchers are drawn so far into the worlds of informants that researchers do not explore other aspects of informants' experience. The result is a limited description of phenomena. Researcher can lose the balance between being in tune and being over-whelmed.

Informants in subsequent cases, however, usually do not focus on precisely what informants from previous cases have focused on. There-fore, over the course of conducting several case studies, researchers can identify multiple aspects of phenomena, and the possible narrowness of findings in one case is corrected by findings in subsequent cases. Most grounded theorists—and qualitative researchers in general—interview informants more than once. This has many advantages, including clarify-ing and extending discussions from previous interviews and comparing what other informants have said, and refining and amplifying emerging understandings.

A second possible pitfall related to closeness to data in GT and DQA approaches is emotional reactions to research findings. Many re-searchers investigate sensitive issues, such as treatment of persons in institutions, death and dying, loss, serious illness, woman physical abuse, rape, and child abuse. Researchers often have strong personal reactions to such content. This, too, can lead to a loss of analytic stance. There-fore, in order to maintain an analytic stance, researchers can benefit from working in teams. Discussion with other team members not only can help researchers deal with personal reactions, but it also can help re-searchers process their findings, leading to further insight into the world of informants, as discussed earlier.

A third pitfall is the possibility of ethical lapses in the conduct of re-search. Social work researchers are bound to the NASW Code of Ethics (Gilgun & Abrams, 2002). Researchers have responsibility for the ethical conduct of their research, no matter what informants might do or appear to do. There are many possible ethical breaches, including boundary vio-lations that researchers commit and boundary violations that researchers permit and even encourage. The first principles of ethical conduct are to do no harm and to protect the well-being of others. The task of Human Subjects Committees is the protection of human subjects, and, of course, every university-based qualitative study must have their approval and oversight. Beyond this, however, social work researchers must under-stand the power differential between themselves and their informants. They must also understand that their status may result in informants complying rather than giving full informed consent. Thus, I recommend that researchers encourage informants not to answer any question they do not want to answer and to stop talking about an issue if they start feeling uncomfortable. I routinely tell informants this and ask them if they'd like to stop if I think they are going outside of their zone of safety.

Researcher self-disclosure, if well-timed, may contribute to the quality of the research. Yet, with the emotion-laden nature of qualitative research, it is important for researchers to make sure that they maintain their analytic stance and not let themselves slide into self-disclosure that is self-indulgent and shuts informants out. Ethically, it is also important not to develop friendships with informants. In addition, sexual relationships are a serious ethical breach and are grounds for serious discipline, such as loss of licenses to practice social work.

Contextualized Findings

The "grounded" nature of qualitative research extends in several directions. Sampling strategies and comparison within and across cases lead to findings that encompass multiple aspects of phenomena. Rarely are concepts defined uni-dimensionally. The goal of describing multiple aspects of phenomena almost automatically leads to embedding phenomena in their contexts. Findings become inextricably linked to context. The "thick description" (Geertz, 1973) characteristic of GT and DQA means that findings are presented multi-dimensionally and in ways that show the phenomena as part of a context (Gilgun, 1992, 2012, 2013; Gilgun & Abrams, 2002).

Patterns and Theories

Theory produced by GT and DQA is pattern theory, which Kaplan (1964) described as hypotheses arranged in horizontal relationships to each other and not hierarchically, with the most abstract first and the later-stated hypotheses as deductions. Pattern theory often is context-specific, and therefore can be at a fairly low level of abstraction. Yet, pattern theory attempts to account for dominant and not so prevalent patterns.

The rich, descriptive data that qualitative methods yield also lends itself to the development of typologies, a strategy for organizing findings that show similarities, differences, and overlaps between and within classes of phenomena. Typologies are particularly helpful in educational and clinical settings, where practitioners are confronted with complex human behaviors. Often interventions, such as medication, educational strategies, and forms of therapy, are linked to classifications that typologies can provide. Robinson et al (200100) used observations of family physicians' responses to patients' emotional distress and developed a four-quadrant typology: the Technician, the Friend, the Detective, and the Healer. They noted that this typology can contribute to physician training, and it can also provide direction to future research that asks such questions such as whether physician style is linked to outcome and whether patients select physicians who suit their personal preferences. A classic example of the use of typologies is E. Franklin Frazier's (1932) *The Negro Family in Chicago* where he classified American "Negroes" as migrants, old settlers, and *nouveaux riches*.

Pattern theory is quite different from hierarchical theory, which is characteristic of much logico-deductive research. Hierarchical theory is composed of a relatively small number of highly abstract principles from which hypotheses are deduced. These hypotheses then are tested, usually using highly complex mathematical formulas on a relatively small number of variables, which are abstracted from context. Hierarchical theory, especially when combined with probability theory, seeks to account only for findings thought to be dominant, and relegates less dominant patterns to the status of error term or outlier. An example of hierarchical theory is the following:

The most consistent findings from studies of family structure and socialization are that single parents exert weaker controls and make fewer demands on children than married parents, while stepparents provide less warmth than do original parents (Thomson, McLanahan, and Curtin, 1992, p. 368).

These general statements are important because they provide an overview of social phenomena, but they are difficult to apply to individual cases unless practitioners are aware of the importance of looking for exceptions to these "normative" statements. Findings stated like this do not account for parents who are exceptions to these patterns, and they invite thinking that one pattern fits all cases. Therefore, they invite stereotyping. Contextual variables and individual experiences and perceptions also are not taken into account. Evidence for such a statement is not based on in-depth studies of parents' experience, but usually on one-time telephone or in-person structured interviews, which, of course, do provide valuable information, but it is not rich and in-depth, a fact that practitioners must keep in mind as they use such findings. Without thinking of exceptions and testing for fit, such statements, when practitioners apply them to practice, risk ignoring individualization and discounting information that is important to specific contexts.

In many senses, therefore, the findings of GT and DQA are more idiographic than nomothetic. They are focused on understanding individual situations and testing to see if findings can illuminate other situations. The process of testing to see if previous findings are relevant to a new situation can be thought of as pattern-matching, where the findings of one case are tested for their fit on succeeding cases (Campbell, 1979). The findings make no claim to be generalizable to all members of a class. Even the findings of nomothetic research cannot claim that their findings will fit a particular situation. This is the ecological fallacy (Rubin & Babbie, 2010). What might be true in general of a group may not be true of individual members of that group (Runyan, 1982). Cronbach (1975) pointed out that findings in any type of research situation must be treated as working hypotheses when applied to local settings. The processes of pattern-matching results in a type of generalizability called *analytic*, which is much different from probabilistic generalizations, which is most commonly taught in research and statistics courses (Gilgun, 1994a; 2005b).

Logico-deductive research, associated with hierarchical theory, is more nomothetic, meaning the search is for general laws, abstracted from time, place, and specific person. Social work practice benefits from both types of research findings-- idiographic and nomothetic. Pattern theory, however, may be more useful to social work practice for three reasons. One, it matches the specificity of the contexts in which social workers practice. Two, it encourages pattern-matching rather than generalizing to situations that have not yet been investigated. Three, it accounts for as many patterns as can be discovered, encouraging the individualization of specific cases.

Even if findings were based on every known type of instance of a phenomenon, however, qualitative theory development is premised on the idea that researchers test each finding for its fit in new situations. The new situation could differ significantly from all other instances on which the findings are based. Because findings of qualitative research are open-ended, they are continually subject to modification.

Parallels to Direct Practice

There are many parallels between direct practice and the procedures of GT and DQA. These parallels are important for at least two reasons. The first is related to research utilization. Practitioner use of research findings may be enhanced when research methods match practice contexts. A second reason for the importance of these parallels is the possibility that, with appropriate training in the use of qualitative methods, social work practitioners can become qualitative researchers. The following are some of the parallels between GT, DQA, and direct practice.

• The focus on the perspectives of informants is congruent with the social work principle to start where clients are and to pay attention to client perspectives throughout the course of practice, with research a form of practice.

• Social work direct practice by definition involves direct engagement with clients. Social workers, like qualitative researchers, strive for empathy, characterized by a balance between being in tune with clients and maintaining an analytic stance. Both the practice of social work and the practice of GT and DQA require this as well.

• GT research and DQA, like social work, often takes place in natural settings; for social workers, in the homes and communities of clients.

• The emphasis on viewing informants as inextricably part of a wider context fits with the social work perspective of focus on the client-environment interface.

• Detailed descriptions of individual cases fit with the social work injunction to individualize assessment, treatment, and evaluation to fit specific client situations.

• The combination of induction and deduction approaches parallels how social workers think about cases. Practitioners use previous research, theory, and practice wisdom while attempting to avoid imposing pre-conceptions on clients. Practitioners want to understand clients in their particularities—the notion of individualization—as do practitioners of DQA and GT.

• Social workers come to conclusions about clients through direct contact and after gathering data from many different sources. The conclusions are tentative, open to modification as new information becomes available.

• Direct practitioners routinely consult with other practitioners to ensure that they have a balanced and comprehensive picture of clients and their situations; this parallels group analysis of data.

* Social workers bring hypotheses with them into new situations, but for the purposes of seeing whether they are helpful in the conduct of practice. They are fully ready to modify these hypotheses to fit the situation. This parallels procedures in GT and DQA.

* The data collection methods of interviewing, observation, and document analysis are used by social workers as well as qualitative researchers.

* The use of field notes, observer comments, and memos are similar to process recording and problem-oriented case record keeping.

Some of the procedures of social work, DQA, and GT, therefore, are complementary. This complementarity bodes well for the future of GT and deductive qualitative approaches in social work research.

Padgett (1998) noted several ways in which "social work practice differs from qualitative research" (p. 374). She makes some good points, such as differences in goals between research and practice, differences between clients and participants in research, training issues, and the multiplicity of underlying assumptions in practice and research. She was concerned some social work researchers appeared to draw potentially problematic parallels between qualitative research and practice. She wanted to provide some balance to an overemphasis on parallels.

Padgett's (1998, 1999) perspectives complement mine. In the earlier version of this chapter, I focused only on parallels and not on differences. As Padgett said, "the parallels are undeniable" (p. 380), but a balanced view is important. I will comment, however, on some of her ideas, those on which I have other perspectives on the fit of DQA and GT with direct social work practice.

Padgett (1998) stated that qualitative approaches do not use pre-existing conceptual frameworks. As I've shown, DQA is designed to do just that. She stated that the ethical responsibilities of researchers and practitioners differ in regard to confidentiality. As I stated earlier, social work researchers must abide by all the mandates of the NASW Codes of Ethics, including reporting laws and duty to warn. Government regulations permit some exemptions from this, but I believe for social work researchers that the Code of Ethics prevails in all research situations.

Although Padgett (1998) makes a good point that social work qualitative researchers learn from research participants, I believe that effective social work practitioners learn from clients. Beyond this, however, researchers do not have responsibilities for attempting to influence client behaviors, and we do not have legal mandates to enforce laws, as child protection social workers do, for example, although researchers are obligated to report to law enforcement actual or threatened harm to informants that we learn about through our research. This actually has been a relief to me. One of the hardest parts of practice for me had been the sense of failure I felt when I seemed unable to be of help to clients. When research informants appear to gain from participating research, I am glad for them, but informant change is not the goal of research. Gathering information is. Clients are not research informants, and research informants are not clients.

I have also shown in the earlier discussion that researchers have a great deal of authority and power in relationship to informants, and that the similar ethical breaches are possible in qualitative research and in direct practice. Padgett (1998), I think, underemphasizes this power. Writing about our own clients poses serious ethical issues, as Padgett noted. However, where would Freud have been if he hadn't done so, and where, in fact, would clinical practice in general be? With this said, if social work practitioners want to write about clients, they must study and follow the NASW Code of Ethics, go through an ethical review within their own agencies, and also review other Codes of Ethics, such as the code of the American Psychological Association. While there are differences between qualitative research and practice, the parallels are clear.

Applications to Practice Research

GT and DQA can facilitate the development of knowledge useful in many types of social work practice settings. My own research, that now spans more than 30 years, has resulted in several types of products that are useful for practice, such as *theoretical models*. These models include one that integrates research on resilience, schema theory, gender studies, and brain research and is meant to guide assessment of families and children where the children have a range of adjustment issues (Gilgun, 2005a), a second that guides practitioners to assess for issues related to neurobiology, executive function, attachment, trauma, and self-regulation (NEATS) in ecological and development perspectives (Gilgun, 2011), and a third that shows the significance of resources in models of risk and that I tested statistically (Gilgun, Klein, & Pranis, 2000).

My qualitative research has resulted in *typologies* related to perpetrators of child sexual abuse (Gilgun, 1994b), effects on adversities on human development (Gilgun, 1996a, 1996b), and effects of sexual abuse on the sexual identity development of men who experienced sexual abuse in childhood (Gilgun & Reiser, 1990).

Another product is *descriptive research* relevant to assessment such as how perpetrators of child sexual abuse view their victims (Gilgun & Connor, 1989), on resilience as process (Gilgun, 1999b), and the multiple effects on me and my thinking that resulted from doing qualitative research on violence (Gilgun, in press b). I've developed and tested *several clinical assessment tools* that are also useful for practice evaluation (Gilgun, 1999a, 2004 a & b) and, with many collaborators, a self-assessment called the RASS, for parents considering adopting children with special needs (Gilgun & Keskinen, 2005). Finally, my research using both GT and DQA has resulted in some practice guidelines for work with children and their families when the children have problematic sexual behaviors (Gilgun, 2006; Gilgun, Jones, & Rice, 2005).

Discussion

Grounded theory and DQA can provide important information that is useful to direct practitioners. Both the procedures and products of these two approaches have parallels to practitioners' experience of their work with clients, although, as Padgett (1998) pointed out, they are differences as well. Thus, these procedures and products are familiar to practitioners, and there is every reason to hope that practitioners will find the products of qualitative research useful to them in their practice. Grounded theory is useful when researchers want to identify lines of research that are significant to informants. To do so, they do what can be considered preliminary studies. Deductive qualitative analysis is the approach of choice when researchers start their research with a conceptual framework, typically composed of a literature review, a précis of the guiding ideas of the research, and research questions to answer and/or hypotheses to test.

My career as a qualitative researcher spans more than 25 years. During this time, I used the procedures of both GT and DQA and focused primarily on the development of violent behaviors, the meanings of violence to perpetrators, and how persons overcome adversities. While doing qualitative research involved enormous challenges and a great deal of on-going learning that continues to this day, its procedures seemed to have come naturally to me. I don't know if my training and experience in direct practice were factors in my easy transition from practitioner to researcher, but after all these years I continue to see parallels between how I did my practice and how I do qualitative research using procedures of GT and DQA.

My research was guided by theory, but, routinely, as best I could, I made attempts to set aside my own assumptions and theoretical orientations and attempted to listen with an open mind to what informants were saying. I purposely sought cases that I hoped would provide evidence that would lead me to modify my findings and even refute them. I sought out co-researchers whose perspectives were different from mine and who therefore could challenge my assumptions and add new ideas to my interpretations. I found that beginning with a conceptual framework was helpful at times; otherwise I may have been unable to identify concrete instances of the phenomena in which I was interested. At other times, my theoretical frameworks were not useful. I was left with a lot of information that was interesting and important in and of itself, but I had little idea as to how to organize it and how to use it. I found at those points, that exploring research and theory that might be relevant.

Thus, over the years, I have read many bodies of research to help me understand the significance of what informants told me. This research includes theories and research on risk and resilience, emotional development, sexual development, social information processing theory, cognitive science, gender theory, theories of human agency, and brain research, to name just a few.

In summary, GT and DQA have much to offer social work research. There appears to be more interest than ever in qualitative approaches, and it is clear to me that social work can never have too much practice-relevant research. Social work direct practitioners already have many of the skills required to do qualitative research. We can never have too many well-trained social work researchers.

References

Abbott, E. (1910). *Women in industry*. New York: Appleton.

Abbott, E. (1950). Grace Abbott and Hull-House, 1908-1921. Part 1. *Social Service Review, 24*, 374-394.

Abbott, E., & Breckinridge, S. P. (1916). *The tenements of Chicago, 1908-1935*. Chicago: University of Chicago Press.

Abrams, L. S. (2003). Contextual variations in young women's gender identity negotiations. *Psychology of Women Quarterly, 27*(1), 64-74.

Becker, H. S. (1953). Becoming a marijuana user. *American Journal of Sociology, 59*, 235-242.

Becker, H. S., Geer, B., Hughes, E. C., & Strauss, A. L. (1961). *Boys in white: Student culture in medical school*. Chicago: University of Chicago.

Ben Ari, A., Winstok, Z., & Eisikovits, Z. (2003). Choice within entrapment and entrapment within choice: The challenge facing battered women who stay. *Families in Society, 84(4),* 53-546.

Benner, P. (Ed.) (1994). *Interpretive phenomenology.* Thousand Oaks, CA: Sage.

Bogdan, R. & Biklen, S. K. (2007). *Introduction to qualitative research for education* (3rd ed.). Boston: Allyn and Bacon.

Bott, E. (1957). *Family and social network.* New York: Free Press.

Blumer, H. (1986). What is wrong with social theory? In Herbert Blumer (1986), *Symbolic interactionism. (pp* (pp. 140-152) Berkeley: University of California Press.

Bulmer, M. (1984). *The Chicago School of Sociology.* Chicago: University of Chicago Press.

Campbell, D. T. (1979). "Degrees of freedom" and the case study. In T. D. Cook and C. S. Reichardt (Eds.), *Qualitative and quantitative methods in evaluation research* . pp. 49-67. Beverly Hills, CA: Sage.

Cook, T. D., & Campbell, D. T. (1979). *Quasi-experimentation: Design and analysis for field settings.* Boston: Houghton-Mifflin.

Corbin, J. & Straus, A. (2008). *Basics of qualitative research* (3rd. ed.). Thousand Oaks, CA: Sage.

Cressey, D. (1953). *Other people's money.* Belmont, CA: Wadsworth.

Crist, J. D., & Tanner, C.A. (2003). Interpretation/analysis methods in hermeneutic interpretive phenomenology. *Nursing Research, 52*(3), 202-205.

Cronbach, L. (1975). Beyond the two disciplines of scientific psychology. *American Psychologist, 30,* 116-127.

Deegan, M.J. (1990). *Jane Addams and the men of the Chicago School of Sociology, 1892-1918.* New Brunswick: Transaction.

Deegan, M.J. (2006). The human drama behind the study of people as potato bugs: The curious marriage of Robert E. Park & Clara Cahill Park. *Journal of Classical Sociology (6),* 101-122.

Dewey, J. (1910). *How we think.* Amherst, NY: Prometheus.

Faulkner, S. L. (2003). Good girl or flirt girl: Latinas' definitions of sex and sexual relationships. *Hispanic Journal of Behavioral Sciences, 25*(2), 174-200.

Frazier, E. F. (1932). *The Negro family in Chicago.* Chicago: University of Chicago Press.

Fuler, T., A. Firpo, L. Guadagno, T. M. Easter, F. Kahan, F., & Paris, B. (2003). Themes from a grounded theory analysis of elder neglect assessment by experts. *The Gerontologist, 43*(5), 745-752.

Geertz, C. (1973). *The interpretation of culture.* New York: Basic.

Gilgun, J.F. (1992). Hypothesis-generation in social work research. *Journal of Social Service Research. 15*, 113-135.

Gilgun, J. F. (1994a). A case for case studies in social work research. *Social Work, 39*, 371-380.

Gilgun, J. F. (1994b). Avengers, conquerors, playmates, and lovers: A continuum of roles played by perpetrators of child sexual abuse. *Families in Society, 75*, 467-480.

Gilgun, J. F. (1994c). Hand into glove: Grounded theory and social work practice research. In E. Sherman and W.J. Reid (Eds.), *Qualitative research in social work*. pp. 115-125. New York: Columbia University Press.

Gilgun, J. F. (1995). We shared something special: The moral discourse of incest perpetrators. *Journal of Marriage and the Family, 57*, 265-281.

Gilgun, J. F. (1996a). Human development and adversity in ecological perspective: Part 2: Three patterns. *Families in Society, 77*, 459-576.

Gilgun, J. F. (1996b). Human development and adversity in ecological perspective: Part 1: A conceptual framework. *Families in Society, 77*, 395-402.

Gilgun, Jane F. (1999a). CASPARS: New tools for assessing client risks and strengths. *Families in Society, 80(5)*, 450-459.

Gilgun, J. F. (1999b). Mapping resilience as process among adults maltreated in childhood. In H. I. McCubbin, E. A. Thompson, A. I. Thompson, & J. A. Futrell (Eds.), *The dynamics of resilient families*. pp. 41-70. Thousand Oaks, CA: Sage.

Gilgun, J. F. (1999c). Methodological pluralism and qualitative family research. In S. K. Steinmetz, M. B. Sussman, and G. W. Peterson (Eds.), *Handbook of Marriage and the Family* (2nd ed.). pp. 219-261. New York: Plenum.

Gilgun, J. F. (2001a), November. Case study research, analytic induction, and theory development: The future and the past, paper presented at the Preconference Workshop on Theory Construction and Research Methodology, National Conference on Family Relations, Rochester, NY.

Gilgun, J. F. (2001b). Grounded theory, other inductive methods, and social work methods. In B. Thyer (Ed.), *Handbook of social work research*, pp. 345-364. Thousand Oaks, CA: Sage.

Gilgun, J. F. (2002). Conjectures and refutations: Governmental funding and qualitative research. *Qualitative Social Work, 1(3)*, 359-375.

Gilgun, J. F. (2004a). Qualitative methods and the development of clinical assessment tools. *Qualitative Health Research, 14(7)*, 1008-1019.

Gilgun, J. F. (2004b). The 4-D: Strengths-based assessments for youth who've experienced adversities. *Journal of Human Behavior in the Social Environment, 10* (4), 51-73.

Gilgun, Jane F. (2005a). Evidence-based practice, descriptive research, and the resilience-schema-gender-brain (RSGB) assessment. *British Journal of Social Work. 35* (6), 843-862.

Gilgun, J. F. (2005b). Qualitative research and family psychology. *Journal of Family Psychology,19*(1), 40-50.

Gilgun, J.F. (2006). Children and adolescents with problematic sexual behaviors: Lessons from research on resilience. In Robert Longo & Dave Prescott (Eds.), *Current perspectives on working with sexually aggressive youth and youth with sexual behavior problems* (pp. 383-394). Holyoke, MA: Neari.

Gilgun, Jane F. (2008). Lived experience, reflexivity, and research on perpetrators of interpersonal violence. *Qualitative Social Work, 7(2),* 181-197.

Gilgun, J. F. (2010a). Methods for enhancing theory and knowledge about problems, policies, and practice. In K. Briar, J. Orme, R. Ruckdeschel, & I. Shaw, *The Sage handbook of social work research* (pp. 281-297). Thousand Oaks, CA: Sage.

Gilgun, Jane F. (2010b). Reflections on 25 years of research on violence. *Reflections: Narratives of Professional Helping,* 16(4), 50-59.

Gilgun, J.F. (2010c), November. The nature of practice in evidence-based practice. Paper presented at the Pre-Conference Workshop on Theory Construction and Research Methodology, annual conference, National Council on Family Relations, Minneapolis, Minnesota, USA, November 2.

Gilgun, J. F. (2010b). Reflections on 25 years of research on violence. *Reflections: Narratives of Professional Helping,* 16(4), 50-59.

Gilgun, J.F. (2011). *The NEATS: A child & family assessment.* Amazon.

Gilgun, Jane F. (2012). Enduring themes in qualitative family research. *Journal of Family Theory and Review, 4,* 80-95.

Gilgun, J. F. (2013). Qualitative family research: Enduring themes and contemporary variations. In Gary F. Peterson & Kevin Bush (Eds.), *Handbook of Marriage and the Family* (3rd ed.) (pp. 91-119). New York: Plenum.

Gilgun, J. F. & Abrams, L. (2002). Commentary on Denzin: The nature and usefulness of qualitative social work research. *Qualitative Social Work, 1*(1), 39-55

Gilgun, J. F. & Brommel, S. (2004). Emotion display rules in the accounts of violent men. St. Paul, MN: University of Minnesota, School of Social Work. Unpublished manuscript.

Gilgun, J.F., & Connor, T.M. (1989). How perpetrators view child sexual abuse. *Social Work.*   *34*, 249-251.

Gilgun, J. F., Jones, D. and Rice, K. (2005). Emotional expressiveness as an indicator of progress in treatment. In Martin C. Calder (Ed.), *Emerging approaches to work with children and young people who sexually abuse* (pp. 231-244). Dorset, England: Russell House.

Gilgun, J.F. & Keskinen, S. (2005). *Readiness to Adopt Children with Special Needs.* Scribd.com.http://www.scribd.com/doc/22159852/Readiness-to-Adopt-Children-with-Special-Needs-User-Manual.

Gilgun, J. F. , Klein, C., and Pranis, K. (2000). The significance of resources in models of risk, *Journal of Interpersonal Violence, 14,* 627-646.

Gilgun, J.F., & Reiser, E. (1990). The development of sexual identity among men sexually abused as children. *Families in Society. 71,* 515-523.

Glaser, B. (1978). *Theoretical sensitivity.* Mill Valley, CA: Sociology Press.

Glaser, B. (1992). *Basics of grounded theory analysis: Emergence vs. forcing.* Mill Valley, CA: Sociology Press.

Glaser, B. (2007). Doing formal theory. In A. Bryant & K. Charmaz (Eds.), *The sage handbook of grounded theory* (pp. 97-113). Thousand Oaks, CA: Sage.

Glaser, B., & Strauss, A.L. (1967). *The discovery of grounded theory.* New York: Aldine

Goldenberg, S. (1993). Analytic induction revisited. *Canadian Journal of Sociology, 18*(2), 161-176.

Kaplan, A. (1964). *The conduct of inquiry.* San Francisco: Chandler.

Konopka, G. (1958). *Eduard C. Lindeman and social work philosophy.* Minneapolis, MN: University of Minnesota Press.

Konopka, G. (1963). *Social group work: A helping process.* Englewood Cliffs, NJ: Prentice Hall.

Konopka, G. (1966). *The adolescent girl in conflict.* Englewood Cliffs, NJ: Prentice-Hall.

Konopka, G. (1988). *Courage and love.* Edina, MN: Burgess.

Lasser, J. & Tharinger, D. (2003). Visibility management in school and beyond: A qualitative study of gay, lesbian, bisexual youth. *Journal of Adolescence, 26* (2), 233-244.

Lenzenweger, M. F. (2004). Consideration of the challenges, complications, and pitfalls of taxometric analysis. *Journal of Abnormal Psychology, 113* (1), 10-23.

Lindesmith, A. R. (1947). *Opiate addiction.* Bloomington, IN: Principia.

Manning, P. K. (1982). Analytic induction. In R. B. Smith & P. K. Manning (Eds.), *Qualitative methods, Vol. II, of Handbook of Social Sciences.* pp. 273-302. Cambridge, MA: Ballinger.

Martin, R. R. (1995). *Oral history in social work: Research, assessment, and intervention.* Thousand Oaks, CA: Sage.

Olesen, V. L., Droes, N., Hatton, D., Chico, N. & Schatzman, L. (1994). Analyzing together: Reflections of a team approach. In A. Bryman & R. G. Burgess (Eds.), *Analyzing qualitative data* (pp. 111-128). London: Routledge.

Popper, K. R. (1969). *Conjectures and refutations: The growth of scientific knowledge.* London: Routledge and Kegan Paul.

Padgett, D. K. (1998). Does the glove really fit? Qualitative research and clinical social work practice. *Social Work, 43*(4), 373-381.

Padgett, D. K. (1999). The research-practice debate in a qualitative research context. *Social Work, 44*(3), 280-283.

Riessman, C. K. (1993). *Narrative analysis.* Thousand Oaks, CA: Sage.

Riessman, C.K. (2008). *Narrative analysis for the human sciences.* Los Angeles: Sage.

Robinson, W. S. (1951). The logical structure of analytic induction. *American Sociological Review, 16,* 812-818.

Robinson, W. D., Prest, L. A., Susman, J. L, Rouse, J. and Crabtree, B. F. (2001).

Technician, friend, detective, and healer: Family physicians' responses to emotional distress. *Journal of Family Practice, 50*(10), 864-870.

Rubin, A. & Babbie, E. (2010). *Research methods for social workers* (7th ed). Belmont, CA: Brooks/Cole.

Runyan, W. M. (1982). *Life histories and psychobiography. Explorations in theory and method.* New York: Oxford University Press.

Shaw, I. & Gould, N. (2001). *Qualitative research in social work.* London: Sage

Strauss, A. L. (1987). *Qualitative analysis for social scientists.* New York: Cambridge University Press.

Strauss, A., & Corbin, J. (1998). *Basics of qualitative research: Techniques and procedures for developing grounded theory* (2nd ed.). Thousand Oaks, CA: Sage.

Taylor, S. J. & Bogdan, R. (1998). *Introduction to qualitative research methods* (3rd ed.). New York: Wiley.

Thomas, W. I., & Znaniecki, F. (1918-1920/1927). *The Polish peasant in Europe and America,* Vol. 1-2. New York: Knopf. First published in 1918-1920.

Thomson, E., McLanahan, S. S., & Curtin, R. B. (1992). Family structure, gender, and parental socialization. *Journal of Marriage and the Family, 54,* 368-378.

Vidich, A. J. & Lyman, S. M. (2000). Qualitative methods: Their history in sociology and anthropology. In N. K. Denzin & Y. S. Lincoln (Eds.), *Handbook of qualitative research* (2nd ed.) pp. 37-84. Thousand Oaks, CA: Sage.

Webb, S., & Webb, B. (1932). *Methods of social study.* Longman, Greens.

Weick, A. (2000). Hidden voices. *Social Work, 5*(5), 395-402.

Witkin, S. L. (1999). Editorial: Constructing our future. *Social Work, 44*(1), 5-8.

Znaniecki, F. (1934). *The method of sociology.* New York: Farrar and Rinehart.

19

ENDURING THEMES
OF QUALITATIVE FAMILY RESEARCH

Contemporary qualitative family research has a rich intellectual heritage that provides researchers with ideas and language that guide them in the procedures of their work and helps them to explain to themselves and to others the traditions on which their work is based. The characteristics of qualitative research that I discuss in this article are understanding experiences in context, immersion, interpretations grounded in accounts of experienced, and research as action-oriented. These characteristics have a strong philosophical base that extends from nineteenth century German philosophy, to American pragmatism and interactionism, and to contemporary research. This article examines this heritage and shows that today's qualitative family researchers stand on the shoulders of giants. This chapter was *first published as Gilgun, Jane F. (2012). Enduring themes in qualitative family research.* Journal of Family Theory and Review, 4, 80-95.

QUALITATIVE FAMILY RESEARCHERS build on a rich intellectual tradition. While many of today's qualitative family researchers feel isolated in the midst of other scholars who do not share their perspectives, we actually have a heritage that not only affirms our identities as researchers but that also provides us with ideas and language that guide us in the procedures of our work and helps us to explain to ourselves and to others what we do, why we do it, and why what we do is important (See Allen, 2000; Allen & Gilgun, 1987; Allen & Pickett, 1987; Ambert, Adler, Adler, & Detzner , 1995, Daly, 2007; Gilgun, 1999c, 2005; LaRossa, 2005; LaRossa & Wolf, 1985; Matthews, 2005; Rosenblatt & Fischer, 1983). The purposes of this article are to examine the origins and history of qualitative family research, to identify some of the enduring characteristics of qualitative family research that stem from this history, and to show their contemporary manifestations and variations.

The four characteristics of qualitative family research that I cover in this article are understanding experiences in context, immersion, interpretations grounded in accounts of experienced, and research as action-oriented. These qualities are linked. In order to **understand the experiences of others in interactive contexts**, researchers practice

immersion. This means researchers do in-depth studies, seek multiple points of view, and often use multiple methods. They seek to understand experiences of others not only because what they learn is interesting, which it usually is, but also because they want their research to contribute to theories, policies, programs, and interventions that affect individuals in families, families as a whole, neighborhoods, and society in general. Thus, qualitative family research typically is action-oriented and sometimes emancipatory, meaning that researchers often want to contribute to **individual, family, and social well-being**.

The materials qualitative researchers produce are **representations** and **interpretations** of what they have observed. Their products are grounded in the perspectives and meanings of the persons who are research informants/research participants. Representations and interpretations are innately theoretical, whether researchers develop explicit theories or concepts or whether they produce narrative descriptions that they organize through concepts. The descriptions and the data on which interpretations are based are not transferable, but the concepts and theories that researchers develop from these particularities are. This means that the findings of qualitative research are generalizable in the sense that theory is. Theory, however, no matter how developed, has to be tested for fit when applied to local settings (Cronbach, 1975). Other qualitative researchers may find that other characteristics are more salient for them than the four I have chosen. That's the nature of qualitative research—it's a matter of perspective.

These ideas are associated with the Chicago School of Sociology in the early part of the twentieth century, although other qualitative research traditions share them. (For overviews of qualitative research from other related traditions see Benner, 1994; Polkinghorne, 1988; Reissman, 2007; Smith, Flowers, & Larkin, 2009; Stake, 2010; Wells, 2011). In 1937, Blumer (1969/1986) named the Chicago School of Sociology perspectives *symbolic interactionism*. There are many varieties of symbolic interactionism and many philosophical principles associated with it (Reynolds, 1993). In this article, I focus primarily on early formulations of interactionism, the time before Blumer attached "symbolic" to the name *interactionism*. As I will show, historically, qualitative family research focused on interactions that persons experienced within their various environments. The notion of experience is central in this early work. Therefore, I spend considerable time on the multiple dimensions of interactionsist understanding of experience and show that inner experiences are inseparable from interactions with others in_multiple contexts.

The scope of the present article includes research that is useful not only for theory-building and for adding to knowledge bases, but also research that may be useful in applied settings, such as family life education, family therapy, and policy analysis. The present article also assumes that family researchers come from a variety of disciplines with diverse agendas that center around interests in families and society. These disciplines include sociology, nursing, social work, psychology, social psychology, anthropology, medicine, and education. Family scholars from several disciplines have a long-term commitment to applications of their research based upon their concerns for individual, family, and social well-being. I also believe that in general family researchers study social issues in order to deepen understandings of family processes and to make a difference for families and, in general, to contribute to social well-being and the common good.

Understanding Experiences in Context

Early in the history of social research, researchers sought to understand human experiences within a variety of circumstances. Daly (1992) explained this aspect of qualitative research when he wrote

In keeping with Weber's (1947) *verstehen* tradition, qualitative methods are suited to understand the meanings, interpretations, and subjective experiences of family members (pp. 3-4).

Notions of understanding and experiences are linked: Researchers seek to understand human experiences. The notion of *verstehen*, or understanding, is an old one, traceable at least to Kant and transmitted through Dilthey (1961). The notion of *erlibnis*, or experience, is traceable to these same sources. Other like-minded philosophers of science have maintained these notions to the present day, including American pragmatists and the Chicago School of Sociology and their theories of interactionism (Gilgun, 1999c, in press; Hamilton, 1994; Reynolds, 1993). Understanding experience includes the assumptions that persons are inseparable from their contexts and thus cannot be understood without taking into consideration the contexts of their accounts and actions, that they interact with others in various contexts, that they espouse beliefs and practices that are widely-held, and that these various interactive processes give rise to socio-cultural beliefs and practices that individuals shape and that shape individuals (Dilthey, 1961; Thomas & Znaniecki, 1919). In interactionist perspectives, human actions and the meanings that individuals attribute to experiences are understood in relation to familial, social, and culture-based themes and practices that arise out of collectivities of thoughts, beliefs, and actions.

Within these perspectives, the intangibles of human experience, such as hopes, emotions, and thoughts, are subject to empirical investigation. Words or language, therefore, take a central place in these philosophies of science because language represents and constructs these "intangibles." In fact, Dilthey (1961) identified philology, or the study of language, as a cornerstone discipline for understanding human experience. He also stated that anthropology, which studies human beings as inseparable from their contexts, is another cornerstone discipline for the pursuit of understanding experience. Anthropology carries expectation that researchers will observe words, other cultural symbols, and human actions.

Words themselves are not neutral but encode culturally-based meanings that individuals interpret. Researchers seek to understand experiences that individuals convey through language, other symbols, and actions. Understanding of the meanings of experiences in Dilthey's (1961) terms requires the study of human actions and also involves observing the effects of human actions on others (p. 71). By observing and interpreting the actions of others and their consequences, viewed as taking place in particular multi-layered systems of meanings, we understand other people's beliefs and our own.

These ideas about language endure to this day and are part of several bodies of thought, including discourse analysis, critical discourse analysis, and semiotics (Wodak & Meyer, 2009). Furthermore, these ideas have contributed to American pragmatism's emphasis on anticipating and observing consequences of human actions for the common good (Dewey, 1958; Menand, 1997; Rorty, 1999).

Examples of Research that Seeks Meanings in Context

While some of the earliest family research was rather short on including accounts of research participants' experiences, it did not take long for the significance of human experiences to become important to researchers. Booth (1899b) and his collaborators rarely shared the accounts of the working poor themselves and when they did, the accounts were brief. For example, Clara Collet's (1889) essay that is a chapter in Booth's volume, while presenting a detailed account of wages, work, and the moral worth of the working women who supplied her with most of her information, spent little time on informants' accounts. She presented many case studies that showed the family and work conditions of the women. She occasionally quoted them, such as when she discussed how some women rejected low-paying jobs while those who were at the point of starvation had no choice. A woman whose husband earned a living wage said she

> just took back work again undone and told the governor that he might try to get some poor women to do it who had nothing to fall back upon; they weren't obliged to work for nothing, thank God (p. 450).

Collet quoted a woman who worked in a factory: "The masters are kind, but the foremen treat us like animals" (p. 466). Collet commented at length on these situations, but did not connect her analysis to widely-held beliefs and practice. She concluded her essay with the statement: "The question of wages is trivial compared with the question of regularity of employment and kind and just treatment" (p. 406). This statement not only shows empathy for the women and perhaps vicarious participation in their difficulties, but also is a statement of value that reveals concern for well-being of the women and their families. However, Collet also appears to have dismissed the importance of reasonably well-paying wages.

Within several years, researchers began to include longer personal accounts. These accounts show the continuity of the emphasis on personal experiences and their inseparability from widely-held beliefs and practices. A good example is the use Thomas and Znaniecki (1918-1920) made of letters that Polish immigrants had written to each other and to family members in Poland (Gilgun, 1999c). Excerpts from these letters are throughout their voluminous work. The following is an example. The speaker is a young Polish man in conflict with his parents over the family business, values relative to the meaning of marriage, and whom he should marry.

> First they [his parents] wanted me to marry any girl whatever provided she had money, and after receiving the dowry they wanted me to give them 300 rubles; then they would go somewhere else and establish a shop and leave me my own bakery. And in leaving they were to take all the contents of the shop. It was well planned, but I was not so stupid as to agree to everything my father wanted. I was rather too good a son, and allowed everything to be done with me, but in the matter of marriage I opposed them positively. I wanted to

marry only a girl whom I could really love and in whom I should have a good companion of life. As to giving money to my parents, I thought that we would talk about it when the time came (Thomas & Znaniecki, 1918-1920, Vol. 2, p. 2174).

Economics versus love and companionship as a basis for marriage, the duties of male children, parental prerogatives, and resistance to parental expectations are themes in this life history. These themes exemplify the young man's lived experience from his point of view as taking place in a historical, cultural context (Gilgun, 1999c). The experience is personal to this young man and his parents, but their beliefs and practices are shared across a wide spectrum of other people who have similar beliefs, experiences, and actions. Family practitioners today who are sensitive to such issues are likely to provide competent services to those who consult them. For example, clients often seek professional services because their personal and family situations are overwhelmingly difficult. They may believe that their private troubles are of their own making. Service providers can do a great service if they have clients reflect upon the social policies that may have affected their particular family and personal situations. For instance, the mortgage and foreclosure policies in this country have greatly affected millions of individuals and families. Millions of people are out of work because of social policies. Self-blame plagues many people and may interfere with creative problem-solving.

Sometimes early researchers sought to have research participants speak for themselves at great length. The third volume of the *Polish Peasant*, for instance, is composed almost entirely a life history that a Polish immigrant wrote, with introductory and concluding analyses by Thomas and Znaniecki (1919). A little more than ten years later, Shaw (1930) asked Stanley, a boy delinquent whom he had known for six years, to write his life history, published in *The Jack-Roller: The Story of a Delinquent Boy*. According to Shaw, life histories of adolescents labeled as delinquent were common during that time. They were the basis of major reforms in the understanding of delinquent young people. Many years later, in the same tradition, Bogdan (1974) worked with Jane Frey to produce Frey's first-person life history account of her experiences with her transgender identity. Most of my research on violence is composed of life histories that I gather through multiple interviews. So, far, however, I have published only one article that is based on one long, first-person, life history narrative (Gilgun, 1999b).

Contemporary autoethnographies (Chang, 2008) appear to be a variation on first-person life history accounts as a means of understanding the intersection of individual experiences and social and cultural milieu at the time of the writing. They are personal narratives that are similar to autobiographies except that researchers provide an implicit or explicit social research analysis. What we now call autoethnographies were common in the introductory sections of books that early researchers wrote, for example, Addam (1895) and Du Bois (1903). The principle was that researchers' biographies provided an interpretive context for their work.

An example of a contemporary ethnography is Kumsa's (2007) personal narrative of her experiences during the Ethiopian civil war when she experienced the loss of her entire family, her home, and her country and what it took for her to find a new life and new sense of belonging in another county. She dug deeply into her own heart to invite readers to share her experiences so that they can understand the catastrophic effects of war. Although a personal story, Kumsa, now an academic, analyzed her own story to show its more general applicability to other similar situations and its contributions to theoretical understandings of the meanings of civil war and its effects on individuals, families, and society.

Researchers' Experiences of Research

In order to understand and interpret the accounts of experiences of others, researchers—and human beings in general—must be reflexive. This means we understand others to the extent that we understand ourselves and that we are aware enough of our own assumptions that we do not impose them on others. Dilthey (1961) articulated these ideas more than 120 years ago when he wrote that understanding the experiences (accounts) of others requires researchers to have clear pictures of the meanings they attribute to their own personal experiences. For Dilthey, such understandings also require empathy and imagination. Since that time, understandings of reflexivity have expanded to include considerations of the power differentials between researchers and research participants, the impact of research on researchers and on participants, and the co-construction of the products of research.

A fundamental issue is researchers' personal perspectives, which are limited, with the consequences that their capacities to understand others and to interpret the beliefs and actions of others are limited, an idea traditional in qualitative research (See Waller, 1934) for an early statement. That is a reason why researchers seek collaborators to help them to gather and interpret research material and why they read the work of others. We push beyond our own perspectives, both personal and theoretical, in order to discover insights, concepts, and theories that illuminate our analyses of other persons' experiences and our own. At the minimum, we desire first to be even-handed about how we depict informants' self-definitions and definitions of their situation and then to analyze their self-definitions even-handedly. We may or may not concur with their definitions of situations, as Thomas and Thomas (1928) pointed out. They gave an example of a man who murdered others who talked to themselves because the man thought that these others were talking about him.

The importance of reflexivity is an enduring theme in qualitative research (Allen, 2000; Finlay, 2002; Gilgun, 1999c; McGraw, Znonkovic, & Walker, 2000). Small (1916), in writing about the first 50 years of sociological research in the United States, pointed out the value of going beyond "technical treatises" and sharing first-person "frank judgments" that will guide interpretations of future generations. He believed that without first-person accounts, "the historical significance of treatises will be misunderstood" (p. 722). Small was the founding chair of the sociology department at the University of Chicago, which at the time encompassed both sociology and anthropology, and recruited the faculty who applied to research procedures the principles that are the subject of this article. Small hired like-minded faculty, such as W.I. Thomas, Robert Park, and Ernest Burgess (Bulmer, 1984; Faris, 1967). Thomas and Park had studied in Germany where they were exposed to ideas of philosophers including Kant, Dilthey, and Simmel. Thomas, Park, and Burgess encouraged the development of findings that incorporated the accounts of the experiences of researchers and the perspectives of informants (Gilgun 1999). They guided their students toward understanding persons and their interactions and not toward axiomatic, explanatory theorizing.

In the Park and Burgess (1921) edited textbook, *The Science of Sociology*, they stated that they wanted the text to "appeal to the experience of the student" (p. v). They advised student researchers to use "their own experience" in writing accounts of their observations and in the reading they did as they conducted their research (p. vi). Park, in particular, was articulate about the centrality of understanding "the meaning of other people's lives" (quoted by Bulmer, 1984, p. 93). This is done, not solely through intellectual processes, but through imaginative participation in the lives of others. Park often quoted the American pragmatist philosopher William James: "the most real thing is a thing that is most keenly felt rather than the thing that is most clearly conceived" (Mathews, 1977, p. 33). He advised Pauline Young (1932) to "think and feel" like the residents of Russian Town, an area of Chicago where Russian immigrants made their homes (Faris, 1967). This advice sounds like an application of Dilthey's (1961) idea that understanding the experiences of others requires both empathy and imagination.

An early example of the applications of this thinking about reflexivity is the work of John Dollard (1937), a graduate of the University of Chicago's sociology department. Dollard wrote a first-person account of race relations in the U.S. south in the 1930s. He incorporated his own experiences into his work. For example, he described the awkwardness of being white in a southern town whose beliefs degraded "Negroes." His shared his fears that other white people watched as he talked to "Negroes" on his front porch, when the norms of other white people at the time viewed the back door as the place for "Negroes." Fearful of transgressing white social norms, he refused to shake hands. He wrote

> My Negro friend brought still another Negro up on the porch to meet me. Should we shake hands? Would he be insulted if I did not, or would he accept the situation? I kept my hands in pockets and did not do it, a device that was often useful in resolving such a situation (p. 7).

This description is full of connotations about the racist social practices of the time and raises questions about the ethics of following these practices or transgressing them. In a footnote, Dollard (1937) said he used "I" reluctantly, but did so because 'it will show the researcher as separate from his data...and it will give the reader a more vivid sense of the research experience" (p. 2). Like Dollard so many years ago, researchers today often want to convey their experiences of the research in order to deepen understandings of situations being researched.

Dollard (1937), too, was aware of his own limited perspectives and the possibility of bias. He devoted a chapter on his biases that included an analysis of encounters with a research informant who had helped him become aware of his biases toward white southerners. He reported that he first became angry when the informant said he had biases, but after observing his responses to white southerners, he realized the informant had a point. His biases were getting in the way of understanding "caste and class in a southern town," the title of his book. It makes sense that he would have to be aware of his biases if he were to write an account that represented the experiences of the persons who were the subjects of his research. He did not want to write an account of his biases toward race relations in the U.S. sought during the 1930s.

Other early researchers also were aware of the effects of biases that include partial perspectives on research. Waller (1934), for example, was one of many who recognized that the concepts researchers already understand are of help in identifying social processes that might otherwise go unnoticed, but that concepts can also be blinders that lead to overlooking what else could be there.

In a similar vein Webb and Webb (1932), who worked on Booth's (1989, 1903) studies of the London poor and conducted other social research over many years, wrote about procedures they had used in dealing with their research team's biases. These procedures included writing down experiences, ideas, preconceptions, and theories before designing and implementing the research. Webb and Webb assured researchers if they put aside even their favorite questions and hypotheses, they would find that the processes of direct involvement in the field results in both answers to questions and to testing and verification of hypotheses. Today we call this procedure accounting for reflexivity.

Some, like Webb and Webb (1932), argue that reflexivity statements increases objectivity, an idea that Harding (1991), among many others, took up decades later when she argued that situating researchers as part of research processes creates a "stronger" and more objective science. Rather than presenting the research through an anonymous narrator whose standpoint is not known, researchers tell much more about their findings when the context the researcher provides is included in research reports.

Early researchers, however, did not always apply principles of reflexivity in order to root out their biases. Booth's (1889) essays on the London poor, while replete with empathy for the plight of the persons whose lives he and collaborators studied in detail, also is replete with judgmental terms such as "loafers," "casual laborers of low character," and "savages" (p. 38). The essay of Beatrice Webb (1899) in the same volume also is insufficiently reflexive at times. She appears unaware of her own judgmentalism, such as her views of English-born Irish people and Irish immigrants. She wrote of "the evil of a growing Irish population" whom she calls "Paddy," a pejorative term. She also saw the influx of immigrants as an "invasion of foreigners" (p. 38).

On the other hand, throughout her essay she shows the empathy and imagination that Dilthey (1961) recommended if we are to understand the experiences of other persons. For example, Webb described in detail how the conditions of work on the London docks result from policies, business practices, and the state of the economy. She viewed some labor practices as unfair and expressed sympathy toward movements for the unionization of workers to negotiate for better wages and regular work. She did not, however, see some of her biases toward the Irish and other immigrants.

A contemporary example of research that includes vicarious participation and researchers' experience is work I have done for more than 30 years on understanding interpersonal violence (Gilgun, 2008, 2010). When I began this research, I was naïve, having no idea of the implications of understanding the meanings of understanding the experiences of others when these experiences are accounts of interpersonal violence. I did in-depth interviews, at least five and as many as 20 per research participant. As I immersed myself in the life stories of persons who had committed violent acts, I was unprepared to deal with the impact of the stories perpetrators told. I vicariously participated in perpetrators' accounts of their experiences, not as a perpetrator for the most part, but as an imaginary survivor. For example, I remember the horror I experienced when a man who murdered and then raped a college classmate described an encounter he had with her the day before (Gilgun, 2008). They were in line at the university's cafeteria. They reached for the butter at the same time. Their arms brushed. He said to her, "Go ahead. You first." I wrote

> The young woman did not realize that she had just touched the man who would strangle her and then rape her early the next morning. I participated vicariously in the dreadfulness of the situation. I had identified with the victim and participated vicariously in the last hours of her life. As I listened to his story, I thought I saw a bullet hole between his eyes. I wondered how the bullet hole got there. I had not moved. I realized that without any conscious thought, I had shot him in my imagination (Gilgun, 2008).

This is unlikely to be what Park meant when he advised students to "think and feel" like their informants. Or maybe it was. I did participate vicariously in their lives.

Stories such as these are important to tell because they show that researchers interact with informants and have experiences to which they give meaning. These stories also illustrate points that Small (1916) and Dollard (1937) made about the inclusion of researchers' perspectives for the purpose of helping audiences, present and future, to interpret the meanings and contexts of research. Dollard's story about shaking hands with "Negroes" and the wisdom of allowing "Negroes" on the front porch are other example of how reflexivity illuminates research reports. Autobiographical accounts are common in reports of qualitative research from the early years until now.

Despite this intellectual heritage, a heritage that provides a foundation for contemporary reflexive accounts of researchers' experiences in the conduct of research, such accounts are rare in family studies (Allen, 2000). In writings, I have done in the related fields of social work and sociology, I published articles that are squarely within this tradition; that is, that accounts of how I and a co-author experienced research with persons who had committed violent acts (Gilgun, 1999b, 2008, 2010; Gilgun & McLeod, 1999). In each of these articles, I used a slightly different approach in sharing my experiences, but each of these approaches sought to show that I am an active interpreter of research participants accounts and that the accounts affected me. For example, in Gilgun (2010), I described a dissociative experience I had when I talked to a friend over lunch about an interview I had just concluded: "I felt myself shoot up into the sky like a helium-filled balloon and saw my friend Mary and me sitting at the round outdoor café table." Experiences such as this provide me with a basis for thinking that we don't know much about the experience and the pleasures of violence to perpetrators because it is so hard to deal with. The difficulties researchers have—that I have—in dealing with the effects of accounts of violence is likely to be one reason we know so little. As Allen pointed out, personal values and experiences influence the data we collect, how we interpret them, and how we represent them. These are enduring themes in qualitative family research.

In summary, understanding human experiences—or accounts of experiences--in socio-cultural/historical contexts is a characteristic of qualitative research in general and qualitative family research in particular. A basic assumption is that human beings are in interactions with various others in their environments. Understanding others involves learning about the meanings they attribute to their interactions with others in a variety of situations. These types of understandings arise from interactions between researchers and research informants. Researchers' subjectivities are part of the research, not only in terms of how informants respond but also in terms of how researchers gain their understandings. Finally, individuals draw upon culture-wide systems of meanings to make sense of and to communicate their accounts of their experiences. These themes have endured over time and are, therefore, part of an intellectual heritage that is alive today.

Immersion

Immersion means sustained engagement with research participants, typically in the settings in which they live. Immersion may involve the use of one method or more than one. Examples of single-method research are interviews with individual or multiple units, such as a family, a couple, or a person to obtain in-depth understandings of persons, contexts, and interactions. Multiple-method research may combine interviews, observations and document analysis, such as personal and historical documents and records (Gilgun, 1999c). Park's advocacy of imaginative participation included the notion of immersion. He advised his students to embed themselves within the situations they wanted to understand. He said

But one more thing is needful: first hand observation. Go and sit in the lounges of the luxury hotels and on the doorsteps of the flophouses; sit on the Gold Coast settees and on the slum shakedowns; sit in the Orchestra Hall and in the Star and Garter Burlesk. In short, gentlemen [sic], go get the seat of your pants dirty" (McKinney, 1966, p. 71).

A typical study used interviewing, observations, document analysis, social mapping, census data, and, in the later years, statistical analysis. Social mapping, discussed earlier, which originated with Booth's (1989, 1903) studies of the London poor (Addams, 1895), involved color coded maps that designated distributions of social problems and locations of residential, business, and undeveloped areas of cities. Social mapping was yet another way of representing social contexts.

Early studies based on principles of immersion, multiple perspectives, and multiple methods include Nels Anderson's (1925) *The Hobo*, Harvey Zorbaugh's (1929) *The Gold Coast and the Slum*, the Mowrers' (1927) *Family Disorganization* and *Domestic Discord* (Mowrer & Mowrer, 1928), *The Jack-Roller: A Delinquent Boy's Own Story* (Shaw, 1929), E. Franklin Frazier's (1932) *The Negro Family in Chicago* and *The Negro Family in the United States* (Frazier, 1939), Charles C. Johnson's (1922) *The Negro in Chicago: A Study of Race Relations and a Race Riot in 1919*, and Warner and Lunt's (1941) *The Social Life of a Modern Community*. One of the main models for this research was Thomas and Znaniecki's (1918-1920) *The Polish Peasant in Europe and America*. Recognized as a landmark in social research (Blumer, 1939/1969; Bulmer, 1984; Faris, 1967; Handel, 1992; LaRossa & Wolf, 1985; Rosenblatt & Fischer, 1993), *The Polish*

Peasant was based upon personal documents, such as diaries, letters, life histories, and public records. A principle underlying these studies was the first I discussed: understanding accounts of experiences in interactive contexts.

Many of these studies had sole researchers, such as Anderson (1925) who practiced immersion because he was homeless for a time himself and lived among the men he researched. As a participant observer, he gave first-person accounts that today might be called autoethnography (Ellis & Bochner, 2000; Jones, 2005. He also interviewed other men and did document analysis. Other studies of the time also involved teams of researchers who engaged themselves for long periods of time in the lives and contexts of the persons of interest. Examples are Johnson's (1922) study of the Chicago race riots and Warner and Lunt's (1941) work on family and community life. Immersion, therefore, involves prolonged stays in the "field," meaning either living with research participants and/or conducting long, multiple interviews, and, typically, using multiple methods.

Studies that continued the tradition of immersion include Hess and Handel's (1965) *Family Worlds*, based upon interviews with five whole families with children, Rainwater's *Behind Ghetto Walls*, Komarovky's (1962) *Blue-Collar Marriage*, and Lopata's (1971) *Occupation: Housewife*, based primarily on in-depth interviews. Stack's (1974) *All Our Children* and Liebow's (1968) *Tally's Corner*. Not only were they participant observers, but they also did in-depth interviews over time and reviewed various policies and the archives of social service agencies. An example of a contemporary study that followed the principle of immersion is the Three Cities Project that combined three waves of surveys, ethnographies, and a child-care provider interaction study (Burton, Purvin, & Garrett-Peters, 2009). The purposes of the ethnographic study of this project fits well with the principles I have discussed so far. The authors of the ethnography said

> we sought to understand the life course experiences of 256 African American, Hispanic, and non-Hispanic white low income mothers of young children in Boston, Chicago, and San Antonio over a 6-year period following the implementation of welfare reform (Burton et al, p. 71).

Three of the four themes of the present article are present in the quote: understanding experiences in context through immersion. The fourth theme, contributions to family and community well-being are implicit, but present because studies of welfare reform examine the consequences of policy-based reforms on individuals, families, and society. Immersion is present because of the length of the studies. Other descriptions of the ethnography showed how immersed the researchers were. They met with the families one or two times a month for a year and a half and then twice a year after that. Not only did they conduct interviews with mothers, fathers, and other caregivers, but they also observed child-caregiver interactions and the interactions in the homes of research participants and in the low-income neighborhoods in which the families lived. Generous funding made this study one of unusual depth and breadth. The US government and private foundations wanted detailed information on the effects a major shift in policy on the quality of life of low-income people.

In summary, immersion provides opportunities to understand individuals and families in depth. It yields the kinds of detail necessary to construct multi-dimensional descriptions of family life in interactive contexts. While some studies involve individual researchers seeking to understanding aspects of family life through a single method, such as interviews, other studies may use multiple methods. Single researchers may conduct multiple method studies such as the work of Stack (1974), but teams of researchers also may be involved in qualitative family research as well. Through immersion, researchers develop in-depth understandings of human experiences. As Atkinson and Delamont (2006) caution, echoing Thomas and Thomas (1928), accounts of experience are not "untrammeled, unmediated representations of social realities," but laden with socially constructed meanings that are subject careful analysis (p. 170).

Findings Grounded in Data

With immersion, researchers become steeped in the meanings that research participants attribute to the events and actions in their lives. They accumulate copious material. It is the job of researchers to make sense of this material. They do so through the use of concepts and theories. Some researchers begin with "sensitizing concepts" (Blumer, 1969/1986) that they identify prior to beginning the research. Sensitizing concepts are abstract ideas that usually are part of theories that researchers may have reviewed for the purposes of the research or are theories with which they are already familiar. Glaser (1978) pointed out that theoretical sensitivity is necessary for researchers to understand and interpret the material that they collect and analyze. The ideas behind theoretical sensitivity and sensitizing concepts have a long history in qualitative research. For instance, Waller (1934), as already discussed, pointed out that concepts with which researchers are familiar are helpful in the identification of social processes that might otherwise go unnoticed.

Sometimes researchers begin with a conceptual framework, which is traditional in the history of qualitative research (Gilgun, 2005). This use of theory is called analytic induction, which an updated version is deductive qualitative analysis. In this approach, researchers seeks to modify and even refute the initial theory through negative case analysis. Grounded theory as a method of theory development is useful when researchers want first to identify a focus through field work and then conduct their research (Bryant & Charmaz, 2007; Corbin & Strauss, 2008). Researchers routinely read related research and theory during the course of data collection to help themselves understand and identify core ideas and processes (Bogdan & Biklen, 2007; Corbin & Strauss, 2008).

In most, but not all reports of qualitative research, any concepts and theoretical statements that researchers make are presented along with some of the material that is the basis of their conceptualization. In this way, they attempt to show the rootedness of their interpretations in the results they report. Most of the data that researchers accumulate do not appear in research reports, even when the reports are book-length. Stack (1974) only shared some of the material that supported her theory of cooperation and mutual aid. Here is one example.

> They [Lily and Bessie] gave some of this money to Cecil and Willie Mae to pay their rent, and gave Willie Mae money to cover her insurance and pay a small sum on a living room suite at the local furniture store. Willie Mae reciprocated later on by buying dresses for Bessie and Lily's daughters and by caring for all the children when Bessie got a temporary job (Kindle edition, no page number).

The patterns of exchange are complex. Through observation and interviews, Stack developed a multi-layered description of the exchanges that occurred routinely among these low-income families, but she could only present part of the concrete instances on which she based her interpretations. Her theory of mutual aid is thus well-grounded in descriptive material. This kind of detail characterizes the material that researchers require as the starting points of their interpretations. Whatever interpretations they make must be linked to concrete descriptions such as these. Such detail is more likely through prolonged engagement.

The work of Abrams and Curran (2009) on post-partum depression is a contemporary example of making sense of complex data and grounding researchers' interpretations in accounts that participants provide. The researchers showed that the women associated their depression as connected with contextual factors, such as poverty, heavy burdens of care for others in addition to children, and little or no contact with biological fathers. The researchers pointed out that the views of the women contrasted with medical wisdom that attributes post-partum depression to cognitive distortions and depressed mood that responds to medication. The researchers based their interpretations of the women's accounts of their subjective experiences and the meanings they gave to their experiences. Here is one excerpt that supported the authors' observations that the women attributed poverty as one of several factors in their depression.

Sheryl related her PPD symptoms to her ongoing financial problems. She described her response to her physician who told her 'not to stress' and to take antidepressant medication, stating. . . they tell me not to stress when I have rent due and electricity, DWP (Department of Water and Power) and a car note and insurance and a baby behind me and you're telling me not to stress (p. 358).

Sheryl and the other women in the study referred to contextual factors that contribute to their stress. How the women interpreted their experiences took center stage. Their meanings are primary throughout the research report.

The researchers' interpretations are rooted in the women's descriptions of the accounts of the experiences of the women themselves. The women's experiences are within socio-cultural contexts that include not only poverty and systems of medical care, but also the contexts and assumptions related to race, ethnicity, and age, since most of the women in the study were young African Americans, who also were poor and newly post-partum. The findings of this study illuminate other similar situations and persons. The findings, therefore, are generalizable through reasoning, analogy, and comparison. The findings could influence public policy, medical practice, and social work practice.

Besides conceptually-rich findings, qualitative researchers also craft their material into many other products that are useful in applied settings and also rooted in rich accounts of human experiences. These applied settings include family life education, family therapy, family policy, social work, nursing, and clinical psychology. Qualitative researchers develop typologies (Chesla, 1994; Frazier, 1932, 1939) that are useful in applied settings such as nursing and social work, various types of instruments including surveys, clinical rating scales, and practice guidelines whose items they draw directly from accounts of human experiences (Gilgun, 2004b). For example, I have developed several sets of clinical assessment tools that are also practice guidelines based upon long-term research on coping with adversities (Gilgun, 1999a; Gilgun, Keskinen, Marti, & Rice,1999; Gilgun, 2004c). I found the development of these instruments to be fairly easy to do because I had spent so much time in the field and was steeped in the meanings that individuals gave to their experiences. On the basis of my experience of immersion that included on-going reading on related research, I was able to develop two sets of instruments that had excellent psychometric properties (Gilgun, 2004c, 1999a) and other instruments that are useful clinically but I did not test psychometrically. Such instruments have the advantage of being based on experiences and meanings, which are the starting points of the applied work of educators, nurses, social workers, counselors, and therapists.

Qualitative methods can also be used in concert with experiments and research on direct practice, such as in social work, nursing, family therapy, counseling, and education, in order to understand how participants experience the interventions (Floersch, 2002; Catalano et al, 2004; Makuau et al, 2008; Rabin, Simpson, Morrow, & Pinto, 2011). Some qualitative researchers create performances (Alexander, 2005), write creative non-fiction (Gilgun, 2004a; Ungar, 2003), poetry (Gallardo, Furman, & Kulkarnit, 2009), and do arts-based research (Finlay, 2005) that use the words of informants so that audience members can understand other people's experiences and participate in them imaginatively.

In summary, the term *grounded interpretations* may fit the various types of products that researchers craft when they do qualitative work. The products of qualitative research are linked or grounded in descriptive material. Researchers first must understand the experiences of those whom they research. Then they write up descriptive material that represents these experiences. After that, they do interpretations of the descriptive material. The word *interpretation* represents the processing of other people's experiences that researcher do, typically in partnership with other researchers and also through reading and using the work of other scholars who have developed theory and research in related fields. Grounded theory (Bryant & Charmaz, 2007; Corbin & Strauss, 2008; Glaser, 1992; Glaser & Strauss, 1967; LaRossa, 2005) is a form of grounded interpretation, but other products of qualitative research are also grounded interpretations as discussed earlier.

Action Orientation

The final enduring theme of qualitative family research is its action orientation, which means researchers want their work to enhance individual, family, and social well-being. Action-oriented research is neither new nor startling. As Rainwater (1974) pointed out, researchers who study social problems for the most part want to contribute to their solutions, goals that both qualitative and quantitative researchers share. While some researchers become advocates for social change once their research is disseminated, others believe their task is done once they have disseminated findings. These variations have endured over time.

Social research began with the work of LePlay (1859) who, in vivid autobiographical writing, described how the revolutions, social upheavals, and economic depressions that were part of the social fabric in France in the eighteenth and nineteenth centuries were formative in his commitment to social research. After completing his research, he expected reform to follow. When it did not, he became an advocate himself for the last decades of his life (LePlay, 1879).

Standards of social research require that researchers separate any desires they have for social reform from the standards they follow to produce credible findings (Ethics Guideline Committee, 2004: Gilgun, 1999c; Hage, Romano et al., 2007; Walker & McGraw, 2000). These standards include researchers making best efforts to be reflexive about their own beliefs and ideologies that may bias their work. As shown in the present article, reflexivity is embedded in the traditions of qualitative research. When practiced well, researchers are able to separate their own beliefs and practices from the accounts and actions of research participants and also include points of view that differ from their own. Walker and McGraw pointed out that advocacy positions of researchers are not problematic when researchers uphold well-established standards of scientific inquiry and practices.

Examples of earlier action-oriented research include those I have discussed in this paper: the Three Cities Project, Stack (1974), LePlay (1855, 1879), and Thomas and Znaniecki (1918-1920). Booth (1889, l903) took frank moral perspectives that showed his desire for social change. Like LePlay (1879) and other reform-minded researchers, Booth lived in the poor communities that he wanted to understand. Rowntree (1901/1902) whose study of the city of York, was based upon Booth's research, also had clear implications for quality of life. In his final chapter, he stated that he had sought facts and not remedies. Yet, he called for the "need for a greater concentration of thought by the nation upon the well-being of its own people" (p. 305).

Addams and colleagues at Hull House in Chicago became familiar with the work of Booth (Addams, 1895, 1912; Residents of Hull House, 1895). Like Booth, the work of Addams and other residents of Hull House were based on concerns for working conditions in factories, child labor, and public education. Addams also contributed to the development of pragmatist philosophy that emphasizes understanding experience, immersion, and social action to promote common and individual good, although scholars have overlooked her contributions until the end of the twentieth century when there was a renewal of the recognition of her influence (Whipps 2010).

The founding members of the Chicago School of Sociology had concerns for improvement of social conditions. Many, such as pragmatist philosopher and education reformer John Dewey (958), were frequent visitors of Hull House some of whose residents were faculty members in the department of sociology and anthropology (Blumer, 1984; Deegan, 1990). The male sociology faculty rejected social reform efforts that involved advocacy and other social actions for reform of social and governmental institutions. Instead, like many social scientists, they thought that their research would influence public opinion so that progress would result (Bulmer, 1984; Deegan, 1990). Faculty members such as Robert Park and Ernest Burgess guided their students to do research with settings and with persons who experienced social inequality (Gilgun, cc). The works cited earlier are examples.

Other researchers mentioned earlier shared the desire to contribute to the social good. Kellogg (1914), for example, wrote that the purpose of the Pittsburgh Survey was to bring together information that would form a "basis for local action" and "for civic advance in other American cities" (p. 497). The purpose of the Unemployment Study of 1928 (Calkins, 1930; National Federation of Settlements, 1931) was to put a human face on the issues and to activate legislative and business support for unemployment insurance.

Various types of action-oriented research based on qualitative approaches continued throughout the twentieth century until today. There are many studies from which to choose as examples. Wax (1971), a graduate of the University of Chicago in anthropology, reported that she and her husband "became moral protagonists of Indian communities" as a result of their research. Wax noted that transformations met with approval by some but "antagonized" those who "defined science as pure" (p. 41). Lindesmith (1947), another Chicago sociology graduate, became an advocate for reform of narcotic laws in response to what he learned from his research on opium addicts.

Examples of contemporary research done on behalf of families is the work of Elizabeth Warren (Sullivan, Warren, & Westbrook, 1989; Warren, 2007; Warren & Tyagi, 2004) who developed the idea of a federal Consumer Financial Protection Bureau based on her research on family bankruptcy and Michal Krumer-nevo who is part of an international group of researchers who have reconceptualized the meanings of poverty. Krumer-nevo (2009) uses critical theory to challenge dominant thinking on poverty that views poor people as inferior, different from other people because of vaguely-defined personal deficits, with nothing to contribute to social policy and social analysis. Critical theory, on the other hand, views people who experience poverty as deprived of material resources and resources related to inclusion in democratic processes. They go unrecognized for the views they have on social policy.

The work of Abrams and Curran (2009) on post-partum depression shows concerns for women who have these issues, but they are not active advocates for policy changes. In their provision of spaces for these women to share their own perspectives on the meanings of their lives, rather than speaking for the women, they are helping to add poorly represented viewpoints to local, national, and international discourses. In this sense, their research implicitly challenges assumptions of who speaks for whom in the areas of policies and definitions of situations.

Any research that allows people to speak for themselves and interpret their own situations to others is inherently emancipatory. Although we have no hard numbers, few researchers probably engage in advocacy efforts in terms of testifying before legislative bodies, mounting letter-writing campaigns, and demonstrating for social reform in response to what they learn in their research. Nonetheless, traditions of emancipatory intent are strong in qualitative research because of its emphasis on understanding the experiences of others in their own terms and then conveying their accounts to larger audiences.

I have stayed with my qualitative research on violence because I believed my work would make a difference in the lives of many individuals, perhaps in programs for survivors of various forms of violence and for perpetrators, and maybe even for public policy. I am not yet finished with this research and have more to publish. The hope that my work has made and will make a difference is what counts for me today and has counted over the years. Without this hope, I would have discontinued the research long ago because of its impact on me (Gilgun, 2008).

Concerns for child and family well-being are shared across multiple disciplines. For example, prevention practice, research, and advocacy among psychologists have become so prominent that the Division of Counseling Psychology of the American Psychological Association has published a set of ethical guidelines called Best Practice Guidelines on Prevention Practice, Research, Training, and Social Advocacy for Psychologists (Hage, Romano, et al., 2007). The first and second guidelines are

1. Psychologists are encouraged to seek ways to prevent human suffering through the development of proactive interventions.

2. Psychologists are encouraged to select and implement preventive interventions that are based on theory and supported by research evidence.

These concerns are central in nursing, social work, family life education, family policy, family therapy and counseling, and many other disciplines concerned with families.

Concern for the well-being of others were foundational to Elliot Liebow. In 1984 when his doctors told him he would die of cancer within a year, he left his position at the federal National Institute of Mental Health to be a volunteer at a shelter for homeless women. When he realized he had more time than doctors had estimated, he did fieldwork with the women and produced his final book, *Tell Them Who I Am* (Liebow, 1993). He died in 1994.

In summary, research that focuses on understanding the experiential accounts of others in interactive contexts, that involves immersion, and that grounds interpretations in data from experiential accounts, in combination with the desire to contribute to individual, family, and social well-being characterizes much of early qualitative research, themes that are present to this day. Such research is inherently emancipatory because it challenges assumptions about who defines situations for whom and, in the longer run, who allocates resources for whom. As Rainwater (1974) noted, researchers interested in social problems want to contribute to their solution, goals shared by most social researchers. Qualitative researchers have a special contribution to make in this regard: By its nature, qualitative research adds under-represented viewpoints to public discourses.

Discussion

The characteristics of qualitative research that I have discussed in this article have a strong philosophical base that extends from nineteenth century German philosophy, to American pragmatism, and to their contemporary manifestations. Throughout this time, researchers have carried on the traditions of understanding experiences in context, immersion, the development of interpretations grounded in accounts of experiences, and contributing to individual, family, and social well-being. The heritage on which contemporary qualitative family research builds is rich and deep.

As I reflect on my own career, the career of other qualitative family researchers, and on the heritage of qualitative family research, I am struck by the intuitive appeal that qualitative approaches to research have to many family scholars. We want to understand families in family members' own terms and within the various contexts in which family members live their lives. Many of us like to be "in the thick of things;" that is, to immerse ourselves in families' worlds in order to understand family processes, experiences in families, and the meanings that family members attribute to these processes. This includes our interest in how family members perceive and interpret social policies and culturally-based themes and practices. Sometimes we are interested in the complexities of affirming family experiences and processes, such as positive child, parent, and couple interactions over time. Sometimes we want to understand problematic situations, such as persistent poverty among families with working parents, child maltreatment, or families who have experienced loss. We are careful and critical scholars who document the basis of our theories and assertions in the accounts of the people with whom we do our research. Whatever the issue, many of us want to inform others about our findings so as to make a difference and thus to contribute to the individual, family, and social well-being. In pragmatist terms, we say we want to contribute to the common good.

While other qualities may also characterize researchers drawn to qualitative family research, these in particular have endured since the mid-nineteenth century origins of social research in general and family research in particular (Gilgun, 1999, in press). I look back at scholars who came before me and have an immediate sense of connection. As I reflect upon younger scholars, I experience similar connections. Somehow, out of the haze of multiple, competing perspectives, we share desires to understand persons in context from their points of view, to be immersed in those contexts, to produce material grounded in human experience, and to have positive influences. These shared meanings constitute a kind of home base for qualitative family researchers and qualitative researchers in general.

Interest in the perspectives of others frees us to accept our own and to pursue what is important to us. The words of Anselm Strauss (1991) apply here. He wrote

> I don't know that my particular career, running as it does through a different set of years and impinging conditions, has any message for anyone today. If there is one I would put the emphasis on having a sense of what fits your own style and temperament, what too you want to get from research—and sticking with resolve to that, and quite as important also attempting to manage conditions to maximize your own creativity and warding off or minimizing those that will lessen or destroy it. If qualitative research lines up with those directives, then do it and keep on doing it (p. 2).

References

Abrams, L. S., & Curran, L. (2009). "And you're telling me not to stress?" A grounded theory of postpartum depression symptoms among low-income mothers. *Psychology of Women Quarterly, 33,* 351-362.

Addams, J. (1895). Prefatory note. In Residents of Hull House (Eds.). *Hull House maps and papers with comments and essays growing out of the social conditions* (pp. vii-vii). New York: Crowell.

Addams, J. (1912). *Twenty years at Hull-House with autobiographical notes.* New York: MacMillan.

Alexander, B.K. (2005). Performance ethnography: The reenacting and inciting of culture. In N.K. Denzin & Y. S. Lincoln (Eds.). *The Sage handbook of qualitative research* (3rd. ed.) (pp. 411-441). Thousand Oaks, CA: Sage.

Allen, K. R. (2000). A conscious and inclusive family studies. Journal of Marriage and the Family, 62(1), 4-17.

Allen, K. R., & Gilgun, J.F. (1987, November). "Qualitative Family Research: Unanswered Questions and Proposed Solutions. " Paper presented at the Theory Construction and Research Methodology Pre-Conference Workshop of the Annual Meeting of the National Council on Family Relations, Atlanta, GA.

Allen, K. R., & Pickett. R.S. (1987). Forgotten streams in the family life course: Utilization of qualitative retrospective interviews in the analysis of lifelong single women's family careers. *Journal of Marriage and the Family, 49,* 517-526.

Ambert, A. M., Adler, P.A., Adler, P. & Detzner, D.F. (1995). Understanding and evaluating qualitative research. *Journal of Marriage and Family, 57, (4),* 879-893.

Anderson, N. (1925). *The hobo.* Chicago: University of Chicago.

Atkinson, P., & Delamont, S. (2006). Rescuing narrative from qualitative research. *Narrative Inquiry, 16(1),* 164-172.

Benner, P. E. (Ed.). (1994). *Interpretive phenomenology: Embodiment, caring, and ethics in heath and illness.* Thousand Oaks: CA: Sage.

Blumer, H (1939). An appraisal of Thomas and Znaniecki's The Polish Peasant in Europe and American. New York: Social Sciences Research Council.

Blumer, H. (1969/1986). The methodological position of symbolic interactionism. In H. Blumer, *Symbolic interactionism: Perspective and method* (pp. 1-60). Berkeley: University of California Press.

Bogdan, R.C. (1974). (Ed.). *Being different: The autobiography of Jane Fry.* New York: Wiley.

Bogdan, R. C., & Biklen, S.K. (2007). *Qualitative research for education: An introduction to theories and methods* (5th ed). Boston: Pearson.

Booth, C. (Ed.) (1889). *Life and labour of the people: East London.* Vol. I. London: Macmillan.

Booth, C. (Ed.) (1903). *Life and labour of the people in London.* Final volume. London and New York: Macmillan.

Bott, E. (1957). *Family and social network.* New York: Free Press.

Bretherton, I (1992). The origins of attachment theory: John Bowlby and Mary Ainsworth. *Developmental Psychology, 28,* 759-775.

Bryant, A. & Charmaz, K. (2007). *The Sage handbook of grounded theory.* Thousand Oaks, CA: Sage.

Bulmer, M. (1984). *The Chicago School of Sociology: Institutionalization, diversity, and the rise of sociological research.* Chicago: University of Chicago Press.

Burton, L. M., Purvin, D., & Garrett-Peters, R. (2009). Longitudinal ethnography: Uncovering domestic abuse in low-income women's lives. In G.H. Elder, Jr.,& J.Z. Giele (Eds.), *The craft of life course research* (pp. 70-92). New York: Guilford.

Calkins, C. (1930). *Some folks won't work.* Rahway, N.J.: Quinn and Goden.

Catalano, R.F., Berglund, L.M., Ryan, A.M.J., Lonczak, S.H., & Hawkins, D.J. (2004). Positive youth development in the United States: Research findings on evaluation of positive youth development programs. *Annals, ASSPSS, 591(1),* 98-124.

Chang, H. (2008). *Autoethnography as method*. Walnut Creek, CA: Left Coast Press.

Collet, C. E. (1889). Women's work. In C. Booth, (Ed.) (1889). *Life and labour of the people: East London*. (pp. 406-477). Vol. I. London: Macmillan.

Corbin, J., & Straus, A. (2008). *Basics of qualitative research* (3rd. ed.). Thousand Oaks, CA: Sage.

Chesla, C.A. (1994). Parents' caring practices with schizophrenic offspring. In P. Benner (Ed.), *Interpretive phenomenology* (pp. 167-183). Thousand Oaks, CA: Sage.

Christians, C. G. (2010). Theories for a global ethics. In Norman K. Denzin & Michael D. Giardina (Eds.), *Qualitative inquiry and human rights* (pp. 45 -65). Walnut Creek, CA: Left Coast Press.

Cronbach, L. 1975. Beyond the two disciplines of scientific psychology. *American Psychologist, 30,* 116-127.

Daly, K.J. (1992). The fit between qualitative research and characteristics of families. In J.F., Gilgun, K.J. Daly, & G. Handel (Eds.), *Qualitative methods in family research* (pp. 3-11. Newbury Park, CA: Sage.

Daly, K. J. (2003). Family theory versus the theory families live by. *Journal of Marriage and the Family, 65,* 771-785.

Daly, K. J. (2007). *Qualitative methods for family studies & human development*. Thousand Oaks, CA: Sage.

Deegan, M. J. (1990). *Jane Addams and the men of the Chicago School, 1892-1918*. New Brunswick, N. J.: Transaction.

Deegan, M. J. (2006). The human drama behind the study of people as potato bugs: The curious marriage of Robert E. Park & Clara Cahill. *Journal of Classical Sociology, 6(1),* 101–122.

Dewey, J. (1958). *Experience and nature*. New York: Dover.

Dilthey, W. (1961). *Pattern & meaning in history: Thoughts on history and society*. (H.P. Hickman, ed.). New York: Harper & Row.

Dollard, J. (1937). *Caste and class in a southern town*. New Haven: Yale University Press.

Du Bois, W. E. B. (1899). *The Philadelphia Negro, Together with a special report on domestic service* by Isabel Eaton. Philadelphia, PA: University of Pennsylvania.

Edleson, J., Lindhorst, T., Mehrota, G., Lopez, L. & Shetty, S. (2010). *Multiple perspectives on battered mothers and their children fleeing to the United States for safety: A study of Hague Convention cases, research report submitted to the National Institute of Justice, Office of Justice Programs, U.S. Department of Justice*. http://www.haguedv.org/reports/finalreport.pdf/.

Edin, K. & Kefalas, M. (2005). *Promises I can keep: Why poor women put motherhood before marriage*. Berkeley: University of California.

Ellis, C, & Bochner, A.P. (2000). In N.K. Denzin & Y. S. Lincoln (Eds), The Sage handbook of qualitative research (2nd ed.) (pp. 733-768). Thousand Oaks, CA: Sage.

Ethics Guidelines Committee (2004). Ethical Guidelines for Managing Conflicts of Interest in Health Services Research. Washington, D.C.: Academy Health: Advancing, Research Policy, and Practice. http://www.academyhealth.org/files/ethics/report.pdf. Retrieved October 3, 2011.

Faris, R. E. L. (1967). *Chicago Sociology 1920-1932*. Chicago: University of Chicago Press.

Finlay, L. (2002). Negotiating the swamp: the opportunity and challenge of reflexivity in research practice. *Qualitative Research, 2(2),* 209-230.

Finlay, S. (2005). Arts-based inquiry: Performing revolutionary pedagogy. In N.K. Denzin & Y.S. Lincoln (Eds.), The Sage handbook of qualitative research (3rd. ed.) (pp. 681-694). Sage: Thousand Oaks, CA.

Floersch, J. (2003). *Meds, money, and manners*. New York: Columbia University Press.

Frazier, E. F. (1932). *The Negro family in Chicago*. Chicago: University of Chicago Press.

Frazier, E. F. (1939). *The Negro family in the United States*. Chicago: University of Chicago Press.

Fry, J., & Bogdan, R. (1974). *Being different: The autobiography of Jane Frey*. New York: Wiley.

Gallardo, H.L., Furman, R., & Kulkarni, S. (2009). Explorations of depression: Poetry and narrative in autoethnographic qualitative research. *Qualitative Social Work, 8(3),* 287-304.

Gilgun, J. F. (1999a). CASPARS: New tools for assessing client risks and strengths. *Families in Society, 80(5),* 450-459.

Gilgun, J. F. (1999b). Fingernails painted red: A feminist, semiotic analysis of "hot" text, *Qualitative Inquiry, 5,* 181-207.

Gilgun, J. F. (1999c). Methodological pluralism and qualitative family research. In M. B. Sussman, S. K. Steinmetz, & G. W. Peterson (Eds.), *Handbook of Marriage and the Family* (2nd ed.) (pp. 219-261). New York: Plenum.

Gilgun, J. F. (2004a). Fictionalizing life stories: Yukee the wine thief. *Qualitative Inquiry, 10 (5),* 691-705.

Gilgun, J. F. (2004b). Qualitative methods and the development of clinical assessment tools. *Qualitative Health Research, 14(7),* 1008-1019.

Gilgun, J. F. (2004c). The 4-D: Strengths-based assessments for youth who've experienced adversities. *Journal of Human Behavior in the Social Environment, 10 (4), 51-73.*

Gilgun, J. F. (2005). Qualitative research and family psychology. *Journal of Family Psychology,19(1),* 40-50.

Gilgun, J. F. (2008). Lived experience, reflexivity, and research on perpetrators of interpersonal violence. *Qualitative Social Work, 7(2),* 181-197.

Gilgun, J. F. (2010). Violence actual and imagined: Reflections on more than 20 years of research. *Reflections: Narratives of Professional Helping, 16(4),* 50-59.

Gilgun, J. F. (in press). Qualitative family research: Enduring themes and contemporary variations. In G. F. Peterson & K. Bush (Eds.), *Handbook of Marriage and the Family* (3rd ed.). New York: Plenum.

Gilgun, J. F., Keskinen, S., Marti, D. J., & Rice, K. (1999). Clinical applications of the CASPARS instruments: Boys who act out sexually. *Families in Society, 80(6),* 629-641.

Gilgun, J, F., & McLeod, L. (1999). Gendering violence. *Studies in Symbolic Interactionism, 22,* 167-193

Glaser, B. (1978). *Theoretical sensitivity.* Mill Valley, CA: Sociology Press.

Glaser, B. (1992). *Basics of grounded theory analysis: Emergence vs. forcing.* Mill Valley, CA: Sociology Press.

Glaser, B., & Strauss, A. (1967). *The discovery of grounded theory: Strategies for qualitative research.* Chicago: Aldine.

Hage, S. M., Romano, J. L. et al (2007). Best practice guidelines on prevention practice, research, training, and social advocacy for psychologists. The Counseling Psychologist, 35(4), 493-566

Handel, G. (1992). The qualitative tradition in family research. In J. F. Gilgun, K. Daly, & G. Handel (Eds.), *Qualitative methods in family research* (21-21). Thousand Oaks, CA: Sage.

Hamilton, D. (1994). Traditions, preferences, and postures in applied qualitative research. In N. K. Denzin & Y. S. Lincoln (Eds.), *Handbook of qualitative research* (pp. 60-69). Frazier, E. F. (1932). *The Negro family in Chicago.* Chicago: University of Chicago Press.

Harding, S. (1991). *Whose science? Whose knowledge? Thinking form women's lives.* Ithaca, N. Y.: Cornell University Press.

Hess, R. & Handel, G. (1959). *Family worlds.* Chicago: University of Chicago.

Johnson, C. S. (1922). *The Negro in Chicago: A study of race relations and a race riot.* Chicago: University of Chicago Press.

Jones, S. H. (2005). Autoethnography: Making the personal political. In N.K. Denzin & Y. S. Lincoln (Eds), The Sage handbook of qualitative research (3rd ed.) (pp. 764-792). Thousand Oaks, CA: Sage.

Kellogg, P. U. (Ed.) (1914a). *Pittsburgh district: Civic frontage.* New York: Russsell Sage Foundation.

Komarovsky, M. (1962). *Blue-collar marriage.* New York: Random House.

Krumer-nevo, M. (2009). From voice to knowledge: Participatory action research, inclusive debate and feminism. *International Journal of Qualitative Studies in Education, 22(3),* 279-295.

Kumsa, M.K. (2007). Home and exile. *Qualitative Social Work, 6(4),* 483-487.

LaRossa, R. (2005). Grounded theory methods and qualitative family research. *Journal of Marriage and Family, 67(4),* 837-857.

LaRossa, R. & Wolf, J. (1985). On qualitative family research. *Journal of Marriage and the Family, 47,* 351-541.

Liebow, E. *Tally's corner: A study of Negro street corner men.* New York: Little, Brown.

Liebow, E. (1993) *Tell them who I am: The lives of homeless women.* New York: Macmillan.

LePlay, F. (1855). *Les ouvriers europeens.* Tours: Alfred Mame.

LePlay, F. (1879). *Les ouvriers europeens* (2nd ed.) Vol 1. Paris: Alfred Mame et fils.

LePlay, F. E. (1866). *La reforme social en France.* Paris: Dentu.

Lindesmith, A. (1947). *Opiate addiction.* Bloomington, IN: Principia.

Lopata, H. Z. (1971*). Occupation: Housewife.* New York: Oxford. McKinney.

McGraw, L A., Zvnonkovic, A.M. & Walker, A.J. (2000). Studying postmodern families: A feminist analysis of ethical tensions in work and family research. *Journal of Marriage and the Family, 62(1),* 68-77.

McKinney, J. C. (1966). *Constructive typology and social theory.* New York: Appleton-Century-Crofts.

Matthews, F. H. (1977). *Quest for an American sociology: Robert E. Park and the Chicago School.* Montreal: McGill-Queens University Press.

Matthews, S. H. (2005). Crafting research articles on marriages and family. *Journal of Marriage and Family, 67(4),* 799-808.

Menand, L. (Ed.) (1997). *Pragmatism: A reader.* New York: Vintage.

Mokuau, N., Brain, K.L., Wong, L.K., Higuchi, Paula, & Gotay, C.C. (2008). Development of a family intervention for native Hawaiian women with cancer: A pilot study. *Social Work, 53(1),* 9-19.

Mowrer, E. R., & Mowrer, H. R. (1928). *Domestic discord: Its analysis and treatment.* Chicago: University of Chicago Press.

National Federation of Settlements (1931). *Case studies of unemployment.* Philadelphia: University of Pennsylvania.

Park, R. E., & Burgess, E.W. (Eds.) (1921). *Introduction to the science of sociology.* Chicago: University of Chicago Press.

Polkinghorne, D. (1988). *Narrative knowing and the human sciences.* Albany: State University of New York.

Rabin, C., Simpson, N., Morrow, K., & Pinto, B. Behavioral and psychosocial needs of young adult cancer survivors. *Qualitative Health Research, 29(6),* 796-806.

Rainwater, L. (1970). *Behind ghetto walls: Black family life in a federal slum.* Chicago: Aldine.

Rainwater, Lee (Ed.) (1974). *Social problems and public policy: Deviance and liberty.* Chicago: Aldine.

Reissman, C. K. (2007). *Narrative methods for the social sciences.* Los Angeles: Sage.

Residents of Hull House (1895). *Hull House maps and papers with comments and essays growing out of the social conditions.* New York: Crowell.

Reynolds, L. T. (1993). *Interactionism: Exposition and critique* (3rd ed.). Dix Hills, NY: General Hall.

Rorty, R. (1999). *Philosophy and social hope.* New York: Penguin.

Rosenblatt, P. & Fischer, L.R. (1993). Qualitative family research. In P. G. Boss, W. J. Doherty, R. LaRossa, W. R. Schummn, & S. K. Steinmetz (Eds.), *Sourcebook of family theories and methods: A* contextual approach (pp. 167-177). New York: Plenum.

Rowntree, B. S. (1901/1902). *Poverty: A study of town life* (4th ed.). London: MacMillan.

Shapiro, V. (2009). Reflections on the work of Professor Selma Fraiberg: A pioneer in the field of social work and infant mental health. Clinical Social Work Journal.

Shaw, C. (1930*). The jack-roller: A delinquent boy's own story.* Chicago: University of Chicago.

Small, A. W. (1916). Fifty years of sociology in the United States, 1865-1915. *American Journal of Sociology, 21,* 712-864.

Smith, J.A., Larkin, F, & Flowers, M. (2009). *Interpretive phenomenological analysis: Theory, method, & research.* New York: Guilford.

Stack, C. B. (1974). *All our kin: Strategies for survival in a black community.* New York: Harper.

Stake, R.E. (2010). *Qualitative research: Studying how things work.* New York: Guilford.

Strauss, A. (1991). A personal history of the development of grounded theory. *Qualitative Family Research, 5(2)*, 1-2.

Strauss, A. (1987). *Qualitative analysis for social scientists*. New York: Cambridge University.

Sullivan, T. A., Warren, E., & Westbrook, J.L. (1989). *As we forgive our debtors: Bankruptcy and consumer credit in America*. New York: Beard.

Thomas, W. I., & Znaniecki, F. (1918-1920). *The Polish peasant in Europe and America*, Vol. 1-2. New York: Knopf.

Thomas, W. I., & Znaniecki, F. (1919). Life record of an immigrant, Vol. 3, *The Polish peasant in Europe and America*. Boston: Badger.

Ungar, M. (2003). Stale. *Toronto Star*. July 29, D15.

Walker, A. J. & McGraw, L.A. (2000). Who is responsible for responsible fathering? *Journal of Marriage and Family, 62 (May)*, 563-569.

Waller, W. (1934). Insight and the scientific method. *American Journal of Sociology, XL*, 285-297.

Warner, W. L., & Lunt, P. S. (1941). *The social life of a modern community*. Vol. 1 of *The Yankee City Series*. New Haven: Yale University Press.

Warren, E. (2007). Unsafe at any rate. *Democracy: A journal of ideas* (5), Summer. http://www.democracyjournal.org/article.php?ID=6528

Warren, E. ,& Tyagi, A. W. (2004). *The two-income trap: Why middle-class mothers and fathers are going broke*. New York: Basic.

Wax, R. H. (1971). *Doing fieldwork: Warnings and advice*. Chicago: University of Chicago Press.

Webb, B. (1889). The docks. In Charles Booth, (Ed.) (1889). *Life and labour of the people: East London. (pp. 184-208)* Vol. I. London: Macmillan.

Webb, S. &, Webb, B. (1932). *Methods of social study*. London: Longman, Green.

Weber, M. (1947). *The theory of social and economic organization* (T. Parsons, Ed.; A. M. Henderson & Talcott Parsons, Trans.). New York: Free Press.

Wells, K. (2011). *Narrative inquiry*. Oxford: Oxford University.

Whipps, J. (2010). Feminist pragmatism. *Stanford Encyclopedia of Philosophy*. http://plato.stanford.edu/entries/femapproach-pragmatism/

Wodak, R. ,& Meyer, M. (2009). *Methods of critical discourse analysis* (2nd ed.). Thousand Oaks, CA: Sage.

Young, P. (1932). *The pilgrims of Russian Town*. Chicago: University of Chicago.

Zorbaugh, H. (1929). *The Gold Coast and the slum*. Chicago: University of Chicago Press.

20

CODING IN DEDUCTIVE QUALITATIVE ANALYSIS

HOW TO CODE when doing deductive qualitative analysis (DQA) is a question that many researchers have. In DQA, researchers begin with theory that guides their work. Theory becomes a source of initial codes that can be thought of as sensitizing concepts (Blumer, 1969; Gilgun 2005, in press). In using sensitizing concepts as codes during analysis, researchers may drop some of them and add new ones. I coined the term *deductive qualitative analysis,* which is an update of analytic induction, an early approach to qualitative research associated with the Chicago School of Sociology (Gilgun, 2005).

In this article, I share questions three student researchers asked me about DQA and my responses. One researcher was a PhD student at the Free University of Brussels, Belgium. The second was a graduate student at Tennessee State University, USA. The third was a doctoral student at the University of KwaZulu-Natal in South Africa. The questions were about sampling, coding, and whether DQA requires theory testing. The short answer is to the third question is no. The defining characteristic of DQA is researchers' use of theory from the onset of their work. In DQA, researchers can either seek to develop theory or simply use concepts from the theory as sensitizing concepts. When there is theory-testing, the testing leads to further development of the theory. The other form is to use concepts from theory to guide the research but not to test theory.

Strauss & Corbin Coding Scheme

Anke Reints, a Ph.D., student in sports psychology at the Vrije Universiteit Brussel, Belgium, emailed me in January 2011, to ask about coding in DQA. She had read two articles I have written on deductive qualitative analysis. One is called "A Primer on Deductive Qualitative Analysis" and the other is "Qualitative Research and Family Psychology."

The following is the email exchange that we had. The article Anke refers to is "Qualitative Research and Family Psychology."

Dear Jane Gilgun, In your article you mention the possibility of using Strauss and Corbin's coding scheme (including open coding, axial coding, and selective coding), while carrying out DQA. I don't really understand this, because isn't it the case that in DQA you already have set your codes *a priori?*

In my case, the components of the model I am testing are my codes. So all the information I gather from the face-to-face interviews are placed under those categories (= components of the model). When I read about grounded theory, I feel here you create your own categories. Do you get my confusion?

This is how I answered Anke. I edited this answer for the sake of clarity and completeness. I did not edit any of the other emails.

Hi, Anke. Good questions. Yes, in DQA you do have prior codes, but you work at trying to improve the ones you started with and developing new ones if what you see in your research material warrants new codes. Negative case analysis helps you to look for exceptions to your emerging analysis so that what you come up with is more inclusive than what you began with. It is easy to find material that supports the prior codes, but it is just as important in many cases to find material that does not fit into your codes. When you find material that does not fit your initials codes, you give names to that new material. In other words, you code the new material. You may also change some of your initial codes if you have material that supports that.

With grounded theory type of coding, you usually first do open coding, which means you simply go through the material and mark up the text with any ideas that come to mind. In deductive qualitative analysis, you also do open coding, but you can do it before or after you code using your prior codes. When you do negative case analysis, you look for any material that does not fit emerging new understandings. You then give names to that new material. In other words, you code that new material.

Negative Case Analysis

You do negative case analysis in at least two points in your research: while you are still collecting data and when you are analyzing data.

Negative case analysis during data collection. While collecting data, it is important to look for and inquire about any exceptions to the general statements that research informants make and any exceptions to the general description of informant actions that you are developing. This is within-case negative case analysis. Also, in choosing your units of analysis—that is, cases to include in your research—it is important to collect data from persons/situations that differ slightly from the cases you have already collected data from and on the basis of which you have already developed preliminary ideas.

Negative case analysis during analysis. When analyzing data, researchers typically develop a story line/narrative/descriptions of processes that they can show fits the material they have collected. In developing these narratives, researchers at some point also look for any material that can show the various patterns that can occur within these descriptions. Typically, researchers look for material that can add to, undermine, and even refute what they so far have described.

Through negative case analysis, researchers will produce a description of processes/concepts that account for patterns, or multiple dimensions of the phenomena of interest.

DQA and Axial and Selective Coding

Axial coding happens naturally in my experience. This involves seeing connections between the various codes. You show what connects to what and what might not connect to other things. You also want to show how they are connected.

Selective coding happens once you have identified the codes or core concepts that you want to concentrate on. This involves coding again, this time using the codes that stand for the concepts you think are really strong. Some of these codes/concepts can be prior codes, but could also have some new codes/concepts that you didn't begin with or you could modify some of the codes you did begin with.

This is Anke's response to the above email.

Awesome, and yes I do get your point. Just one more (little) thing. Is it true that by using maximum variability (in my sample I have selected a variety of types), I am following the idea of negative case analysis. Namely that because there are many different types of participants, the chance is there that several cases will not fit my prior codes.

The following is my answer.

Yes. The sampling procedures you are thinking of following would give you a variety that would challenge your coding scheme. Typically negative case analysis involves doing a series of cases that are similar and then choosing a negative case, but if you are clear about your sampling, variations are fine.

Hypothesis Testing & DQA

On June 5, 2013, Ben Duncan, a student at Tennessee State University, USA, emailed me to ask whether he has to test hypotheses in doing DQA. This is what he wrote.

I have a question concerning deductive qualitative analysis (DQA). I am using the Park and Oliver (2008) pedagogical content hexagon conceptual model composed of six components : (1) Knowledge of Science Curriculum, (2) Knowledge of Students' Understanding in Science, (3) Knowledge of Instructional Strategies, (4) Science Teaching Orientation, (5) Teacher Efficacy, (6) Knowledge of Assessment in Science.

I am using open, axial, and theoretical coding. My objective (and this is where I need some reassurance) is to produce codes through open coding, develop categories through axial coding, and then using theoretical coding to group the categories under the appropriate component from the Park and Oliver (2008) model.

Do I need to state a hypothesis to be classified as DQA? I have not done this. I perceive my analysis to be classified under your described DQA because I have a predetermined concepts derived from my theoretical framework that I will use in coding. Therefore, this is technically not grounded theory. Also, my goal in the results section is to formulate assertions based on my participants and the nature and sources of pedagogical content knowledge.

I was thinking DQA is a perfect fit, since I am not inductively creating my own codes, categories, and concepts throughout the analysis.

This is how I responded.

I'm happy to see that you are using a prior framework. They are very important in qualitative research. I suggest that you consider the prior categories a set of sensitizing concepts--that is concepts that are helping you see in your data what you might not otherwise have seen. The coding scheme you are using is generic--the scheme names processes that researchers have done since research began and that people do in their everyday life as they attempt to make sense of their experiences.

While coding within the broad categories of your framework, I suggest that you look for data that could add to your prior concepts in a variety of ways, such as adding dimensions to the concepts (or adding patterns that were not part of the concept until you did your research) and that might challenge and even undermine what you thought you were finding and what other people said were part of the concepts. This is negative case analysis, which you can think of as a serious of conjectures and searches for refutations of your conjectures. The conjectures in your case are likely to be the contents of the categories (concepts) you began with and that you are developing further.

No, you do not need a hypothesis for deductive qualitative analysis. The sole issue for a study to be DQA is for researchers to have prior explicit concepts [that guide the research initially] and/or theories that they want to test and further develop.

Axial and Selective Coding

On July 13, 2013, Ansuya Naguran, a doctoral student at the University of KwaZulu-Natal in South Africa, emailed me with questions about axial and selective coding. This what she wrote.

I read your article entitled "Coding in Deductive Qualitative Analysis." I found the article very helpful. Thank you for sharing it.

I have a question. Is it is always necessary to conduct axial and selective coding when using DQA? Selective coding makes some sense to me in terms of my data, but the criteria of axial coding (causal conditions, context etc.) doesn't. Perhaps I am not understanding axial coding correctly. Is it possible to use DQA without doing axial coding (Strauss and Corbin) and still discuss the relationships between categories and properties?

I would greatly appreciate your help.

This is how I answered.

No, it is not necessary to do axial coding and follow the steps of causal conditions, context, etc, in. Strauss and Corbin developed those steps in response to students who wanted concrete, specific guidelines to follow. Both grounded theory and deductive qualitative analysis are actually open-ended and adaptable. You don't even have to do open and selective coding. They started using these names after many of us were doing our own style of coding, which often does involve variations on what they have called open, axial, and selective. These names are handy in that they characterize what many already do when they code. but the conditional matrix and so many of the details are optional. What is important is that you state simply and clearly what you have done.

One day, I will write a detailed description of DQA. In the meantime, these kinds of questions and answers bring out issues that I usually haven't thought of.

Discussion

Deductive qualitative analysis is different from how many people think researchers are supposed to do qualitative research. Beginning with theory and with pre-established codes is unusual. On the other hand, a surprising number of qualitative researchers do theory-guided research. They typically are not clear about the procedures they follow. This article and others I have written on DQA seek to articulate and clarify procedures for doing theory-guided and theory-testing qualitative research.

How to do DQA raises questions for researchers. This article responds to questions of three students from three countries.

References and Further Reading

Bulmer, M. (1984). *The Chicago School of Sociology: Institutionalization, diversity, and the rise of sociological research*. Chicago: University of Chicago Press.

Charmaz, Kathy. 2006. *Constructing grounded theory: A practical guide through qualitative analysis*. London: Sage.

Corbin, J., & Straus, A. (2008). *Basics of qualitative research* (3rd. ed.). Thousand Oaks, CA: Sage.

Covan, Eleanor Krassen (2007). The discovery of grounded theory in practice: The legacy of multiple methods In Antony Bryant & Kathy Charmaz (Eds.), *The Sage handbook of grounded theory* (pp. 58-93). Thousand Oaks, CA: Sage.

Cressey, D. R. (1953). *Other people's money*. Belmont, CA: Wadsworth.

D'Cruz, H.,Gillingham, P. & Melendez, S. (2007). Reflexivity, its meanings and relevance for social work: A critical review of the literature. *British Journal of Social Work, 37(1)*, 73-90.

Dilthey, W. (1961). *Pattern & meaning in history: Thoughts on history and society.* (H.P. Hickman, ed.). New York: Harper & Row.

Faris, R. E. L. (1967). *Chicago Sociology 1920-1932.* Chicago: University of Chicago Press.

Finlay, L. (2002). Negotiating the swamp: the opportunity and challenge of reflexivity in research practice. *Qualitative Research, 2(2),* 209-230.

Gilgun, J. F. (1999). Fingernails painted red: A feminist, semiotic analysis of "hot" text, *Qualitative Inquiry, 5,* 181-207.

Gilgun, Jane F. (2005). Qualitative research and family psychology. *Journal of Family Psychology,19(1),* 40-50.

Gilgun, Jane F. (2007, November). The legacy of the Chicago School of Sociology for family theory-building," Pre-Conference Workshop on Theory Construction and Research Methodology, National Council on Family Relation, Pittsburgh, PA, USA.

Gilgun, Jane F. (2009). Deductive qualitative analysis and family theory building. http://www.scribd.com/doc/26474669/Deductive-Qualitative-Analysis-Family-Theory-Building

Gilgun, Jane F. (2010). A primer on deductive qualitative analysis and family theory building. http://www.scribd.com/doc/26474669/Deductive-Qualitative-Analysis-Family-Theory-Building

Gilgun, Jane F. (2010). A primer on deductive qualitative analysis: A slideshow. http://www.scribd.com/doc/40014289/A-Primer-on-Deductive-Qualitative-Analysis-A-Slideshow

Gilgun, Jane F. (2010). Case-based research, analytic induction, and theory development: The future and the past. http://www.amazon.com/Case-Based-Research-Induction-Development-ebook/dp/B004D4YMRQ/ref=sr_1_29?ie=UTF8&m=AG56TWVU5XWC2&s=digital-text&qid=1295639501&sr=1-29

Gilgun, Jane F. (2010). The intellectual roots of grounded theory. http://www.amazon.com/Intellectual-Grounded-Qualitative-Research-ebook/dp/B004D4ZOVO/ref=sr_1_67?ie=UTF8&m=AG56TWVU5XWC2&s=digital-text&qid=1295639644&sr=1-67

Gilgun, Jane F. (2012). Enduring themes in qualitative family research. *Journal of Family Theory and Review, 4,* 80-95.

Gilgun, Jane F. (in press). Writing up the results of qualitative research. In Patricia Leavy (Ed.), *Oxford handbook of qualitative research methods.* Oxford, England: Oxford University Press.

Glaser, B. (1978). *Theoretical sensitivity.* Mill Valley, CA: Sociology Press.

Glaser, B., & Strauss, A. (1967). *The discovery of grounded theory: Strategies for qualitative research.* Chicago: Aldine.

Park, R. E., & Burgess, E.W. (Eds.) (1921). *Introduction to the science of sociology.* Chicago: University of Chicago Press.

Lindesmith, A. (1947). *Opiate addictions.* Bloomington, IN: Principia.

Strauss, A. (1991). A personal history of the development of grounded theory. *Qualitative Family Research, 5(2),* 1-2. Available at http://www.scribd.com/doc/44659994/Anselm-Strauss-Writes-A-Personal-History-of-Grounded-Theory-Other-Articles

Sutherland, Edwin H. (1937). *The professional thief.* Chicago: University of Chicago Press.

Thomas, W. I., & Florian Znaniecki. (1918-1920/1927). *The Polish peasant in Europe and America*, Vol. 1-2. New York: Knopf. First published in 1918-1920.

Webb, S. &, Webb, B. (1932). *Methods of social study.* London: Longman, Green.

Young, P. (1932). *The pilgrims of Russian Town.* Chicago: University of Chicago.

Znaniecki, Florian (1934). *The method of sociology.* New York: Farrar & Rinehart.

Note: Field researchers are individuals who do in-depth work with informants in the settings in which informants live their lives. If they do interviews, the interviews are in-depth and seek to understand individuals within their particular situations.

APPENDIX

WE SHARED SOMETHING SPECIAL:
THE MORAL DISCOURSE OF INCEST PERPETRATORS

AT FIRST GLANCE, suggesting that incest perpetrators have moral perspectives on incest seems like an oxymoron, a contradiction in terms. Yet, incest perpetrators are embedded in cultures that view incest as morally repugnant, and laws make incest illegal. Along with other members of their cultures, incest perpetrators are socialized in varying degrees to understand the proscriptions against incest. Consequences for perpetrators can involve repugnance and shame heaped upon them, social ostracism, loss of family relationships, and legal sanctions. In addition, for victims and other family members, incest brings great harm (Armstrong, 1978; Briere, 1992; Browne & Finkelhor, 1986; Finkelhor & Dziuba-Leatherman, 1993; Friedrich, 1990; Gilgun, 1990, 1991; Herman, 1992; Rush, 1980; Russell, 1983; Wyatt, Newcomb, & Riederle, 1993).

Self-interest, fairness, and concern for doing no harm, especially to persons in close family relationships, would appear to provide sufficient motivation to deter incest in those who might consider it. Yet, incest occurs in one in six families in the United States (Russell, 1983, 1986), and about 100,000 new cases occur each year (Williams & Finkelhor, 1992). Perpetrators are members of victims' nuclear and extended families. These figures demonstrate the ineffectiveness--for a large number of persons--of moral repugnance and consequent sanctions as deterrents. These figures also suggest an ability of incest perpetrators to suspend, reinterpret, or neutralize moral principles which enjoin them to promote the welfare of others and to avoid incest.

In this paper, I used the concepts of justice and care to analyze the narrative accounts of incest perpetrators. These concepts are fundamental ideas in moral philosophy and theories of moral development and were brought to wide-spread attention by the work of Carol Gilligan and her colleagues (Brown & Gilligan, 1992; Gilligan, 1982; Gilligan, Ward, & Taylor, 1988; Lyons, 1983). Data were gathered through open-ended life history interviews. Through narrative accounts, informants give meaning, value, and coherence to a sequence of events, or stories. Their moral values are infused in their accounts (Tappan, 1991). The method of data analysis and interpretation was modified analytic induction.

MORAL DOMAINS

Justice and care are central concepts in moral philosophy and theories of moral development (Bloom, 1986; Manning, 1992; Noddings, 1984). Though sometimes considered a set of prescriptions based on conceptions of justice (Kohlberg, 1984; Smetana, Kelly, & Twentyman, 1989), morality also is associated with a capacity for care. Controversy exits over whether care or justice is morally preferred and represents a higher level of moral development (Cortese & Mestrovic, 1990; Gilligan, 1982; Gilligan et al, 1988; Kohlberg, 1984; Manning, 1992; Noddings, 1984). Gender enters this controversy because the justice perspective is associated with men's moral decision-making and care with women's (Gilligan & Attanucci, 1988; Larrabee, 1993).

Currently emerging is the perspective that justice and care orientations are complementary. The integration of both perspectives characterizes not only morally mature and responsible individuals (Gilligan, 1982; Gilligan et al, 1988; Manning, 1992), but also morally sensitive political systems and policies that, in the words of Bloom (1986), "contributes to the personal, intellectual and moral growth of its citizens" (p. 97). Criteria for making moral judgments often are implicit and involve interpretations of whether behaviors are just and caring in their intent and consequences and whether individuals take responsibility for the acts and for consequences (Bloom, 1986; Gilligan, 1982; Gilligan et al, 1988; Noddings, 1984; Manning, 1992; Smetana & Kelly, 1989).

Care

Care encompasses concern, loyalty, and love for self and others (Gilligan, 1982; Dewey, 1908/1980; O'Neill, 1989). Grounded in relationships and responsiveness, care arises, in the words of Manning (1992), from a "sympathetic identification with others." She continued, "When we see someone suffering, for example, we feel the suffering almost as if it were our own. Our desire to do something to relieve the suffering springs naturally from this empathic response" (p. 67). This view has wide support in moral philosophy. Bloom (1986) wrote that what Gilligan and colleagues mean by care and response, what the Chinese mean by jen, and what he means by empathy all involve efforts to connect with unique and concrete others in deeply personal ways and thus to identify with them and to understand them. This level of identification leads individuals to resist hurting others, to protect vulnerability, and actively to promote the welfare of others in the others' own terms (Bloom, 1986; Gilligan & Attanucci, 1988; Lyons, 1983). Care, then, is more than simply showing concern in particular situations, but represents responsiveness based on principles (O'Neill, 1989). Awareness that interpersonal acts have consequences for networks of care, such as families, is part of the care framework (Manning, 1992).

Taken to extremes of either too much or too little, caring can be defective because of its negative consequences. In a discussion of "intelligent sympathy," which is an analogue to care and empathy, Dewey (1908/1980) pointed out that sympathy can degenerate into "immediate indulgence of a dominant emotion," which overcomes concern for consequences for the self or for others (p. 107). Showing love and empathy in a self-centered way--that is, without considering what others might need and want--is an example of "immediate indulgence." Not considering the impact of behaviors on others exemplifies too little caring. Tendencies to provide too much or too little care are tempered by principles of justice, such as adherence to rules and to fairness. In moral conduct, then, care, does not stand alone, but is joined with notions associated with a justice orientation (Houston, 1990).

Justice

An ethic of justice is grounded not in connection and empathy but in duty and obligation (Lyons, 1983). Fairness, equal treatment, respect, rights, impartiality, and the applications of abstract principles and procedural rules are associated with a justice orientation. Status variables such as age, gender, sexual orientation, and race are important because they render persons vulnerable to unfair treatment--e.g., oppression. Emphasis on fairness necessitates the modification of procedural rules to accommodate ability and other attributes related to status. For example, laws throughout the United States now are being modified to accommodate child witnesses in courts.

Some moral philosophers view rules associated with a justice framework as a sort of safety net when caring cannot be mustered. Manning (1992) said that rules represent "socially recognized moral minimums" to be applied when "moral attention flags." Below that minimum, conduct is morally condemned. Rules can provide some protection for the rights of vulnerable others in societies characterized by "large-scale selfishness and inattention" (p. 82).

Finding a balance between care and justice for self and for others is an on-going challenge (Dewey, 1908/1980; Gilligan, 1982; Manning, 1992). Dewey argued that theories of moral behavior recognize "the necessity of acting sometimes with especial and conscious regard for oneself" while simultaneously being accountable, responsible, and "responsive to the needs and claims of others" (p. 170). In Dewey's (1908/1980) framework, seeing the continuity between individual acts and long- and short-term consequences is the basis of moral decision-making, while the isolation of acts from consequences suggests a tendency toward evil. In Dewey's words, "Every act has potential moral significance" (p. 11) because of its possible consequences. Moral significance of individual acts emerge, not in abstract discussion, but in terms of consequences for concrete persons in concrete situations (Bloom, 1986; Dewey, 1908/1980; Manning, 1992).

Moral Philosophy

Moral philosophers rarely have addressed interpersonal relationships, especially family relationships (Okin, 1989; Manning, 1992). Traditional Western philosophy has focused on the ethics and morality of the public sphere, such as medicine, war, apartheid, discrimination, and the obligations of the state. The more private spheres of friendship and family have not been identified as moral problematics.

Within psychology, moral developmentalists have been of two minds. Kohlberg, Levine, and Hewer (1984) represented the view that relationships are not the proper domain of moral inquiry, although they are of concern to women and girls. Piaget (1932), on the other hand, said there would be no morality without relationships. Recently, feminist scholars from several different disciplines (e.g. Houston, 1990; Miller, 1986; Noddings, 1984; Okin, 1989; Ruddick, 1989; Tronto, 1987) have begun to address the moral dimensions of family relationships. Many of these scholars have posited a gender bias in choices of moral problematics.

Moral Dimensions of Incest

It is ironic that family relationships are not part of traditional moral theorizing and are sometimes overlooked and even undervalued in research on human development. Families are permeated with inequalities in terms of age, size, gender, developmental level, status, knowledge, and power. Children, in particular, are vulnerable to abuse of power because of their unequal status in relationship to adults. When parents and others with authority over children choose to disregard principles related to justice and care, children have few resources with which to prevent harm to themselves. Their behaviors and verbal protests have impact only on those who are receptive to them. They need both care and respect of their rights as persons in order to develop to their full potential. Moral considerations may be factors in constraining parents and others who have power over children from committing incest and other forms of abuse of children. The absence of a public discourse on the moral dimensions of family relationships may account partially at least for the common occurrence of incest.

Philosophers are not alone in ignoring the moral dimensions of families. Research and theory on incest also have paid little attention to these domains. For example, a recent and otherwise informative study of incest perpetrators (Williams & Finkelhor, 1992) and a review of research (Williams & Finkelhor, 1990) did not touch upon moral dimensions, nor did a well-received edited volume on incest fathers (Horton et al, 1990). The one place where moral considerations are present at least implicitly are in definitions of incest. These considerations have been consistent over the recent history of child sexual abuse research. For example, the definitions of Groth (1979) and of Wyatt, Newcomb, & Riederle (1993) recognized the inequality of children and adults and the disregard of adults for the impact of sexual abuse on children. Other than implicitly in definitions, however, the moral dimensions of incest are slighted. A major missing piece in our understanding of incest is how perpetrators apply or avoid applying principles related to justice and care to their incestuous acts.

Definition of Incest

For this research, incest is defined as sexual behaviors between family members who legally are prohibited to marry. Prohibitions are based primarily on age differences and biological and legal ties. Incestuous behaviors include touching the sexual body parts of children and inducing or forcing children to touch perpetrators' sexual body parts. These body parts include the vulva, vagina, anus, buttocks, breasts, testicles, and penis. A comprehensive definition includes non-touch incest, such as looks and talk. In the present research, both types of incest occurred in many cases, and touch incest was present in all cases.

Perpetrators are assumed to experience sexual gratification through incestuous acts (Gilgun & Connor, 1989; Williams & Finkelhor, 1990, 1992).

Given the inequalities that characterize families, children cannot give informed consent to sexual relations, except perhaps in cases of mutually agreed-upon explorations between generational equals. Their status as children and their lack of understanding of the nature and consequences of sexual behaviors precludes informed consent. Their freedom of choice is further compromised and the probability of covert coercions is present because of the authority and physical size of the older person. In this definition of incest, family members include the following: adults who are biological and adoptive parents, other adults who have parental roles with children, brothers, sisters, aunts, uncles, grandparents, and cousins. Male perpetrators--adults, adolescents, and children--and a younger female child is the most common configuration. Although figures vary from study to study, fathers and stepfathers may account for about one-quarter of all incest, uncles may account for another one-quarter, with the other fifty percent may be committed by brothers, sisters, cousins, grandparents, and aunts, with women infrequently identified as incest perpetrators (Russell, 1986).

Hypotheses

The hypotheses of this study were derived from the literature on justice and care and shaped by my assumptions about incest.

• Incest perpetrators have special regard for themselves and do not have regard for the impact of incest on their victims.

• Incest perpetrators are not morally integrated, and, if they have a moral focus it will be on justice.

The first hypothesis draws heavily on notions of care and uses the language of Dewey (1908/1980). It assumes that children suffer when they are victimized incestuously and that perpetrators disregard this suffering. Furthermore, this hypothesis assumes that incest perpetrators are selfish and inattentive to others, language borrowed from Manning (1992). As discussed earlier, notions of care include identification with the suffering of others, resisting hurting others because of this identification, responsiveness, loyalty, the protection of vulnerability, and the active promotion of the welfare of others.

When persons are morally integrated, they apply principles of both care and justice in their moral decision-making. The second hypothesis assumes that incest perpetrators are not morally integrated, and, if they have any moral perspective on incest, they will focus on justice. In moral conduct, when caring fails, justice provides a safety net. In incest, caring appears to have failed, and notions of justice do not take up the slack. The assumption that justice will be emphasized is based upon wide-spread findings that men are more likely to emphasize justice and women care. Since most incest perpetrators are male, I assumed that they would emphasize justice in their discussions of their own incestuous behaviors. As discussed earlier, notions related to justice include fairness, equal treatment, attention to rules, and respect for status variables such as age, gender, and race.

METHOD

Modified Analytic Induction

The method used in this research is based upon the procedures of analytic induction. Similar to grounded theory (Glaser, 1992, 1978; Glaser & Strauss, 1967; Strauss, 1987; Strauss & Corbin, 1990) in some method-ological procedures, analytic induction differs in the timing of the use of concepts. Both stem from the Chicago School of Sociology. Rather than pre-selecting hypotheses and the concepts on which they are based, grounded theory seeks to discover them through processes of emer-gence, which occur over the course of data analysis and interpretation.

The procedures of analytic induction, too, are based on emergence over the course of the analysis. In analytic induction, however, research-ers develop hypotheses, sometimes rough and general approximations, prior to entry into the field, or, in cases where data already are collected, prior to data analysis. These hypotheses can be based on hunches, as-sumptions, careful examination of research and theory, or combinations. Hypotheses are revised to fit emerging interpretations of the data over the course of data collection and analysis. Researchers actively seek to disconfirm emerging hypotheses through negative case analysis, cases that hold promise for disconfirming emerging hypotheses and which add variability to the sample. In this way, the originators of the method sought to examine enough cases to assure the development of universal hypotheses.

Originally developed to produce universal and causal hypotheses (Manning, 1991; Robinson, 1951; Znaniecki, 1934), contemporary re-searchers have de-emphasized universality and causality and have emphasized instead the development of descriptive hypotheses which identify patterns of behaviors, interactions, and perceptions (Bogdan &

Biklen, 1992; Denzin, 1978; Gilgun, 1992). Bogdan and Biklen call this approach modified analytic induction. Several classic qualitative studies produced by members of the Chicago School of Sociology (Bulmer, 1984) used analytic induction (e.g., Angell, 1936; Becker, 1962; Cressey, 1953; Lindesmith, 1947). This method rarely has been used in contemporary studies of families.

The present research used modified analytic induction. My goal was to test hypotheses derived from the literature on care and justice and to modify them to fit in-depth subjective accounts of incest perpetrators. I assumed that the concepts would serve to sensitize me to concrete indicators and processes related to justice and care. While research based on analytic induction is guided by hypotheses and concepts, researchers assume that through processes of emergence, they will discover concepts and hypotheses not accounted for in their original hypotheses; in fact, that is the point of analytic induction.

Informants

Informants were 11 incest perpetrators, 10 men and one woman, recruited on a volunteer basis from maximum and medium security prison sex offender treatment programs and from snowball sampling from among persons in community treatment and self-help groups. They ranged in age from 32 to 54, and they were predominantly white working and middle class. Nine were married at the time of the interview, and two were divorced. They abused both boy and girl children. Several abused brothers and sisters and other relatives such as cousins and nieces during adolescence.

As adults, they primarily victimized their biological children, with two cases of stepfather-stepchild incest and one case of abuse of a niece. The woman perpetrator stopped abusing children in adolescence. Some abused children inside and outside of the families, but all were incest perpetrators. The variability of informants provided several opportunities to do negative case analysis, which, as explained earlier, seeks to disconfirm emerging hypotheses and creates samples which have major variabilities. For example, the woman perpetrator, the man who abused his nieces when he was an adolescent and his son and daughter when he was an adult, and the four men who abused children to whom they were not related as well as those to whom they were related added variability to the sample. In terms of their relationships to the victims, the gender of their victims, and the ages during which they perpetrated, they are fairly representative of identified incest perpetrators (Abel et al, 1988). I was not seeking to develop universal hypotheses, but the variability in the sample suggested that they hypotheses might be illuminating in several types of incestuous families. Informants signed a detailed informed consent, were encouraged not to answer any questions they did not want to answer, and were assured they could withdraw without prejudice from the research at any time, procedures approved by the institutional review board of the university with which I am affiliated.

Data Collection and Analysis

Data were collected through open-ended life history interviews. I interviewed each informant an average of six times each for a average interview time of 12 hours per informant, except for the woman perpetrator for whom there was opportunity for one three-hour interview. This totals more than 120 hours of interview time. I conducted all interviews. Although a general topical interview guide was used, the timing and wording of each question was individualized in order to capture the perspectives of informants in their own words. The interview primarily was a dialogue, where I frequently checked my understandings and interpretations of the informants' words and meanings. I introduced my interpretations by saying, "I want you to know how I'm thinking about what you're saying. Let me know if I'm not understanding what you're saying." This approach, in combination with the length of the interview process, resulted in an in-depth look at the subjective interpretations of informants.

The interviews were tape-recorded, transcribed verbatim, and coded using the justice-care framework. I compared the conceptual definitions and hypotheses with concrete indicators in the data. I analyzed each case individually, identifying themes, codes, and dimensions of the concepts of care and justice. I carefully noted variations within each of the dimensions, and, I sought to challenge each emerging finding with other findings. My intent was to create as complete a picture as possible of the moral discourse of the perpetrators in this study. Two research assistants worked with me. Not only did they reanalyze several of the cases, but we discussed in depth the possible meanings and interpretations of the data.

The data were collected and transcribed before I applied the justice-care framework. Although I was there to hear every word of each interview, I was and continue to be amazed at how helpful the analytic framework was to alerting me to instances of care and justice, distortions of justice and care, the absence of justice-care considerations, and findings that were not part of the care-justice framework. The framework truly was sensitizing because its concepts gave me a sharply focused intellectual context, or template, on which to place the informants' narratives (cf., Campbell, [1979]). It guided the entire analysis.

RESULTS

A defining procedure of analytic induction is the modification of hypotheses during the conduct of the research. To fit the perpetrators' narrative accounts, I reformulated the hypotheses to such an extent that I have new sets of statements. They are not relational hypotheses--that is, hypotheses positing clear and possibly causal relationships between two or more concepts--and only loosely can be called descriptive hypotheses (cf., Kerlinger, 1973).

Most striking about the perpetrators' accounts was that almost all of them defined incest as love and care. The types of love they expressed ranged from sexual and romantic to care and concern for the welfare of the children. These were unanticipated findings. I did not hypothesize that perpetrators would view incest as caring and as romantic love. Rather, I assumed incest represented lack of care and, implicitly, an inability to love. It did not occur to me that perpetrators would equate incest and romance, or even incest and feelings of sexualized caring. From previous research cited earlier, I did assume that incest perpetrators would experience profound sexual gratification through incest. Ironically, their professed love of whatever type was contradicted by many other aspects of their accounts, such as continuing the incest when the children wanted to stop, withholding permission to do ordinary things until the children submitted sexually, and letting others think the children were lying when the incest was disclosed. These perpetrators, therefore, did not view incest as harmful to victims, did not reflect upon how they used their power and authority to coerce children to cooperate, and even interpreted their behavior in many cases as forms of care and romantic love.

Care

The first hypothesis as originally formulated was

Incest perpetrators have special regard for themselves and do not have regard for the impact of incest on their victims.

As a result of the analysis, I reformulated the hypothesis as follows.

Perpetrators have special regard for the deep pleasure they find in incest. Concepts of romantic love and mutuality are prominent in many but not all incestuous relationships. Many interpret their behaviors as promoting children's welfare and not hurting them. The sense of love and caring that many perpetrators express for the children are contradicted by behaviors that are sometimes unresponsive and cruel.

Dewey's (1908/1980) phrase of "immediate indulgence of a dominant emotion" (p. 107) fits all 11 perpetrators. This notion is one of several that I found to be sensitizing. The idea of special regard for themselves held up throughout the analysis. While there are nuances of difference in how informants described their experiences, the emotions in which they indulged represented degrees of pleasure in incest. "Bliss," "thrilling," "thrill," "exciting," "rush," "high," "fix," "good feelings," and "release" are words they used. As one example of an informants' discourse in this regard is that of a father talking of his sexual relationship with his 13 year-old daughter:

To me, it's [meaning the incest] not the same as having an orgasm. I mean, it was thrilling, and it was exciting, but it wasn't what I was looking for. Bliss is the word that I would identify with that. There's a really satisfying feeling of everything is kind of relaxed. There doesn't seem to be any pressure. It's a real nice place to be.

Love. For most, their high pleasure extended to considering the incest love. Four different patterns relating to experiences of love emerged during the analysis: expressing no love, expressing sexualized affection, believing themselves to be in love, and experiencing an intense love meant in "every fiber of my body." The rarest style is having no feelings of love, and this occurred with an incestuous father who also abused his nieces for about five years when he was a teenager. He said, "They were just something to use, really," because "It [the sexual behavior with his nieces] was the only thing I could use as a safe release, you know." These children, then, were objects, not persons to be cared for and treated in just ways.

The perpetrators experienced degrees of caring and affection for the children. Even the man who expressed no caring for his nieces expressed concern and caring for his children, sentiments which he said "took second place" to the good feelings he got from the incest. A typical statement of affection is the following, provided by the sister about her two brothers, younger than her by five and seven years, whom she abused for about four years, when she was 12 to 16: "Fondling, just touching, sleeping with, touching, sort of a nurturing thing" is how she talked of her incest with them. An uncle perpetrator said, "I felt close to the kids while I was doing that." The expression of care, in these cases appeared to be sexualized and experienced in contexts where notions related to justice--such as respect for differences in status variables--had no place.

Some of the fathers and stepfathers saw themselves as in love, two to the extent that they often thought of running away with the children to start new lives. A stepfather said:

> I know there were points there where I thought I could leave my wife and take my daughter with me, and we would go off to wherever. It was like I had two wives.

He abused his stepdaughter for 11 years, from age five to 16, and he was 25 years older than her. Another stepfather described a "love affair" with his stepson, whom he abused when the boy was 12 to 14 years old:

> To me, to me, when I was having my relationship with my son, it was a love affair. It really was. It was, it was real.

A biological father said he had a better relationship with his three year-old daughter than he did with his wife. He was, however, talking about the non-sexual parts of his relationship, which he described as playful and affectionate, consisting of spending time with her, reading her stories, and playing with her "at her level." He talked of his sexual abuse of his daughter as separate from the playful, affectionate parts of his relationship. Sex with his daughter was a high, something he sought intently. Toward the end of his abuse of this daughter, he experienced feelings of high intensity and a drive for connection. This is a fourth pattern related to love. This father said:

> The feeling was, it's not a feeling--it's a thought. The thought was so doggone strong about making that connection with my daughter, that she understand that this is love...Wow. It was strong....I meant it with every fiber in my body. It was really important that she understand, and I make some connection from her to me, too.

He reported this happening the last few times he abused his daughter. Afterward, but not during the incest, he reported feeling confused and scared about these feelings.

Though not accounted for in my original hypothesis, notions of affection and romantic love are prominent in the discourse of the incest perpetrators in this study. Care, as it is discussed in moral philosophy and theories of moral development, does not encompass romantic love, although caring and promotion of the welfare of others can be components of romantic love. The perpetrators apparently experienced what they thought was caring. For some, the caring was sexualized affection, for others romantic love, and for still others a drive for connection so deep so deep and powerful it scared and confused them. While using the discourse of care and romantic love, the perpetrators in this study were disdisconnected from the implications of their status variables--age, gender, size, and role in family--for the power they had over children.

Mutuality. About half claimed that the love was mutual. Words such as "we were close," "we shared something special," "I loved her--she loved me," "mutual care, "he enjoyed it as much as I did," and "I trusted them and they trusted me," characterized all but a few accounts. Some were concerned that the sex be mutually enjoyable. A stepfather said, "Sometimes I would feel guilty because Mary [not her real name] didn't have an orgasm."

The stepfather who said he had a love affair with his son provided several examples of what he considered mutuality with his son, such as the following:

> When I got home, he always had the heater in, you know, the shed going, and it's the first thing he'd say when I'd come in the house. He'd say, 'Dad, I've got the heater plugged, plugged in.' He just as well said, 'Dad, I'm ready to go make love.'

He abused the child in the tool shed in back of the house. The sexual acts, too, he interpreted as mutual love:

> There was caring there, you know. I, we, used to talk while we were doing it, and I'd ask him if he enjoyed this or that. He'd say, 'Yes, Dad, I love it,' and I'd say, 'Do you want to quit? Do you want to stop?' He, he'd say, 'No,' and when he would masturbate me or fellate me, he would tell me, 'I'm going to make you feel good.'

He reported Jack [not his real name] used to wait for the mail each day for a letter from his biological father, who never wrote nor sent presents for birthdays and holidays. This stepfather did not see Jack as vulnerable, as craving affection and attention from a father figure, and he did not interpret his behavior as taking advantage of this vulnerability. When he told me that Jack currently is suicidal, he said Jack's depression is related to Jack's enjoying sex with him and not being able to handle that the love was homosexual. He could not see all the other possible factors leading to Jack's suicidal thinking.

Of those who discussed mutuality related to sex, some conceded that while the children loved them, they might not have liked the sex. As a father said:

> It was the love and affection she was getting from me is what she liked. It might have been the acts she didn't like....What was between Beth [not her real name] and I was something real special, something that was just ours."

This emphasis on mutuality can be challenged by notions related to justice. Relationships can be mutual when parties to the relationship are equal in status or, when differences exist, respect is paid to the implications of these differences. In incest, age, experience, and authority related to role in the family are the status variables of interest. Gender could have played a significant role for the victims as well, since most of the perpetrators were male and most of the victims were female.

When status differences are taken into account, mutual relationships are possible between persons who are not equal in status variables. Mutually loving relationship between parents and children and mutually respectful relationships between professors and students are examples. In these cases, persons in authority make appropriate demands on those with less authority and are vigilant about the potential for abuses of authority and the power that goes with it. Incest perpetrators, on the other hand, do not take into account the differences in status variables and the implications these variables have for freedom of choice, autonomy, and, thus, mutuality. From the perspectives of justice orientations, the perpetrators' constructions of their relationships with children as mutual can be challenged.

Promoting the children's welfare. Many not only saw incest as love, but stated they were promoting the children's welfare. Words such as "teaching her," "satisfying her," "showing her," "trying to make her aware of what boys do," making her a better lover than her mother, "showing her he loved her," "comforting," "consoling," and "helping kids out of their own mess" are some of the words informants used. The following quote from a biological father demonstrates the theme of consolation:

> I honestly believe that during the abuse that I was showing, that I was feeling sorry for Beth, because of the way Margaret [mother and wife, not her real name] used to nag and bitch at her [the child victim] all the time, and it was like I was comforting her at the same time she was comforting me. That, oh, I was showing her a type of love.

The language of these this perpetrator is infused with notions related to care. Empathy and responsiveness to suffering are implicit, while he was explicit about the comfort he believed he was giving. Yet he took these notions, sexualized them, and then evaded the injustice of his behaviors by stating this was a mutual sexual relationship.

The theme of "helping kids out of their own mess," means that some informants said they showed children that sex could change their sad and depressed moods and make them feel better. For example, a biological father gave his daughter a vibrator, not only to help her alter her moods, but to satisfy herself sexually and to keep boys away. He said:

> I gave her the vibrator, that was one of the things I said, you know, you can use this when you want to be sexual, and you don't have to go out and get a boyfriend and pick some guy up in school or whatever. You can use this instead. If you wake up at night--I taught her some things--if you're feeling frustrated, or you feel angry, this will always calm you down. I recognized it at that time, that some of those things can be satisfied through sexual means, and I told her that, and I showed her how to use it.

In the guise of showing compassion for suffering and promoting his daughter's welfare, certainly important components of care, this father was encouraging his daughter to use masturbation to cope with stress and to avoid peer heterosexual relationships.

 Using cognitive-behavioral theory, researchers on child molesters found that perpetrators develop cognitions and beliefs which support their behaviors (Abel, Becker-Cunningham-Rathner, 1984; Stermac & Segal, 1989). Yet, as poststructuralism points out, these perpetrators also can be viewed as shaping language to fit their behaviors. For example, Leahy (1994) noted that poststructuralists see persons as "molding and creatively adapting discourses as they act" (p. 48). The incest perpetrators of this study, then, co-opted and molded the language of care while pursuing their incestuous relationships. Human beings, however, live in community, and there are limits to the freedom persons have, both in how they act and in how they use language to mold their interpretations of their behaviors. The moral philosophers cited earlier would interpret incestuous behaviors as short-sighted and selfish, having immediate positive consequences for perpetrators and negative consequences for the children, and as violating principles of justice and care, this despite perpetrators' self-descriptions as caring and their love as mutual.

Promoting the welfare of others is an example of another sensitizing concept in my analysis of these data. Prior to constructing the analytic framework, I was only vaguely aware that this was a component of care. The framework helped me to identify within informants' narratives those stories that showed distortions in the promotion of children's welfare.

Unresponsiveness. While all but one professed having great care for the children, they betrayed some of the fundamental principles of care. Not only were they unresponsive to the children's attempts to stop the incest, but they often were cruel in trying to keep the children from telling anyone. They appeared to disconnect from their professed deep caring. Self interest, regardless of the consequences for the child, took over.

Unresponsiveness appeared in most of the informants' stories. A biological father who abused his daughter in his bedroom cajoled her out of her resistance:

I'd go into Beth's room at night, you know, and I'd ask if she'd want to come in to watch tv, you know, in my room. Sometimes she'd say, 'Yes,' and she'd come. Sometimes she'd say, 'Well, I don't know.' I'd tickle her, you know, and goof around with her a little bit, and then I'd pick her up and carry her into our room.

Several were coldly manipulative and deceptive. A stepfather said his stepdaughter learned in school that a father should not have sex with his daughter. Many times she said,

'We shouldn't do this,' and I'd tell her, 'Yeah, I know that. I'm sick, and someday I'll get help, and that was being a con. If I'd tell her that, then she would usually leave her guard down and we'd....[He didn't finish the sentence.] I think I told her it was wrong because that's what she wanted to hear. I didn't really feel it was wrong.

Responsiveness was yet another instance of a sensitizing concept. Prior to familiarizing myself with the justice-care framework, I was not clearly aware that moral philosophers and developmentalists had identified responsiveness as a component of care. In the cases just discussed, informants showed an absence of responsiveness.

The incest perpetrators in this study were similar to many other men in our culture in their lack of responsiveness of the tactics they used to gain sexual access to the objects of their choice, in their case, children. For example, in her study of fraternity gang rape, Sanday (1990) discovered the term " working a yes out," used by men to describe their manipulations to be sexual with women. In addition, as widely reported in the national press, a study released in 1994 reported that almost one third of the women surveyed stated they engaged in first intercourse against their will, either by being pressured or through physical force (Greeley, 1994). The unresponsiveness in the discourse and conduct of the incest perpetrators in this study were consistent with models of behavior and language that are part of some wider gender-based cultural practices.

Cruelty in keeping the children from telling. Some were cruel in keeping the incest secret. Instilling fear in the children, such as warning that their mothers would leave if they ever found out, was a common tactic. One man let his daughter believe that if she told, her mother--and his wife--would kill him:

> A couple of times, [my wife] would say, 'If I ever found you you were touching the girls, I'd kill you'....saying that in front of the victim and the abuser, and the victim feeling close to the abuser, and [the victim] kind of says, 'I ain't, I sure ain't going to say anything because, if I say anything now, Ma will kill Dad.'

The professed caring of these perpetrators was contradicted by their behavior. As Manning (1992) pointed out, when caring fails, then the rules of justice provide a safety net. This did not hold true for the incest perpetrators in this study.

Sexual relationships between clients and therapists often have been compared to incest (Bates & Brodsky, 1988; Luepker, 1989; Twemlow & Gabbard, 1989; Smith, 1989). Abusive therapists may view their sexual relationships with clients as love and as promoting the welfare of clients. Basing their estimate on a review of research, Twemlow and Gabbard stated that the "lovesick therapist" is the most common type, conservatively representing about half of all abusive therapists. Like the incest perpetrators in this study, abusive therapists often view the relationships as therapeutic and healing; in short, as promoting the welfare of clients (Pope & Bouhoutsos, 1986; Smith, 1989; Twenlow & Gabbard, 1989). These researchers observed that in actuality, despite their professed love and care, therapists not only were abusing their power but they were satisfying their own drives and acting in their own self-interest while denying and overlooking effects on clients. Researchers also pointed out the innate cruelty of therapists' exploitation of clients; while, on the one hand, professing great love, they may be behaving cruelly and sadistically in maintaining sexual contact with clients.

The experiences reported by the incest perpetrators in this study, then, are analogous to experiences of therapists who perpetrate against their clients. Like the incest perpetrators, abusive therapists take advantage of the trust and dependency which characterizes many therapeutic relationships. Taking advantage of others while using the discourse of care, then, are occurrences which go beyond parent-child relationships and may be issues in any relationship where there is an imbalance of power.

Justice

> Incest perpetrators are not morally integrated, and, if they have a moral focus, it will be on justice.

Almost immediately, I found this hypothesis inadequate. It was based on Gilligan's (1982) thesis that men tend to focus on justice and women on care and my assumptions that incest perpetrators are unlikely to integrate justice and care. Since all but one of the perpetrators were men, I assumed they would emphasize the justice aspects of their moral understanding of incest, particularly incest as the breaking of a major social rule. Instead, beyond stating that they knew incest was wrong, informants were almost inarticulate about the meaning of breaking the social rule against incest. Their interpretations of justice were embedded in their stories. For example, rather than respecting age as a status which renders children vulnerable to exploitation and oppression, they took advantage of children's vulnerability. As shown in the earlier discussion of care, they interpreted their sexual exploitation as romantic love and care. As will be discussed below, some also said what they were doing was not incest but love. About a third, possibly to avoid seeing themselves as exploiting children, asked children's permission to continue with the incest.

To respond to these findings, I formulated three statements related to justice:

1) Incest perpetrators are aware that incest is wrong.

2) Incest perpetrators take advantage of children's vulnerability, but many do not see their behavior this way.

3) Some incest perpetrators try to diffuse their authority and responsibility by making children the pseudo-gatekeepers of the incest.

Incest as wrong. Incest perpetrators are like other members of their culture in their understanding of proscriptions against incest. The evidence is both direct and indirect. The direct evidence is in their statements that incest is wrong. Indirect evidence came from the precautions they took to avoid detection. Furthermore, about half stated that what they were doing was not incest. Most stated explicitly they knew incest was wrong and all the others implied they knew. Some explicit statements include: "I knew incest was against the law," "The incest taboo was a big thing for me," "I knew if I continued this way, I'm going to prison," "Morally and religiously, I knew it was wrong," and "I knew I'd get locked up if I got caught."

Informants provided many more examples of implicit recognition that they thought incest is wrong. A stepfather avoided eye contact with his stepdaughter during the abuse because he was afraid he would lose his erection. Other examples include informants who made sure no one was around when they perpetrated, such as husbands who waited to be sexual with their daughters and sons until their wives went grocery shopping and the stepfather who took his stepson camping in remote woods accessible only by a two-hour walk. He said, "I knew we were alone and everything. So I wasn't worried about that [being discovered]."

A few informants, however, were inconsistent in their statements that incest is wrong. The stepfather who said he "conned" his stepdaughter by agreeing incest was wrong but who "really didn't feel it was wrong," also said he felt guilty about having sex with a child. The man who took his son to the remote woods had other contradictory thoughts, such as: "The incest taboo was a big thing to me" and "My son and I had a love affair." He saw the wrongness in his relationship with his stepson as "teaching him the wrong kind of love," meaning homosexual love. Yet, he also said that "Knowing it was wrong made it more exciting."

Like the man who had a "love affair" with his stepson and also thought it was wrong to be teaching him homosexual love, other perpetrators were confused about what was wrong in their sexual behavior. Reflecting on his divided self as a teenager, an informant was aware of his confused ideas. Speaking ironically about his own beliefs, he said, "It wasn't okay to bring Playboy into the house, but it was okay for me to be sexual with my little sister."

Not incest. Some informants explicitly stated their sexual acts with the children were not incest. One father said incest perpetrators should be hung, shot. Another father said:

> I viewed it as, what was between Beth and I was something real special...The guy next door was a police officer, and he abused his daughter. It came out in treatment that he abused another daughter in a previous marriage, too. I found it real disgusting.

When other fathers had sex with their daughters, that was incest, said another informant. "What I was doing was different. I was making love to my daughter...to my son," he said. Yet another informant reported:

> We never had penile intercourse. I don't know why. I had it stuck in my brain that I couldn't have that. That was incest to me.

Other researchers have found that perpetrators against children differentiate their behaviors from others whose behaviors are similar. McCaghy (1967) noted that child molesters often thought other offenders were "weak," "had no excuse," "off their rockers," and "very different from myself" (p. 67). McCaghy called these interpretations denial. The present study has an additional perspective; namely, that incest perpetrators are like other members of their culture and share cultural proscrip- proscriptions against incest. Like others who abuse their power, incest perpetrators redefine what their behaviors. In their minds, what they were doing was not incest but love and care.

These perpetrators showed a split awareness or fragmentation, where they held inconsistent and logically incompatible views, without making connections between their multiple perspectives. This phenome- non is mentioned in early research on child sexual abusers (e.g., Apfelberg, Sugra, & Pfeffer, 1944; Weiner, 1962) where terms such as "schizoid" and "split" were used but not elaborated. The fragmentation may be a partial response to conflicts between the moral proscriptions against incest and the tremendous pull they experienced toward commit- ting incest. Like others in their culture, these informants believed incest was morally repugnant. Moral considerations, then, may have resulted in contradictory discourses and behaviors. Ptacek (1988), who found similar contradictions and inconsistencies in the accounts of men who batter women, came to a similar conclusion. Following Scott and Lyman (1968), he wrote that the men's contradictory accounts were attempts at "face- saving or avoiding judgment" (p. 149).

Children's vulnerability. In their drive to keep the incestuous rela- tionships going, incest perpetrators took advantage of children's lack of knowledge, trust, and dependence, and they, therefore, misused their au- thority. There are many facets to informants' taking advantage of children's vulnerability. Some told the children that incest is okay, while knowing they were using children's naivete and trust. The following illus- trate this pattern:

To me, she was accepting that [incest] being okay. She was only 13, very easy to think that, to make her think that what she was doing was all right, because she doesn't have a whole lot up there yet at that age.

Another father said:

In your daughter's eyes, Dad can do no wrong, you know. If Dad says it's okay, it's okay.

Peters (1976) also found that some incestuous fathers relied on their authority to keep the incestuous relationships going.

Some not only consciously used children's trust, but experienced a sense of power stemming from the trust:

She was so willing. It's like the control that I had, sense of power, or whatever. She trusted me.

A few misused their authority and bargained to keep the children involved sexually. A stepfather said:

When she started to resist, it was more, it turned into threats and manipulation with money, or 'You're grounded,' or 'You're not going to get anything,' or 'You can't go there if you don't do this for me.'

A sense of entitlement also came through in a few of the narratives. An informant "once or twice" had thoughts of being entitled to sex with his daughter: "She's my daughter. She needs to take care of my needs." The incestuous father who, as an adolescent, also abused his younger sister starting when she was three, said: "She's part of the family. What I'm doing is not wrong." Like other informants, he immediately said, "I knew it was wrong," again illustrating the characteristic fragmented sense of right and wrong. Some men's belief in their entitlement to sexual access to females has been noted in feminist writing about male sexual abuse of females (cf. Armstrong, 1978; Bart, 1983; Rush, 1980; Sanday, 1990). Researchers on male batterers have pointed out similar patterns of entitlement (Ptacek, 1988). Rich (1979) believed that male entitlement is embedded in the discourse of the general culture.

Children as gatekeepers. Not only did the informants violate principles of an ethic of justice by taking advantage of children's vulnerability, but many abused their authority by asking the children to be gatekeepers for the incestuous acts. The perpetrators, being adults and parent and parent figures, clearly had the authority in these relationships, and to delegate their authority in circumstances where children had virtually no freedom of choice had to be highly confusing to the children, as well as unfair and harmful. As one man said to his stepson, "Anytime you want to quit, we'll quit." At another time, he said, "If like he, if he had said, 'No, Dad, I don't want to do this' we wouldn't have done it." In response to his daughter's protests that incest is wrong, an informant developed the following convoluted reasoning:

She began to realize as she got older, how wrong it was, you know, and I had [done] a bad thing. I had told her, you know, that it come to a point where I was afraid that it was going to come to actual intercourse, and I told her at that time that if I made any advances to her that she was to reject them.

A few "gave" authority over the incest to the children and then took it back. As a stepfather said:

I'd just say, I don't want to do this anymore. Now matter what I do, just say no or something like that...but I'd talk her into it somehow. A couple of weeks later, or a month later.

Placing the authority with the children is a form of role reversal; in age stratified systems, older persons have authority over younger. In this case, the older gives pseudo authority to the younger.

Placing responsibility for gatekeeping sexual relationships on the weaker person is a theme of our culture. In child sexual abuse prevention programs, for example, almost all of the attention is teaching children how to avoid being abused, and little if any emphasis is placed on the responsibility for potential perpetrators not to perpetrate. In dating relationships, too, women are taught to feel responsible for putting the brakes on male sexual advances. This re-alignment of the gatekeeper function becomes a "technique of neutralization" (de Young, 1988; Sykes & Matza, 1957) that is, a way of evading responsibility for one's own behavior. The discourse of incest perpetrators, then, is part of the larger social discourse on female responsibility for male sexual behavior.

In some cases, perpetrators neutralized the age discrepancies by experiencing themselves as the same age as the children. Either they thought of the children as older or themselves as younger. One man said incest with his daughter was like being a kid again. A stepfather said:

I was having a sexual affair that I'd never had before. You know, that age was important to me because I hadn't had a girlfriend then, and I think, I think, I started looking at that as a relationship instead of just how fucked up it was.

For him, the 20-year age gap and her pre-adolescent status was not an issue, except that it compensated him for something he earlier had wanted and did not acquire.

Incest perpetrators violated every aspect of justice discussed in the moral philosophy and moral development literature. Rather than seeing the children as meriting special consideration because of the status variables of age, they took advantage of status differentials. While they were in incestuous relationships, they sometimes realized what they were doing was wrong, but they could not articulate why. Knowing it was wrong did not stop their behavior.

DISCUSSION

The incest perpetrators in this study gave contradictory, inconsistent, and fragmented accounts, which could accurately reflect their experiences. The drive for deep pleasure and, for most, their experience of incestuous sex as love and care, impelled them to over-ride the constraints of the incest taboo and the moral principles of justice and care. Conflicted, they knew they were breaking a highly sanctioned rule. In response to this conflict, they co-opted some of the discourse of justice and care and invoked discourses characteristic of perpetrators of predatory behavior toward women. Their fragmented and contradictory accounts belied and distorted the moral principles woven into their accounts.

The narratives provided enlightenment on experiences of incest. Informant after informant defined incest as romantic love and testified to the deep pleasure, bliss, and sense of intimacy they sought and found in incest. Incest as romantic love was an unexpected finding, and it provides new insights. This finding may help would-be perpetrators and active perpetrators recognize that what they are thinking of doing or are doing is still incest, no matter how much meaning and peace it may bring to their lives. In addition, part of the pleasure could be the power of the secret that incest is pleasurable. Making this private pleasure public could diffuse the power of the secret. Shock, horror, disbelief, and our own taboos about talking about incest as pleasure or even bliss are barriers to this public moral discourse. Researchers on therapists' sexual exploitation of clients also have found wide-spread denial as barriers to understanding and prevention. They recommend public discourse and education of therapists as remedies (Pope, Sonne, & Holroyd, 1993).

These narratives also suggest that we may lack a public moral discourse on children's vulnerability and the power older persons have over children. Some informants appeared not to understand that incest takes advantage of children's vulnerability, and it brings great harm. Many seemed to think they were in a mutual relationships and believed they were being fair because they did not physically force children. There is no magic in being able to do what we want with children. Not only are children raised to obey adults, they are aware of possible dire consequences if they disobey (Gilgun, 1986). Force, therefore, is more than physical, and can arise from authority stemming from roles in the family, gender, and physical size. These considerations generally are not part of the moral discourse on families and might not be well known among those who have hegemony over children.

Analytic Induction as Method

The procedures of analytic induction in conjunction with my reading of the justice and care literature provided a useful map through the complex narratives of the incest perpetrators in this study and an intellectual template for the analysis. Had I begun the study with an interest in moral discourse but without an immersion in the literature, in other words, as a grounded theory study, I might have arrived at similar findings. I would have been reading the literature simultaneously with data analysis and interpretation. Taking this approach made little sense, however, because moral reasoning, though a vast field, centers around the two main concepts of justice and care. The literature was readily available, and I felt more prepared for the analysis by doing the reading first. In retrospect, I think the analysis was made more efficient by my prior knowledge of the notions of justice and care. Equally important was developing hypotheses prior to the analysis. Incest is highly-charged emotionally, and to attempt to do research as if I had no prior hypotheses about the moral discourse of incest perpetrators seemed impossible. Those hypotheses, while based on the literature on care and justice, also represented my personal perspectives.

Finally, I have found that using analytic induction did not preclude discovery, a major reason researchers are interested in grounded theory. Like grounded theory, the procedures of analytic induction are based on openness to new understandings. I was anchored by my knowledge of the relevant literature, while at the same time, I found I was discovering information I did not anticipate. Analytic induction, then, combines the discovery aspects associated with grounded theory, while anchoring research processes to prior research and theory.

Hypotheses and Descriptive Statements

Modified analytic induction has the goal of developing descriptive statements of relationships among concepts and makes no claim of universality. As formulated, the hypotheses are analytic generalizations (Gilgun, 1994), which, though stated in universalistic language, are not intended to account for all incest perpetrators, but only for the perpetrators in this study. These hypotheses may illuminate and perhaps help in understanding other incestuous situations and will be useful in theory development, policy, primary prevention, program development, and family therapy. When applied to other similar situations, they may have to be modified. The current findings, then, are open-ended, subject to reformulation in other circumstances, but useful at the same time for the new insights they provide. The theoretical generality of the findings has been increased through showing how the discourse of incest perpetrators is part of many other social discourses, such as therapists' abuse of clients and male college students' manipulations of young women for sex.

Future Research

In the narratives of incest perpetrators, this research unexpectedly discovered a discourse of romantic love interlaced with discourses related to male manipulations and pressure of women to gain sexual access, and vocabularies of care and justice. As research on abusive therapists suggests, these discourses may be found in other abusive relationships. For example, Levinson (1989), quoted a "love" poem which extolled physical violence as life-giving and unifying. A piece of it reads: "If you kick me, it is my pulse and rice,/The more you beat me with your shoes,/The more we are united" (p. 9). Research on other types of abuse might help clarify whether the use of the language of justice, care, manipulation and pressure, and romantic love are generally found in discourses on abusive relationships.

Another possible approach to research on the discourse of power relationships in families is to use a vocabulary of motives framework. Briefly, the principles of investigating vocabularies of motive directs researchers to analyze the meanings of speech used by persons in "delimited social situations" (Mills, 1940, p. 904). By accounting for the meanings of vocabularies of motive that are typical in several specific contexts, we can contribute to a sociology of knowledge. Examples of a vocabularies of motive approaches can be found in sociological analyses of deviance, such as rapists (Scully & Marolla, 1984), child molesters (de Young, 1988), and parents who kill their children (Margolin, 1990). The present research, though not by intent, appears to be within the vocabularies of motive research tradition.

Postmodernism offers yet another potentially fruitful perspective that can be applied to research on incest perpetrators in particular, and in the more general area of abusive power relationships in families. The fragmentation in the discourse of incest perpetrators fits well with postmodern views of the world as paradoxical, ambiguous, and inconsistent. An explicit post-modernist analysis of narratives of persons who commit incest or other abusive acts could illustrate and elaborate this aspect of postmodernism, whose components, as Graham and Doherty (1992) pointed out, remain open to further elaboration.

A second reason to undertake a postmodernist analysis of narratives of persons who commit abusive acts is the potential to demonstrate the limits of the plasticity of discourse. For some, postmodernism leads to solipsism, where "anything goes" and universal standards of truth or moral conduct can not exist. Rosenau (1992) termed this trend a position of "skeptical postmodernists," while she called those who posit standards independent of individual interpretations "affirmative postmodernists." Feminists such as Baber and Allen (1992) and Hare-Mustin and Maracek (1990) fit into the "affirmative postmodern" category when they challenged this slide toward solipsism by stating that oppression is oppression regardless of how some persons interpret it. To my knowledge, the limits of individual interpretations within a postmodern framework have yet to be demonstrated within a research report. The present study touched upon these issues, but much more can be done with these ideas.

Finally, much of the research done on families, especially research that involves in-depth interactions with informants, such as interviews and observations, can be emotionally evocative for researchers and informants. While reflexivity and subjectivity have been viewed with both alarm and intrigue for their implications for the meanings of findings, there is a great deal more we could understand about subjectivity and research. Dealing with incest perpetrators in long interviews was emotionally challenging to me, and, at times, to the informants. I would like to write about reflexive processes in my research, closely tying my accounts with sections of the narratives that were evocative. For researchers to do this is an important next step in our understanding of reflexivity and research.

Note: First published as Gilgun, Jane F. (1995). We shared something special: The moral discourse of incest perpetrators. *Journal of Marriage and the Family, 57*, 265-281.

References

Abel, G., Becker, J. V., & Cunningham-Rathner, J. (1984). Complications, consent, and cognitions in sex between children and adults. *International Journal of Law and Psychiatry, 7*, 89-103.

Abel, G., Becker, J. V., Cunningham-Rathner, J., Mittleman, M., & Rouleau, J. L. (1988). Multiple paraphilia diagnoses among sex offenders. *Bulletin of the American Academy of Psychiatry and the Law, 16*, 153-168.

Apfelberg, B., Sugra, C., & Pfeffer, A. (1944). A psychiatric study of 250 sex offenders. *American Journal of Psychiatry, 100*, 762-770.

Angell, R. A. (1936). *The family encounters the Depression.* New York: Scribners.

Armstrong, L. (1978). *Kiss daddy goodnight.* New York: Hawthorne.

Baber, K. M., & Allen, K. R. (1992). *Women and families: Feminist reconstructions.* New York: Guilford.

Bart, P. (1983). Why men rape. *Western Sociological Review, 14,* 46-57.

Bates, C., & Brodsky, A. (1988). *Sex in the therapy hour.* New York: Guilford.

Becker, H. (1953). Becoming a marihuana user. *American Journal of Sociology, 59,* 235-242.

Bloom, A. A. (1986). Psychological ingredients of high-level moral thinking. *Journal for the Theory of Moral Behavior, 16,* 233-250.

Bogdan, R. C., & Biklen, S. K. (1992). *Qualitative research for education* (2nd ed.). Boston: Allyn & Bacon.

Blumer, H. (1986). *Symbolic interactionism.* Berkeley: University of California Press. (Original work published 1969)

Briere, J. (1992). *Child abuse trauma: Theory and treatment of the lasting effects.* Newbury Park, CA: Sage.

Brown, L. M., & Gilligan, C. (1992). *Meeting at the crossroads: Women's psychology and girls' development.* Cambridge, MA: Harvard University Press.

Browne, A., & Finkelhor, D. (1986). Impact of child sexual abuse: A review of the research. *Psychological Bulletin, 99,* 66-77.

Bulmer, M. (1984). *The Chicago School of Sociology.* Chicago: University of Chicago Press. Campbell, D. T. (1979). Degrees of freedom and the case study. In T. D. Cook & C. R. Reichardt (Eds.), *Qualitative and quantitative methods in evaluation research* (pp. 49-67). Beverly Hills, CA: Sage.

Cortese, A. J., & Mestrovic, S. G. (1990). From Durkheim to Habermas: The role of language in moral theory. In J. Wilson (Ed.), *Current perspectives in social theory* (Vol. 10, pp. 63-91). Greenwich, CT: JAI Press.

Cressey, D. (1953). *Other people's money.* Glencoe, IL: Free Press.

Denzin, N. (1978). *The research act* (2nd ed.). New York: McGraw-Hill.

deYoung, M. (1988). The indignant page: Techniques of neutralization in the publications of pedophile organizations. *Child Abuse and Neglect, 12,* 583-591.

Dewey, J. (1980). *Theory of the moral life.* New York: Irvington. (Original work published 1908)

Finkelhor, D., & Dziuba-Leatherman, J. (1993). The victimization of children. Unpublished manuscript, University of New Hampshire, Family Violence Research Laboratory. Friedrich, W. N. (1990). Psychotherapy of sexually abused children and their families. New York: Norton.

Gilgun, J. F. (1986). Sexually abused girls' knowledge of sexuality and sexual abuse. *Journal of Interpersonal Violence, 1,* 113-125.

Gilgun, J. F. (1990). Factors mediating the effects of childhood maltreatment. In M. Hunter (Ed.), *The sexually abused male: Vol. 1. Prevalence, impact, and treatment* (pp. 177-190). Lexington, MA: Lexington Books.

Gilgun, J. F. (1991). Resilience and the intergenerational transmission of child sexual abuse. In M. Q. Patton (Ed.), *Family sexual abuse: Frontline research and evaluation* (pp. 93-105). Newbury Park, CA: Sage.

Gilgun, J. F. (1992). Definitions, methods, and methodologies in qualitative family research. In J. F. Gilgun, K. Daly, & G. Handel (Eds.), *Qualitative methods in family research* (pp. 22-40). Beverly Hills, CA: Sage.

Gilgun, J. F. (1994). A case for case studies in social work research. *Social Work, 39,* 371-380.

Gilgun, J. F. & Connor, T. M. (1989). How perpetrators view child sexual abuse. *Social Work, 34,* 349-351.

Gilligan, C. (1982). *In a different voice.* Cambridge, MA: Harvard University Press. Gilligan, C., & Attanucci, J. (1988). Two moral orientations: Gender differences and similarities. *Merrill-Palmer Quarterly, 343,* 223-237.

Gilligan, C., Ward, J., & Taylor, J. (Eds.). (1988). *Mapping the moral domain.* Cambridge, MA: Harvard University Press.

Glaser, B. (1978). *Theoretical sensitivity.* Mill Valley, CA: Sociology Press.

Glaser, B. (1992). *Basics of grounded theory analysis.* Mill Valley, CA: Sociology Press. Glaser, B., & Strauss, A. (1967). *The discovery of grounded theory.* Chicago: Aldine.

Goffman, E. (1963). *Stigma: Notes on the management of spoiled identity.* Englewood Cliffs, NJ: Prentice-Hall.

Graham, E., & Doherty, J. (1992). Postmodern horizons. In J. Doherty, E. Graham, & M. Malek (Eds.) *Postmodernism and the social sciences* (pp. 197-241). New York: St. Martin's.

Greeley, A. M. (1994, October 24). A national survey on sex raises some troubling questions. *Minneapolis Star Tribune,* p. Al 1.

Groth, A. N., with J. Birnbaum (1979). *Men who rape.* New York: Plenum.

Hare-Mustin, R. T., & Maracek, J. (Eds.). (1990). *Making a difference: Psychology and the construction of gender.* New Haven: Yale University.

Herman, J. L. (1992). *Trauma and recovery.* New York: Basic Books.

Horton, A. L., Johnson, B. L., Roundy, L. M., & Williams, D. (Eds.). (1990). *The incest perpetrator: A family member no one wants to treat.* Newbury Park, CA: Sage.

Houston, B. (1990). Caring and exploitation. *Hepatica, 5,* 115-119.

Kerlinger, F. N. (1973). *Foundations of behavioral research* (2nd ed.). New York: Holt.

Kohlberg, L. (1984). *The psychology of moral development.* New York: Harper & Row.

Kohlberg, L., Levine, C., & Hewer, A. (1984). The current formulation of theory. In L. Kohlberg, *The psychology of moral development* (pp. 212-219). New York: Harper & Row.

Larrabee, M. J. (Ed.). (1993). *An ethic of care: Feminist and interdisciplinary perspective.* New York: Routledge.

Leahy, T. (1994). Taking up a position: Discourse of femininity and adolescence in the context of man/girl relationships. *Gender and Society, 8,* 48-72.

Levinson, D. (1989). *Family violence in cross-cultural perspective.* Newbury Park, CA: Sage.

Lindesmith, A. R. (1947). *Addiction and opiates.* Chicago: Aldine.

Luepker, E. T. (1989). Sexual exploitation of clients by therapists: Parallels with parent-child incest. In G. R. Schoener, J. H. Milgrom, J. C. Gonsiorek, E. T. Luepker, & R. M. Conroe (Eds.), *Psychotherapists' sexual involvement with clients: Intervention and prevention* (pp. 73-79). Minneapolis, MN: Walk-in Counseling Center.

Lyons, N. P. (1983). Two perspectives: Self, relationships, and morality. *Harvard Educational Review, 53,* 125-145.

McCaghy, C. H. (1967). Child molesters: A study of their careers as deviants. In Marshall B. Clinard & Richard Quinney (Eds.), *Criminal behavior systems: A typology* (pp. 75-88). New York: Holt, Rinehart.

Manning, P. K. (1991). Analytic induction. In K. Plummer (Ed.), *Symbolic interactionism: Vol. II. Contemporary issues* (pp. 273-283). Brookfield, VT: Elgar. (Reprinted from *Qualitative methods*, pp. 401-430, by R. Smith & P. K. Manning, Eds., 1982, Cambridge, MA: Ballinger)

Manning, R. C. (1992). *Speaking from the heart: A feminist perspective on ethics.* Lanham, MD: Rowman & Littlefield.

Margolin, L. (1990). When vocabularies of motive fail: The example of fatal child abuse. Qualitative Sociology, 13, 373-385. Miller, J. B. (1986). *Toward a new psychology of women* (2nd ed.). Boston: Beacon.

Mills, C. W. (1940). Situated actions and vocabularies of motive. *American Sociological Review, 6,* 904- 913.

Noddings, N. (1984). *Caring: A feminist approach to ethics and moral education.* Berkeley: University of California Press.

Okin, S. M. (1989). *Justice, gender, and the family.* New York: Basic Books.

O'Neill, 0. (1989). Virtuous lives and just societies. *Journal of Social Philosophy, 20,* 25-30.

Piaget, J. (1932). *The moral judgment of the child.* London: Kegan Paul.

Pope, K. S., & Bouhoutsos, J. C. (1986). *Sexual intimacy between therapists and patients.* New York: Prager.

Pope, K. S., Sonne, J. L., & Holroyd, J. (1993). *Sexual feelings in psychotherapy.* Washington, DC: American Psychological Association.

Ptacek, J. (1988). Why do men batter their wives? In K. Yllo & M. Bograd (Eds.), *Feminist perspectives on wife abuse* (pp. 133-157). Newbury Park, CA: Sage.

Rich, A. (1979). *On lies, secrets, and silences: Selected prose 1966-1979.* New York: Norton.

Robinson, W. S. (1951). The logical structure of analytic induction. *American Sociological Review, 16,* 812-818.

Rosenau, P. M. (1992). *Post-modernism and the social sciences.* Princeton, NJ: Princeton University Press.

Ruddick, S. (1989). *Maternal thinking: Toward a politics of peace.* Boston: Beacon.

Rush, F. (1980). *The best-kept secret.* New York: Prentice-Hall.

Russell, D. E. H. (1983). The incidence and prevalence of intrafamilial sexual abuse of female children. *Child Abuse and Neglect, 7,* 133-146.

Russell, D. E. H. (1986). *The secret trauma.* New York: Basic Books.

Sanday, P. R. (1990). *Fraternity gang rape: Sex, brotherhood, and privilege on campus.* New York: New York University Press.

Scott, M. B., & Lyman, S. M. (1968). Accounts. *American Sociological Review, 33,* 46-62.

Scully, D., & Marolla, J. (1984). Convicted rapists' vocabulary of motive: Excuses and justifications. *Social Problems, 31,* 530-544.

Smetana, J. G., & Kelly, M. (1989). Social cognition in maltreated children. In D. Cichetti & V. Carlson (Eds.), *Child maltreatment: Theory and research on the causes and consequences of child abuse and neglect* (pp. 620-646). New York: Cambridge University Press.

Smetana, J. G., Kelly, M., & Twentyman, C. T. (1984). Abused, neglected, and nonmaltreated children's conceptions of moral and conventional transgressions. *Child Development, 55,* 277-287.

Smith, S. (1989). The seduction of the female patient. In G. 0. Babbard (Ed.), *Sexual exploitation in professional relationships* (pp. 57-69). Washington, DC: American Psychiatric Association.

Stermac, L. E., & Segal, Z. V. (1989). Adult sexual contact with children: An examination of cognitive factors. *Behavior Therapy, 20,* 573-584.

Strauss, A. (1987). *Qualitative analysis for social scientists.* New York: Cambridge.

Strauss, A., & Corbin, J. (1990). Basics of *qualitative research.* Newbury Park, CA: Sage.

Sykes, G. & Matza, D. (1957). Techniques of neutralization: A theory of delinquency. *American Sociological Review, 22,* 664-670.

Tappan, M. B. (1991). Narrative, authorship, and the development of moral authority. *New Directions for Child Development, 54,* 5-25.

Tronto, J. C. (1987). Beyond gender difference to a theory of care. *Signs, 12,* 644-663.

Twemlow, S. W., & Gabbard, G. 0. (1989). The lovesick therapist. In G. O. Babbard (Ed.), *Sexual exploitation in professional relationships* (pp. 71-87). Washington, DC: American Psychiatric Press.

Weiner, I. B. (1962). Father-daughter incest: A clinical report. *Psychiatric Quarterly, 36,* 607-632.

Williams, L. M., & Finkelhor, D. (1990). The characteristics of incestuous fathers: A review of recent studies. In W. L. Marshall, D. R. Laws, & H. E. Barbaree (Eds.), *Handbook of sexual assault* (pp. 231-255). New York: Plenum.

Williams, L. M., & Finkelhor, D. (1992). The characteristics of incestuous fathers (Report to the National Center on Child Abuse and Neglect, the U.S. Department of the Navy, and the North Star Fund). Durham: University of New Hampshire, Family Research Laboratory.

Wyatt, G. E., Newcomb, M. D., & Riederle, M. H. (1993). *Sexual abuse and consensual sex: Women's developmental patterns and outcomes.* Newbury Park, CA: Sage.

Znaniecki, F. (1934). *The method of sociology.* New York: Farrar & Rinehart.

ALSO BY JANE GILGUN

Children's Books

Busjacked!
Emma and her Forever Person
Five Little Cygnets Cross the Bundoran Road
Patrick and the Magic Mountain
Salamander: The Story of Two Boys
The King's Toast
The Little Pig Who Didn't go to Market
The Picking Flower Garden
Thorns Have Roses: A Story of Recovery from Clergy Abuse
Turtle Night at Playa Grande
Will the Soccer Star

Books

Child Sexual Abuse: From Harsh Realities to Hope
Children with Serious Conduct Issues
Hannah Robinson: The Celebrated Beauty of Her Day (play)
I Want to Show You: Poems
On Being a Sh*t: Unkind Deeds & Cover-Ups in Everyday Life
The NEATS: A Child & Family Assessment

Manuals

Lemons or Lemonades? An Anger Workbook for Kids
Leomons or Lemonade? An Anger Workbook for Teens
Readiness to Adopt Children with Special Needs with Sue Keskinen
The CASPARS: Clinical Assessment Tools for Client Risks & Strengths

ABOUT THE AUTHOR

JANE F. GILGUN, PHD, LICSW, is a professor, School of Social Work, University of Minnesota, Twin Cities, USA. She does research on the meanings of violence to perpetrators, the development of violent behaviors, and how persons overcome adversities. She has published widely in these areas and on qualitative methods within the Chicago School of Sociology tradition.

She worked at a public Rhode Island child welfare social service agency for several years, returned to graduate school, and then became a professor. She also writes children's books, non-fiction, and articles that are available on Amazon and other internet booksellers. She has many videos on YouTube that include the landscapes in Northwest Ireland, trail riding in Minnesota and elsewhere, horse racing, pig racing, and more.

Her interests include her horses, Padron's Elegante (Ellie) and Finn MacCool, who are mother and son, her dog Jazz, gardening, photography, cooking, the arts, and spending time in County Leitrim and County Sligo, Ireland.

Jane has a bachelor's and master's in English and American poetry from the Catholic University of America and the University of Rhode Island, respectively, a master's in social work from the University of Chicago, a licentiate in family studies and sexuality from the Catholic University of Louvain, Belgium, and a Ph.D. in child and family studies from Syracuse University. She is a licensed independent clinical social worker.

Lightning Source UK Ltd.
Milton Keynes UK
UKOW06f1823070615

253057UK00009B/140/P